THE POWER OF NAMES

THE POWER OF NAMES

Uncovering the Mystery of What We Are Called

Mavis Himes

ROWMAN & LITTLEFIELD
Lanham • Boulder • New York • London

Published by Rowman & Littlefield
A wholly owned subsidary of The Rowman & Littlefield Publishing Group,
Inc.
4501 Forbes Boulevard, Suite 200, Lanham, Maryland 20706
www.rowman.com

Unit A, Whitacre Mews, 26-34 Stannary Street, London SE11 4AB

British Library Cataloguing in Publication Information Available

Library of Congress Cataloging-in-Publication Data

Name: Himes, Mavis, author.
Title: The power of names : uncovering the mystery of what we are called / by Mavis Himes.
Description: Lanham : Rowman & Littlefield, 2016. | Includes bibliographical references and
    index.
Identifiers: LCCN 2015039185| ISBN 9781442259782 (cloth : alk. paper) | ISBN 9781442259799
    (electronic)
Subjects: LCSH: Names, Personal--Psychological aspects. | Identity (Psychology)
Classification: LCC CS2309 .H56 2015 | DDC 929.4001/9--dc23 LC record available at http://
    lccn.loc.gov/2015039185

™ The paper used in this publication meets the minimum requirements of
American National Standard for Information Sciences Permanence of Paper
for Printed Library Materials, ANSI/NISO Z39.48-1992.

Printed in the United States of America

To the memory of my parents
Louis ben Moishe v' Chaya and
Miriam bat Hymie v' Bertha

When, as a child, I wrote my name for the first time,
I knew I was beginning a book.
—Edmond Jabès, The Book of Questions, vol. 1

NOM, "name," should be read twice, from left to right
and from right to left.
Because two words compose it: NOM and MON, my name.
This name is mine. All names are personal.
—Edmond Jabès, The Book of Resemblances, vol. 2

CONTENTS

PREFACE

I wrote this book to interact with my own name through an exploration of names and naming more generally. Naturally, my thoughts and ideas about names and naming have been influenced by my work as a practicing psychoanalyst. Throughout my adult life and now in writing this book, my clinical practice and theoretical orientation have deepened my appreciation of the power of speech and language, in general, and of names, in particular. As a result, I have come to value the broad impact of proper names and the significant role they play in our lives.

Most of us do not stop to question our name; it is simply a given. Rarely do we stop and explore its meaning or significance, as if assuming a predetermined and fixed nature that requires little thought. In our current times, an explosion of genealogical research, courtesy of the Internet, may change this and bring names into a topic of interest. Moreover, a more recent trend of name-changing may also provoke some people to become more aware of the name they have been assigned.

In discovering the web of influence woven by my own name, I also realized the extent to which I have been formed by my own Jewish heritage. Consequently, detailed illustrations of my own ethnic roots have found their way into these pages. I hope my journey will inspire others to question and reflect on their own unique ancestral histories.

As I considered the forms and structures of names, I also became increasingly fascinated by the derivation of word meanings. To consider the lingering traces of word usage from their first appearance to the

transformed yet subtle changes in meaning that occur over time in-
trigued and entertained me. Bastardizations and extensions of particular words and their reappropriated connotations added a further dimension of understanding. Also finding their way into this book are the
narratives and vignettes of my patients and the friends and colleagues
who sustained me during my research. It never ceased to amaze me
how often those with whom I spoke on this subject had a story to share
with me, if not about their own name then about the name of a friend,
relative, or acquaintance. The spelling of names, the pronunciation of
names, the meaning of names and name changes—all made their way
into a variety of conversations.

I discovered that people were comfortable sharing personal stories
in social settings; talk of the proper name inevitably led to conversations
about families and their origins. If I was at table with a group of ten
friends, there would be ten stories; twelve people and there would be
twelve stories. Some people claimed a deep attachment to their name,
while others demonstrated disdain or indifference. Some said their
name had a significant impact on their life, opening doors or creating a
certain confidence, whereas others shied away from their name, dislik-
ing the sound or pronunciation, the associations or the history. I am
indebted to all those people who, knowingly or unknowingly, contrib-
uted in some way to this work and helped me recognize the power of
the proper name as a shorthand and metaphor for one's personal life.

This book is a journey into the power and significance of this proper
name, a name proper to each unique individual. While I have included
some mention of First Nations and African cultures, these are certainly
outnumbered in these pages by names, naming rituals, and etymological citations related to Western culture. However, I hope readers' imag-
inations will carry them to other associations and places with which they
may be familiar.

Finally, due to the sensitive and personal nature of this material, I
did not include personal stories without permission and, in many cases,
without certain modifications. Any references to my patients and their
names have also been modified and disguised to protect confidentiality.
In certain cases, I have had full consent to use exact name spellings.

Mavis Himes
Toronto, September 2014

PROLOGUE

In my dream, I am shaking hands with Jacques Lacan. I ask him his name and he replies, with a smile, "Why, my name is Jacques Lacano-vitch."

This may seem a strange person to appear in one's dreams, but for me it was not a surprise. At the time I was undergoing my analytic formation in Lacanian psychoanalysis, and Lacan was in the forefront of my thoughts. Jacques Lacan was an iconoclast, a rebel, a radical thinker and a brilliant psychoanalyst, a man whose name was synonymous with originality, creativity, and innovation in the field of Freudian psycho-analysis. Often referred to as the French Freud, he read and reread, worked and reworked, the texts of the venerable old man of psychoanal-ysis, creating a new way to talk about and practice psychoanalysis. Nor was it surprising that I would have dreamed of Lacan with those letters appended to his name. During that phase of my personal analysis, I had been speaking about my name, Mavis Himes, and had looked into the fact that my father and his siblings had legally changed their surname from Heimovitch to Himes. Wouldn't you know it but those missing letters had gone and attached themselves in my dream to this grand old master. The dream rekindled my interest in my name and its impact on my life, to research the question of the proper name: How does the proper name function? And how does a name change, either voluntary or by coercion, affect the bearer of the name?

Most of us take our names for granted. Yet our first name—both an introduction and a greeting—is one of the first words we learn. Assigned to us by our parents with love, it is freighted with their expectations and hopes for our future. Our surname, meanwhile, carries our collective history: It is a branding of transmission and affiliation, linking us to our ancestral past.

Our name rolls off our tongue with ease and familiarity. It is a signifier around which our identity is intimately linked. It travels with us like a passport, testifying to our unique presence on this earth. It is a permanent marker that functions as a shorthand for who we are, conjuring up a mosaic of associations: Kennedy, Shakespeare, Einstein, Stalin, Muhammad. Lacan once said that a search for origins was a mythic journey, a return to a legendary past. The proper name returns us to that beginning and brings us closer to that mythic first step. From birth to death, our name is the signature of our personal journey through life. Our name accompanies us as a faithful and, in most cases, permanent marker of identification, that permanent abode in which we live.

Part I

Called into Existence

I

AN INVITATION INTO BEING

At the moment of conception, and even earlier, when our existence is only a fantasy in the minds of our parents, we are assigned a name. Your name will be Elizabeth Mary Ferguson, born on this September 7, 2014, in the city of Toronto, Canada. This is the name by which you will be called. And through this naming, Elizabeth Mary Ferguson will be inscribed into a world of speech and language, symbolized by her name. Just like the physical cut from the umbilicus that separates us from our mother, so our given name creates a first psychological scansion, or division, from our biological parents and heralds us into the world with a particular mark of identity.

And so it is that when we are asked the question "Who are you?" it is by pronouncing our name, that kernel of our most intimate identity, that we first respond. Through our proper name we greet the world, and the world, in turn, greets us. The prominence of our name is conspicuous in its enunciation. As a patient of mine once said, "I live within the confines of my screwed-up family matrix, and my name is simply a relic, all that is left of a washed-out historical fact. And I am confronted with it every day when asked the question: And what is your name, sir?" This name, assigned at childbirth, is the ongoing birthplace in which we live. We savor our name as we speak it; it rolls around in our mouth and off our tongue in a familiar, facile way. Even the accent with which we pronounce the unique combination of syllables is particular to our very intimate sense of self.

Our name is also the physical substrate of our being, of both the internal and external passport we carry through life. As a record of our birth in a country of origin, it allows us to freely enter and depart from foreign lands. Without a name, there is no passport, no social security or social insurance number, no identification papers to give us admission to many social institutions. Documents link geography, history, and personal identity to a name. Without these, we become *persona non grata*, a being on the fringes of society.

Our name is that passport which records our internal private world, a world that does not always mirror the intent with which the name was given. A secret world in which we dream, argue, make love, whisper, and shout; the *dit-mansion* (Lacan's play on words, "house of the said") of our being, a space of familiarity and shelter. We consider this metaphorical home a sphere of intimacy, shaped by our unique experiences and memories. It houses our memories and souvenirs, our illusions and fantasies, our certainties and our misgivings. The French philosopher Gaston Bachelard describes the characteristics of our first childhood home in his book *The Poetics of Space* as our "first universe, a real cosmos in every sense of the word . . . All really inhabited space bears the notion of home."[1] And like the permanent imprint of this first universe, our name resounds within us throughout our life.Unlike the color of our hair or the freckles and beauty spots that may dot our skin—courtesy of the genetic coding of our physical being that marks each of us as unique—our name is an invitation into our being. Naming is not a random act. Names are not chosen and assigned indiscriminately. In many cultures a sacredness surrounds not only naming rituals but also the names themselves, which are endowed with an inviolability that marks their wearers from its first utterance.

Our proper names mark our entry into life; given name and surname are the symbolic talismans by which our unique life story begins. They inevitably return us to a question of origins. Yet childhood amnesia makes us strangers to our own beginnings. We accept without question the stories we have been told about our first stirrings and early days. Their mythic origin is told, repeated, and inscribed in our memory; it forms the foundation of our life's narrative. As the Egyptian-born poet Edmond Jabès writes, "Beginning is a human invention, an anguished speculation about origins. Animals—like plants—do not even have an inkling of it."[2]

* * *

The day I was born, winds howled across the Montreal sidewalks, as snowblowers, churning their way up and down the streets, spewed piles of fresh snow onto front yards. According to my mother, my birth was premature by a few days. At the first sign of contractions, she called my father, who returned from work as quickly as he could. Anxious to get my mother to the hospital, he steered his way around snowdrifts and parked cars, speeding down the hill to the Herbert Reddy Hospital.

"Slow down," my mother implored, but he maintained his speed all the way to the emergency entrance. The obstetrician, a forty-year-old bachelor still living at home with his mother, warned my father not to leave.

"Mr. Himes, this one is going to be fast."

Apparently, this handsome bachelor, the target of much gossip and women's glances, had also delivered my sister, whose delivery had been slow and laborious. "You just shot out," my mother frequently told me over the years. "You were just anxious to get going. Right from day one. Always impatient, just like the way you are today."

She also told me that the obstetrician married a staff nurse shortly following my birth—and just a few weeks after his mother's death. She always concluded her story with, "The women were lined up, but somehow he wouldn't marry until his mother died."

In my mind, my birth was linked to the fate of this doctor whose dependency on his mother interfered with his maturity.

When I was a little girl, my mother often read to me before my bedtime. Most of the stories began the same way. I would immediately be drawn into another world . . . a world of bygone times, perhaps an imaginary world, a crepuscular, shadowy world between light and darkness. I would nod off to sleep, transported by images of a beyond, a world populated by figures and caricatures dancing in my head as my mother's voice lulled me into the Land of Nod. In a time long and faraway in the past . . . There was and there was not . . . A very, very, long time ago . . . In the oldest of days and ages and times . . . Long before your time . . .

* * *

And so each of our own stories begins: *Once upon a time . . .* We are a new entry on the stage of life. A birth, a breath, a cry of being. A mass of physiological, neuroanatomical, and biochemical cells and neurons wrapped in a blanket of human skin.

Tumbling out of the birth canal and tossed into this world, the newborn lands into the hands of those who have preceded him. In time, he will be molded and shaped by those adults, themselves imperfect, insecure, anxious. They will caress, feed, nourish, fondle, and sustain him. In moments of frustration and suffering, they will bundle him up too tightly, smother him, elude him. At the mercy of their moments of triumph and sorrow, he will bend to their demands, forever trying to carve out the shape of their desire, their wants, their hopes. Amidst the lallation, the cooing and babbling and the earliest vocalizations between infant and mother, the as-yet-not-completely-formed infant will be bathed in the love of his parents. Having been given a name and having responded positively to its demand to come alive, he will begin to recognize the repetition of this word in these earliest interactions. In the intimate embrace of his parents, his name will be uttered—in a whisper or a murmur, a clamor, or a shout. Nestled against the breast, he will derive pleasure and comfort from the repetition of this word that makes of its sound a familiar rhythm. Within the shelter of this intimate bond, this sounding of his name, his being will be informed.

The first sounds the infant hears come from the soul of the mother's being—whispers and lullabies, words of endearment—in a voice punctuated by intonations and modulations in rhythm, pace and timbre, and cadence. A voice that later will be recognized by its familiarity, its sweetness, its exclamations and expletives. Perhaps a voice that pulls with seductiveness or pushes with forlornness. This first language of private communication constitutes a preliminary code between mother and child that does not enter the universe of shared speech and language. The vocal apparatus is flexed with the oral pleasure of producing sounds. The voice will begin to shape itself into letters, repeated phonemes of sound that gradually take on meaning by their consistency and repetition. For example, the universal forms of "mama" and "papa" constitute the beginnings of a common code of symbols in languages around the globe, yet in the early months these phonemes also partake in the pleasure of sound play.

Soon the infant will scan the musical notes of his mother's voice. These sounds will no longer be only a source of comfort, or of emptiness, but also of information and signification. And very quickly, he will recognize those particular and distinctive sounds that form smoothly into a regular sequence. The labels that he hears and to which he responds become repetitive language patterns. And with increasing familiarity, he hears his own name as a melody of sweetness, or at times bitterness, to which he orients himself without hesitation. Conversely, the infant will also discover the power of his own sound. Within weeks, he will begin to recognize the impact of his own voice, his own cries, on the person who hears the cries as a call. The mother, interpreting the sounds of her infant as a demand for food, for comfort, for warmth, responds in haste, in panic, or in time, gradually attributing particular meanings to her baby's sounds.

In this way, our little newborn will become a speaking being, a *parlêtre*, who will enter the world of desire and determination, drive and enthusiasm. His life will be honored and commemorated, lived with his named presence, until its end.

❁ ❁ ❁

But even before any of this, the infant will be called into existence with a name, his birth followed by an act of nomination. This act of naming is a summoning, an awakening of the human infant into being. The little darling, the one whose life has just been revealed, must be called into being, and it is with his name that he will be summoned to respond. With joy and glee, with tears and howls, with an upturned smile or a downturned scowl, with legs circling the air or with fists pounding, respond he must. And like God's calling to Abraham at the beginning of the story of his near-sacrifice of his son Isaac and Abraham's response, *Hineini* ("Here I am"), so too the newborn responds symbolically: I am here. I hear you. Yes, that is me.

The birth name animates us, creates us, and demands of us a certain responsibility. We are each of us invited to take a name, to infuse our name with élan and vigor, to bring our name into circulation with vitality, to make our name come alive with our own life-affirming energy.

Unfortunately, there are instances where a name is not taken, when it is not permeated with spirit or passion. Either by a deliberate or unconscious act of refusal or by a significant impairment, the call is unheard, unheeded, avoided, or foreclosed, and there is no reply—for example, in the extreme cases of autism, of disrupted development or genetic anomalies, or in the nascent structure of a psychosis. In these cases, a rupture occurs in the shared use of language. Or consider the child born after the death of a sibling in which the bereaved parents choose to give this child the same name as the deceased one. Exposed to the weight of grieving parents and the unconscious wish on the part of parents to fulfill the hole left absent by the child, the "replacement child" cannot accept the given name without serious limitations, and may withdraw into mental illness.

Research on how language is acquired describes how parents use the given name as a means of calling. With a modulated, high-pitched voice pattern, they call: *You, Barbara! My sweetheart! Pay attention. Barbara! Look! Here! You come and see Mummy!* First the exclamations and then the name uttered to catch the attention of the busy baby: *Sally, Bob, Barbara, Michael—stop what you are doing, I am calling you, I want your attention. Look at me, look at Mummy.* And then the response: the turning and looking, the verbal and nonverbal replies, the chuckles and vocalizations.

As we grow, we will follow the pattern of this first call, this appeal from the external world. The call by name puts each of us in a position to respond definitively. Consider an example from everyday experience. To know someone, to use their name, is to stand in relation to that person, to call in such a way that the other person must respond. Even in a casual encounter, when we address someone by their name, we are asking for a response:

> "Alice!" [I am calling you.] "Yes?" [I am listening, I am here.]
> "Please put your shoes away (or do such-and-such)." [a request]
> "Okay." [a response]

Or consider the times when we use someone's name in anger or frustration, as if the use of the name exerts an additional force or will grab more attention. Parents often assert their power and control by calling their children by name:

> "Come to dinner now, please." [no response]
> "*Johnny*, I said come to dinner right now." [response]

As adults, we continue to be called on to respond in various situations. We do not always do so: We may refuse to go to school, to enlist in the army, to take a test. We may not answer the phone or the door, denying our response to a social convention or demand. We can choose to avoid the stack of bills piling up in the mailbox or consumer surveys. There are innumerable opportunities to avoid responding to the call of our name.

Once a name is assumed at birth, it becomes a part of us, interwoven with the fabric of our innermost being. Why do we sometimes feel uncomfortable when we are speaking to someone we do not know very well or whom we have just met—a car salesman comes to mind—and that person begins to use our first name? Why do we cringe when our first name is used repeatedly in a conversation? Because the speaker is assuming the existence of a relationship that in fact is either lacking or absent altogether. *Susan, you know that when I met you, I was reminded of another friend of mine. And Susan, this person looked just like you . . .* The discomfort of a transgression, a line crossed without permission. To use someone's first name in casual conversation is to assume a particular relationship to that person. We do not enter such intimacy without implicit permission, nor are we always prepared to grant this privilege to others. Sometimes, the familiar use of our name becomes a trespassing of boundaries.

By contrast, the tenderness with which we call each other through a private code or through terms of endearment expressed only in private moments attests to the way in which names become infused with a libidinal charge and a certain *jouissance*, or sensual pleasure. Each of us can probably remember or continue to experience being embraced and called by a name unique to a particular love relationship. In the most intimate of moments, we sense the eroticism of the name, of the name saturated with a life-filled energy. These names of affection invite a reciprocity of offering and receiving; at these special moments, we experience the intimacy and sexual desire with which our name can become imbued.

A given name is never random. It trickles down through the unconscious of the name-givers. While life and birth circumstances, moral qualities, physical characteristics, and simple preference (we just liked the sound of it) may contribute to the choice of a given name, it is rarely that neutral in its selection. Sometimes the latent meaning can be discerned if parents are pressed or asked directly. However, even in cases where parents insist on its neutrality, behind the so-called neutral name hide the hopes, aspirations, and dreams of each set of parents.

Fashioned after a movie star, named after a prophet, forged in the memory of an aunt, an uncle, or a lost child, the newborn is endowed with the fantasies and desires of those whose name he receives. And having received this nomination, he will be created out of what he has been given.

✿ ✿ ✿

It is almost inconceivable for us to imagine not having a name, for to be without a name is to be without form or qualities, without shadows, without dreams, without imagination, without a soul. And worse, without a home.

To live without a name would be to live on the margins of life. It would be to belong to the kingdom of animals that roam through their world nameless and anonymous (with the exception of domesticated pets, which we name as surrogate members of our family).

To remain without a name is to live on the periphery of life without access to others, for our name links us to a community of speaking beings, each of whom also bears a name. As the king of the Phoenicians says to Ulysses, "Tell me the name you go by at home—what your mother and father and country men call you. For no one in the world is nameless, however mean or noble, since parents give names to all children they have."[3] To endure in a nameless condition would be to survive life as inhuman, not-yet-human, or subhuman. When we stop using the names of individuals, they become the anonymous, faceless mass of men and women. When we want to disconnect or when we want to objectify, we eliminate the individual by referring to a trait or quality: "the boy," "the slave," "the mother," "the ugly one," "the one with the dark skin"; or to the plural: "those skinheads," "the slanted eyes," "the rednecks," "the blacks," "the Jews." Similarly when we want to classify people, we refer to the collective: "the gypsies," "those Romans," "the Serbs," "the infidels." We create distance by collapsing singularity into an indeterminate horde.

In 1938, at the time of Kristallnacht, Jews were stripped of their actual names when Hitler instituted law #174 whereby Jews were forced to assume a name considered Jewish from a published list of names. As part of this decree, all Jewish men were to assume the middle name Israel and all women the middle name Sarah. Thus Hitler first robbed the Jewish people of their individual identities by eliminating their actual names and limiting their unique trait of identification to a generic status. Then he stripped his victims even more by branding them with numbers, further robbing them of any semblance of humanity. The obliteration of names was an intentional weapon to reduce a segment of humankind to the nonhuman.

A recent news article reported on frightening incidents of abuse carried on in a residential center for the developmentally disabled in southern Ontario. To add to the horrific practices of the institution, now facing charges for the alleged abuse of its residents, was the burial practice of children who had died while in its care. In a TV news clip, the camera rolls slowly over the marked graves of the cemetery, a panoramic view of rows and rows of gravestones—numbered and nameless.

The state of namelessness produces a sense of mental confusion and disarray; the nameless remain anonymous social pariahs. In medieval and romantic literature, the creation of characters without names reinforced a feeling of mistrust and suspicion bordering on contempt. Whether in fiction or in reality, it is always more reassuring to know with whom you are dealing than with an unnamed figure.

To be named is to occupy the spirit of one's identity, no matter who one's parents and grandparents may be and no matter how one's life will unfold. And to inhabit one's name is to enter the shared universe of discourse and activity with other speaking beings.

2

NAMES WITH POWER

The name written on my birth certificate is Mavis Carole Himes. This is my English name, the name with which I greet the world, and the name by which I am acknowledged in return. In my opinion, an unexciting name. An unusual name, perhaps, but one that announces nothing about the person it represents. My name does not carry the weightiness of Angustias (anguish), Magdalena (the saintly "Mary"), Amelia (industriousness), Martirio (martyrdom), or Adela (a "going forward"), the five daughters in Federico Garcia Lorca's *House of Benarda Alba*, nor the lightness of a name like Joyce or Gloria.

My first name, Mavis, is defined in the dictionary as "song-thrush," the bird *Turdus musicus*, a word of Middle English origin. My surname, Himes, is also brief and diminutive. It gives nothing away; it shields me from my ancestral history, unlike such family names as O'Leary or McInerney, Rostropov or Katchachurian, which announce their ethnic origins.

Had I been born prior to the Edict of Napoleon I in the eighteenth century, I would have been named Mavis, daughter of Louis and Miriam, for that was a time when family names were not required by law and offspring were identified by the names of their parents alone. Or, had I been born at an even earlier time, I might have been named simply Mavis, daughter of Louis the tailor.

In Judaism, an infant is given both a Hebrew and a Christian, or secular, name. Frequently this secular name bears a resemblance to the Hebrew name by sharing the same initial letter (Leon/Lavan), by being a translation from Hebrew to English (Shoshana/Rose), or by bearing a resemblance in both languages (Dvorah/Deborah). The Hebrew name may be retained as a middle name in honor of a deceased relative, like my sister whose middle name, Ann (Chaya), commemorates our paternal grandmother. While the secular name is for everyday use, the Hebrew name is reserved for all festivities and rituals associated with the Jewish community: It is the one used for a call to the Torah in synagogue, for recording in a marriage certificate (*ketubah*), and for commemoration on a tombstone. It is usually kept separate from its secular counterpart.

My Hebrew name is Malkah, or *Malkah bat Leib v'Miriam* in full, as Jews are still defined in relation to their parents' given Hebrew names. Considered an old-fashioned name in Israeli circles today, Malkah means "queen" in English. My parents tell me I carry a regal name!

As a young girl, I learned that I had been named after my great-aunt, my maternal grandmother's sister, who had died tragically in a car accident. I learned only later, as a teenager, that this particular sister had been considered the "wicked" one who had match-made my grandmother in order to get her out of the marital home. I carry a tarnished regal name!

My family name, Himes, is an abbreviation of the patronymic of my paternal grandfather, Morris Heimovitch. Haimovitch, Haimowitz, Hajmowicz, Chaimovitch, Haimevici, Chajmovicz—all variations on this name as influenced by geographical location and local pronunciation (i.e., Russian, Polish, Ukrainian). The Hebrew word *chaim* expresses the essence of life. It first appears in the Bible when God creates man out of dust and breathes *nishmat chaim*, "the breath of life," into his nostrils (Gen. 2:7). Jews frequently add a suffix or prefix to their father's name to indicate "son of" or "descendant of"; these vary in different languages and countries: Wolfson, Rubenovitch, Markowitz, ben-Yehuda, or ibn-Gvirol. Through my father's patronymic, I cherish the vitality of life and incorporate its life-affirming energy. In the Middle Ages, it was not uncommon for Ashkenazi Jews to add *chaim* to a given name in the event of sickness or danger in order to ensure long life and health.

※ ※ ※

My father's full name was Louis Frank Heimovitch. He was one of seven brothers and two sisters all carrying the surname Heimovitch. As my father and uncles entered the world of business during the 1940s in Anglophone Montreal, they decided to drop some letters and abbreviate their name to Himes. Why did they drop these letters? What was the significance of this name change for them? And what is the significance of this name change for me and my ties to an abbreviated, misshapen name?

Perhaps, like many Jews around the world, my father and uncles did not wish to announce their ethnic identity in a city with residues of anti-Semitism; Himes conceals whereas Heimovitch reveals. Perhaps it was also a pragmatic, financial decision; perhaps they thought the new name would be less troublesome and more profitable for business purposes. Perhaps they wished to appear more assimilated. Perhaps they wanted to separate themselves from those other Jews, those strange-looking men with anemic complexions and long sideburns who scurried about Friday afternoons in their black top hats and long, black topcoats to get home before Sabbath began, at sunset, in Outremont, a neighborhood whose name means "beyond the mountain," originally beyond the mountain from the main settlement of Montreal. This neighborhood, once characterized by a cultural mosaic of struggling ultra-orthodox Jews, established and wealthy Francophones such as the Trudeaus, and a mixed Anglophone population, to this day is a thriving hub of mixed ethnic identities. The Heimovitch boys from Grubert Lane may have imagined that, as the Himes brothers, they could blend more easily among those who strolled along Sherbrooke and Dorchester, the major arteries of the largely Anglophone downtown, or up and down the aisles of the James A. Ogilvy store, a bastion of the English establishment with its tartan boxes, its grand chandelier brought from Her Majesty's Theatre a few blocks away, and the piper whose music filled the store. Whatever the motivation, the name change stuck and would be transmitted to all the offspring of my generation and on.

I have often wondered: *Did the brothers all agree? Was there a vote? Did they argue? Was it a hasty decision or one discussed over a period of time?* I never asked my father those questions. My interest in names surfaced after his death, and today there are no surviving siblings of his generation.

Seven Heimovitch boys—they of the scrawny legs and torn leggings, mismatched socks, and unlaced shoes—must have filled a row of their own through spring, summer, fall, and winter, as they turned the crumpled pages of the prayer book, or *mahzor*. Was it on the way from this place of worship, prayer books tucked high under their armpits, that the seeds of change were strewn—seeds of hatred tossed about in the teasing and taunting of name-calling by the French Canadian *gamins* fomenting and echoing the hate-filled refrain from thousands of miles across the ocean? We and they and we and they and we and they and we and they? Jews and Arabs and Jews and Poles and Jews and Cossacks and Jews and Germans and Jews and the French, the Québécois, the Francophones?

Was it only in a self-imposed exile that the chorus could be changed? Was it on the homeward return from that holiest of brick buildings that a new name was forced into creation, forged from the rocks that landed on the pavement? A new, abbreviated name in a new country: Himes. So my full name is Mavis Carole Himes. English on the outside, Jewish on the inside. Or is my name *Malkah Heimovitch*? A foreign name, an unfamiliar name, a name that announces its strangeness and ethnicity. My Anglicized name, an amputation from the original, is a name in exile, a name that has been lifted, removed from the soil, and transplanted to live or die.

I am the rightful inheritor of this abbreviated surname. As a Himes, I am the product of a union between my father and mother, and, as the custom in this country, I choose to carry the inscription of my paternal surname, in spite of my marital status. And yet this name, modified by my father and his brothers, conceals my true identity. For it erases all ethnic markings and removes all traces of my cultural roots. It hides the intergenerational chain that binds me to a wandering tribe of nomads in the Land of Ur over five thousand years ago.

When people meet me, they often question the derivation of my name. They are never sure of my background. I have been told that Mavis is an English name, frequently employed for servants and maids; I have been told that Mavis is the name of African Americans in the southern United States; I have been told that my name is old-fashioned, outdated, and idiosyncratic.

* * *

The ancient worlds of the Ancestors danced and sang with the exultation of naming. A new life, a new personality, a new destiny. A birth, a name, a celebration of naming. The close connection between a person's essence and his being was infused with the force and intensity of permanence encapsulated through the letters of a name. Over and over again, the Ancestors insisted that we remain true to the essentialism of our name, this moveable home we carry wherever we roam. They also understood that to name was to bring something into existence. They too believed that to name was to put into real circulation the stuff of life, the scenes and acts of the lived experience.

In this timeless worldview, the process of naming was not only a summoning into existence, but also a calling from and by an-Other; not to possess a name was tantamount to nonexistence. Name-giving was always and necessarily a calling forth of a force associated with creation and domination.

The history of man as name-giver goes back to time immemorial. And with the power to name came a belief in the power of names themselves. Not only was power invested in the person bestowing the name, but a certain power and magic was also believed to reside in the name itself. To know someone's name could also be to have access to a secret knowledge about that person.

As was believed in many cultures, to know a person's name was to gain an intimate knowledge of their being, the secrecy of their innermost thoughts and desires. For example, Egyptian mythology believed in the existence of a supradivine force, principle, law, or essence, referred to as *ma'at*, which means "truth" or "justice." By partaking of this essence, a human magician could acquire power over men and gods. Accordingly, the great secret of the gods was said to reside in their name.

Treacherous Isis, a mortal, aspired to become a goddess by laying hold of the sacred name of Ra. When the great god Ra was old and almost dead from a poisonous snakebite, Isis approached him, offering him her aid. In delirium, he recounted the story of his life, revealing a parent's prohibition of revealing his name. Slippery Isis agreed to help him survive, but only on the condition that he reveal this name. In desperation, Ra consented. His name was taken away from him, and Isis became "the great goddess, the queen of gods, who knew Ra by his own name."[1]

In the holy books of Judaism, it is written that the name by which a person is called constitutes that person's soul and vital force. When a soul inhabits a body, it draws life into it by means of its name; that is, by the correct joining and enunciation of its letters. The Hebrew name by which all things are called constitutes the literal speech of the Ten Sayings by which the world was created. It is believed that each person embodies this life force through the manipulation and formation of letters. According to one tractate in the mystical writings of a Chassidic text (*Shaar HaYichud VehaEmunah*), the name is the vessel that contains the vital force inherent in the letters of the name. The letters of the name are a channel through which life is drawn into the body. Even the word *shem* (name) has the same numerical value as the word *tzinor* (pipe). If someone faints, he will be called by his Hebrew name in order to arouse the life force at its source.

Jewish tradition has always insisted on the power of the name. Jewish law forbids man to utter the name of God, the ultimate One, the supreme master, for man is prohibited to enter the essence of the Divine. As incontrovertible evidence for this commandment, orthodox Jews turn to the biblical episode in which Moses asked God to reveal his name so the children of Israel might know whose authority their leader was following. In the account, God refuses Moses, instead giving only an indication of his power: *Ehyeh-Asher-Ehyeh*, I-Am-Who-I-Am, or, according to other interpreters, "I-Am-Who-Brings-into-Being" or even "I Will Be What I Will Be" (Exod. 3:13–14). The condensed form of this name, the Tetragrammaton, YHWH, can only be read by its replacement Adonai (Lord), Elohim (God), or HaShem (the Name). The ineffable name of God must be protected and preserved and is thereby condensed into writing that can only be read in the unending repetition of an unsayable sound.

Just as the Egyptians knew that the essence of the gods resided in the secret power of their name, so the Jews believed that to know the name of God was to assume an intimate knowledge prohibited to man. Man can never presume to know what is reserved for God. To know a name was to have access to a suprahuman power that could result in danger or death. It is also interesting to note that the Hebrew word for "to know" or "knowledge" is also a euphemism for sexual knowledge, suggesting a further taboo associated with the name. To know intimately is to enter into the realm of life's mysteries—the sacred and the taboo, the holy and the profane.

Kabbalistic (or Jewish mystical) thought brings us closer to certain anthropomorphic conceptions and primitive beliefs that we associate with the Ancients. Not only was it believed that each person was named in accordance with his origin or destiny, but it also was accepted that certain unforeseen events could control man's fate.

We can see this in relation to the practice of name-changing that was common in the Middle Ages. A person who was dangerously sick might be advised to change his name in the hope that the angel of death, who was said to summon people by their name, would be confused. This custom, known as *meshanneh shem* (to give a person additional names at any time in his life), became widespread among Ashkenazi Jews. Some names could be temporary and might last until a time of marriage, while others might stick for life. It was also advised that Jews of the same name should not live in the same town or permit their children to marry into one another's families. Men were urged not to marry a woman of the same name as their mother, or the woman was required to change her name, lest the fate of the two women become intertwined. In Russia, as late as the twentieth century, it was considered unlucky for a father-in-law to have the same name as the bridegroom.

A certain leaning toward superstitious beliefs and a naive, perhaps irrational, respect for the unseen and the unknowable clings to the history of my ancestors and my ancestors' ancestors. Superstitious beliefs have trickled down into current traditions. Today, in East European Jewry, when several people have died in a family, a newborn child is named after one of them, a name that is never uttered so as not to give the spirit any opportunity to harm the child. Instead, a nickname is used: "little one" or "old one." The custom of naming a child after a deceased relative is similarly based on a belief that to name a child after a living person might confuse the angel of death, who might mistake the child for the adult and thereby take the wrong person. And to adopt the name of a living relative may also rob the adult of their own unique soul.

Jewish tradition also holds that God inscribes each person's destiny in his record by name. If a person is so critically ill that there is no hope for him or her, a ritual called *shinui hashem* (name change) is performed. A copy of the Holy Scripture is opened at random, and the first name that appears is given to the dying person to replace the old name. If God had determined that person "A" should die, then his decree need not affect the person now called "B." A change of name, a change of fate.

In both Muslim and Jewish traditions, a person experiencing a tragedy in life may ask a religious leader in the community to change their
given name: Their name has become too powerful and cursed; therefore, it must be changed.

I met a man recently who introduced himself as Kirk Rothstein.
Noting the incongruity of an English-sounding first name and a Jewish-
sounding family name, I asked him about it, explaining my interest in
the topic. His explanation was overshadowed by a throwaway comment
as he walked away: "But I have another name, a secret name. When I
was young, I was extremely sick and the doctors were not convinced
that I would survive, so the rabbi gave my parents, who had always
remained secular Jews, another name for me, which to this day I do not
know. It was given to confuse the angel of death, and I guess it worked!"
And in a passage from the book *Divisadero* by Michael Ondaatje, one of
my favorite Canadian writers, I read:

> He was enjoying the man's company, as well as the woman's singing
> in the mornings. Which had come first, he asked, her name, which
> was Aria, or her pleasure in singing? "Who knows," the husband said,
> "she's Romani, they have so many names. The secret name, which is
> never used but is her true name, which only her mother knows, that's
> hidden to confuse supernatural spirits—it keeps the true identity of
> the child from them. And the second name, which is a Roma name,
> is usually used only by them. And that one is Aria."[2]

✼ ✼ ✼

The fact that a person's name was imbued with powerful significance
and contained within it a force essential to one's personality had many
implications, including evil ones. During the Rabbinic period of Baby-
lonian Jewry (70–500 CE), demonology pervaded the thoughts of most
men and women. This was a time when gods, angels, demons, and
spirits hovered and interfered, populating the minds and beliefs of the
living. While some demons were beneficent and helpful, others were
mischievous and malevolent: They inhabited the air and the trees, flew
through the skies, and perched atop houses, frequently hiding in corners and outhouses. No wonder these supernatural beings needed to be
appeased. They could wreak havoc on daily life, creating minor mishaps
and major catastrophes.

Both Gentiles and Jews wanted to be spared the fate of demons, wishing to exorcise ghosts and, especially, to preserve the happiness of their marital life. Both groups believed demons had a particularly ill effect on these matters, and both looked forward to a salvation consisting of good health, sexual satisfaction, and a normal daily life unmarred by inexplicable accidents or bad luck. At that time, no one seems to have enjoyed an abundance of such blessings. Magical incantations patterned after human models of obligation were used in the rituals to counteract these troublesome demons, forcing them to swear vows and oaths and perform the bidding of man.

The Jews, surrounded by the cultural climate of the Persians, whose belief in demons was widespread, were known to have defended themselves against threats from the world of the demonic not only with incantations but also with amulets and prayers, the study of Torah, and an adherence to their faith's commandments. It was believed that demons, not the deities or God, implemented curses activated by people's abused vows or oaths, and that, when a person swore an oath or when a magician conjured up a hostile vow, the demon himself had simultaneously undertaken an oath to carry out the curses. Rabbis, while remaining the religious leaders of their community, were expected to settle disputes and perform judicial duties. It was believed that, by virtue of their knowledge of the Torah and divine names, these "lawyer-magicians"[3] could work miracles, interpret dreams, exorcise demons, compose healing incantations, and manufacture amulets.

It is the rich interplay of culture and sacred writings that influenced the Jews in their conception of and use of names—and thereby influenced naming conventions in the West.

3

GO OUT AND NAME

"People of the Book, that's what we are called," my father often told me when I was growing up. "There is a reason for that, Mavis. The book is our most precious commodity. You can take away our land and our possessions, you can exile us and scatter us in the four directions of the wind, you can transplant us wherever you will, you can strip us of our names, but there is one thing you absolutely cannot do—you cannot take away our knowledge and our laws. To be a Jew is to belong to the world of this text and these writings: the Book of Books. This is our inheritance."

People of the Book—the book carried by the Jewish people, the book memorized in their souls, the book written into their flesh. The book with words that promise survival and longevity. A book written in Hebrew and Aramaic, an ancient tongue no longer spoken. These words embrace and contain the essence of a people used to living in a state of perpetual exile.

The Torah scrolls, the words of the Unnamable One, are dressed in velvet, adorned with filaments of gold embroidery. They dwell in the sanctuary of the ark, the *aron kodesh*. Another *dit-mansion* of words, a dwelling place of the said/spoken; another *bayit* (house), *bayit shel millim* (a house of words).

        * * *

This is the line of descendants from which I trace my roots. My name, Mavis, daughter of Louis and Miriam (Malkah bat Leib v'Miriam), follows a thread, a filament that binds me to this tribe of

men and women wandering in the desert. My lineage flows from the
Ancients: Hebrews, Maccabees, Pharisees. No pure evidence supports
a direct lineal descent from the historic Abraham, son of Terah of the
rediscovered Ur of Sumeria, although many scholars have attempted to
argue this claim.

For example, Dr. Neil Rosenstein, a noted genealogist and author of
The Lurie Legacy, attempts to demonstrate historically that the Lurie
lineage, which includes such luminaries as Sigmund Freud and Martin
Buber, the eleventh-century sage Rashi, and many other revered Jewish
scholars from Hillel to Hezekiah, extends to King David of the tenth
century BCE. In fact, Rosenstein conjectures that this oldest-known
living family, which reads like a celebrity column of prominent historical and contemporary figures (the Prophet Isaiah, Karl Marx, the violin-
ist Yehudi Menuhin, and even the Rothschilds), would possibly connect
most Ashkenazi Jews. My scepticism about such matters predominates.
I would prefer to say that the bond of a common origin based on soil, if
not blood, unites me with fifteen million other people who call themselves Jews.

Twenty years ago, my first readings of the psychoanalyst Jacques
Lacan forced me to consider the enigma of my own beginnings and the
traces of my own ancestral roots. In my first personal psychoanalysis in
the 1970s (a process required in the formation of an analyst), religion
was not a topic for interpretation. An implicit taboo on religion and
politics within analysis at that time, combined with my age and stage of
life, made the immediacy of my issues take precedence over what appeared inconsequential.

In my second analysis, during the 1990s, these matters emerged as
an opening, another point of entry into my past, but one I was not ready
to traverse. But during my third analysis, I chose to open that door and
enter this unfamiliar terrain. It was not religious theology or nationalist
idealism that announced itself in that opening, but a connection to my
Jewish heritage. And it was through the missing letters of my name that
I sought out what my ancestry and my own hidden inheritance, represented by my name, meant to me.

Being Jewish, I came to see more clearly, is about believing in a
world that is consequential and in which all events are infused with
meaning. Religion, after all, is about the inner world, a spiritual sense of
peace and gratitude for the world around us. The outward signs of a

traditionally Jewish life—the close observance of Shabbat, regular synagogue attendance, community prayer—might be signs of religiousness, but then again, might not. *Keva*, the letter of the law, must be balanced with *kavannah*, the intent, the spirit of the practice. To follow most of the commandments of Judaism mechanically for the sake of a required practice without soul and commitment is considered worse than the honest and meaningful establishment of a limited number of practices. Moving one's lips in synagogue so that others may see a devotion to prayer holds less value than the prayer of one who struggles and questions the meaning of prayer.

Being Jewish is also about maintaining a link to a community of wanderers and nomads, tracing one's genealogy to a descendant of one of the Twelve Tribes of Israel. It demands an unwavering connection to a chain of historical events that span over five thousand years. The narrative begins in the valley of Ur in Mesopotamia with the birth of a family: the patriarchs, Abraham, Isaac, and Jacob; the matriarchs, Sarah, Leah, Rachel, and Rebecca; and all of their descendants. And it continues with the birth of a nation, the children of Israel, led by their devoted leader, Moses, out of slavery in Egypt and into the promised land.

Being Jewish means struggling under the weight of this history, both symbolic and real. It demands an accounting of this history whose more recent past in the twentieth century has been filled with horror and genocide, racism and prejudice. A struggle fraught with uncertainty, loneliness, ambiguity, and a concern for survival that is repeated not only through each generation, but within each member of its community. And it acknowledges its instrument of transmission as the family unit, with all of its blemishes and foibles, for, as Rabbi Hartman, the Jewish scholar, reminds us, without parents, there is no Abraham, no covenant, and no Sinai. While my inheritance as a Jew placed me squarely within this heritage, one that was embraced by my parents and grandparents, I chose an alternative route to express my ethnic inheritance: an academic pursuit of anthropology and philosophy, psychology and psychoanalysis, a secular tradition of study and research.

If anything, I had shied away from any association with my ancestral roots. My life, both professionally and personally, eschewed any obvious affiliation as if the outward expression of Judaism had become unacceptable to me. And yet, my ancestral home, the one I carried through my name, repeatedly brought me back. Immersion in my analytic studies further reinforced a distance from any religious roots. Instead, I unabashedly viewed myself as standing in the great tradition of those secular humanists—Walter Benjamin, Franz Kafka, Sigmund Freud—who were to "put themselves positively on the fringe and then to use their fringe position as a declared vantage point to look into the depths of history and the psyche,"[1] as the psychoanalyst David Meghnagi has put it.

All of these writers were products of a process of cultural secularization that had swept through the Jewish world from the late seventeenth century, finding their precursor in the figure of Baruch Spinoza. In all these cases, the position as outsider was turned around and used to break through into novel and revolutionary ways of imagining life.

For Freud personally, the historical and mythical-symbolic dimensions of Judaism were a source of struggle and conflict, as well as an unconscious source of inspiration on his lifework of establishing psychoanalysis as a science. And these influences were not lost on Lacan, whose work is also interspersed with multiple biblical references.

✳ ✳ ✳

But what of this journey of names? What do we know about the history of naming?

Hereditary family names were established in much of Western Europe by the end of the sixteenth century, though in more remote areas, pockets of resistance remained and archaic forms of names continued to spread. Jews and gypsies, the nomadic and the landless, always lived on the margins of Christian society. They had always been exempt from the requirement of a fixed surname. As described above, the Jews traditionally used dual given names: a Hebrew religious name (*shem hakadosh*, or sacred name) for family and communal usage and a non-Jewish name (*shem hakinuim*, or secular name) by which they were known in gentile milieus. The significance of the given name is well ingrained in Judaism. Historically, the chosen given name "connected a Jew of any period with his forebears, his religion, his whole heritage and the Bible,"[2] as Feldbyum writes, resulting in a proliferation of names chosen from the Bible.

Some biblical names, such as Samuel, Joshua, and Eliezer, contain specific references to God, whereas others reflect birth circumstances (Isaac, or "he laughs/will laugh," a reference to Abraham being told he would have a child by his wife Sarah, who was significantly past her child-bearing years); commemorations of an event (Eliezer, or "my God has helped me"); or family relationships (Benjamin or Batsheva, with the prefix *ben* meaning son and *bat* meaning daughter).

Gradually, given names were replaced by post-biblical names of Semitic origin, a few appellations of Greek origin, and modifications of names reflecting the host culture. Beginning in the mid-nineteenth century, Christian names began replacing Hebrew names: Arnold for Aron and Leon for Leyb. The custom of naming children after deceased relatives had already existed by the Middle Ages and has continued, either as the first or second name, over the centuries.

Until the emancipation of the Jews in the late eighteenth century, most Jews used the traditional system of patronymics noted above in terms of European names in general—that is, the first name followed by *ben-* (son of), *bar-* (son of, in Aramaic), or *bat-* (daughter of) and then the father's name—to indicate ancestry and birth history.

The period from the eighteenth to the twentieth centuries saw tremendous changes in naming laws for Jews, with a cascading effect in the various Eastern and Central European countries, as well as in Russia. Beginning with the decree *Das Patent über die Judennamen*, issued on July 23, 1787, by Franz Josef II, emperor of the Austro-Hungarian Empire, Jews living under his reign were required to acquire a surname. Initially this decree stipulated that family names were to be assigned from a list of German names; a prior decree had also limited Jews of this region to choose personal names from a list of 123 male and 31 female names. In an attempt to easily identify the Jews from the rest of the population, these names were mainly German forms of biblical names, a small number of German Christian names, and a few Yiddish appellations. Resistance to this legislation was led by middle-class Jews in Prague who wanted to give German names to their children. In 1836 a new law permitted the choosing of any German name but prohibited name changes. With the proclamation of a general civic rights law in December 1867, all naming restrictions came to an end.

Only in the early nineteenth century, through the Napoleonic decree of July 20, 1808, and with Napoleon's victory marches through Russia, Poland, and Germany, were Jews living in lands west of the Rhine required by law to acquire surnames. Whether names were adopted or imposed on this community is still unclear. A known example is the family history of Ludwig Wittgenstein, the renowned Austrian philosopher. Ludwig's great-great-grandfather Meyer Moses had a son named Moses Maier (alternate spellings: Maier, Meyer) who became a steward, or land agent, for the aristocratic Seyn-Wittgenstein family in the county of Wittgenstein in Westphalia, Germany. Moses Maier, Ludwig's great-grandfather, later married Brendel (alternate spellings: Breindel or Bernadine) Simon and built up a large trading business. In compliance with the Napoleonic decree, he took the name of Wittgenstein.

In Central and Eastern Europe, many patronymics were frozen into second names with the addition of suffixes (Mendelson, Levinson, Silverman). Surnames, bought from the state, emerged from a variety of sources: from rabbinical surnames, toponyms (place names), occupations, and personal characteristics. Names were also foisted on others by impatient and intimidating officials incapable of decoding difficult- and foreign-sounding names. Those who were unable to pay for their name were assigned names of an undesirable nature: Klutz (clumsy), Billig (cheap), Beckmesser (knife beak), or Drek (shit).

Many Jewish surnames were German compounds. The first part was sometimes based on nature, such as flora and fauna: Apfel (apple) and Blum (flower); or metals: Silber (silver) and Kupfer (copper); or the heavens: Licht (light) and Stern (star); or colors: Braun (brown) and Schwartz (black). The second parts included topographical terms, such as Berg (mountain), Feld (field), or Stein (stone); habitations, such as Haus (house) and Heim (home); or words related to plants, such as Baum (tree) or Zveig (branch). Variations of these patterns existed in other Jewish communities in other parts of Europe as well.

The acquisition of certain surnames served the interests of the state by presenting the Jews as an assimilated population. In many cases, names sounded similar irrespective of religious affiliation. Names ending in topographical and toponyms sometimes coincided with place names in Central Europe and surnames of nobility who owned the localities, such as Grunberg, Rosenberg, or Rosenthal.

At the end of the eighteenth century, with the various partitions of Poland and a steady stream of anti-Jewish laws, Russia acquired a large Jewish population. In 1791 czar Catherine II the Great established a territory for Russian Jews to live. Created under pressure to rid Moscow of the business competition of the Jews and its evil influence on the

Russian masses, the Pale of Settlement, as it was called, included the territory of present-day Poland, Latvia, Lithuania, Ukraine, and Belorussia. More than 90 percent of Russian Jews were forced to live in the poor conditions of the Pale from 1835 to 1917. With the establishment of the Pale, legislation was passed demanding Jews retain a hereditary or assumed family name without change. To comply with state demands, authorities within the communities quickly created special naming patterns. In the region of Belarus, one-third of names were created by adding the suffix *-in* to female given names (Dvorkin, Malkin, Shifrin); in northern Ukraine, nearly half of the names ended in *-man* (Silverman); and in many other places, names were based on place names ending in *-ski* (Chepelevski, Albertinski).

In the French republic, a letter from an irritated bureaucrat to a prefect prompted an imperial decree of July 1808 requiring all Jews to adopt and declare a fixed first and second name. In the same year, the French mayor of Metz, exasperated with trying to regulate the *état civil*, wrote: "Nothing is more common . . . than to find a son bearing a different surname from his father, a brother from a brother, and to discover individuals having but one name decide to take another . . . But this is nothing compared to the situation of women: at least half of them do not know themselves what their real names are, and it is not possible to establish that they really have second names."[3]

And so, like dominoes falling, the same legislation regarding naming was imposed by the governments of Austria, Prussia, and Russia, as well as those in Western Europe, as part of their regulation of their Jewish population. However, in certain countries (e.g., France, Prussia), this was accompanied by a degree of emancipation and forced modernization.

* * *

The Bible provided Western civilization with a template for the act of naming. As many thinkers and scholars have pointed out, humankind's naming mimics God's act of creating. Made in the image of God, man creates and names. In the first version of the creation story, found in Genesis 1, the universe is called into being by the force and power of words. God conceived the universe and all of its animate and inanimate creatures by invoking a series of letters into which he blew life, fashioning the design of life.

Bereshit bara Elohim et ha'shamayim v'et ha'aretz. "In the beginning, God created heaven and earth." Bold and lucid words. A calling forth into existence. Through these acts of speech, life not only was produced but also was sustained. The voice names and a world of life is brought into existence. In the words of one Torah commentary, "God said: and the divine word shatters the primal cosmic silence and signals the birth of a new cosmic order."[4] From the utterance "Let there be . . . ," the universe was born.

In his founding acts, God calls forth light; then the sky; then dry land, with its vegetation; then the luminaries; then the fish and fowl; then the land creatures, including humankind, of whom it is said in verse 27: "And God created man in His image, in the image of God He created him; male and female He created them." Man and woman appear as the last creatures after all the other animals have appeared on earth. Man and woman share in the bounty of the garden and its creatures, as God commands them to be fruitful and multiply and rule over the animals: "Be fertile and increase, fill the earth and master it; and rule the fish of the sea, the birds of the sky, and all the living things that creep on earth."

And in the second version of the creation story, found in Genesis 2, God gives man the opportunity to name. One possible reading suggests that because man had been created alone, God, all-knowing and considerate father figure that he is, reevaluated his decision and recognized that he had made a grave mistake. In order that man not be isolated and lonely, he decided to assign man a helper. And so we read:

> The Lord God said, "It is not good for man to be alone: I will make a fitting helper for him." And the Lord God formed out of the earth all the wild beasts and all the birds of the sky, and brought them to the man to see what he would call them; and whatever the man called each living creature, that would be its name. And the man gave names to all the cattle and to the birds of the sky and to all the wild beasts . . . (Gen. 2:18–20)

Beginning with the naming of common objects (plants, animal, stars), we move to the proper name that follows the birth of man: Adam - Adamah - Adam. Man - Earth - Adam. And these words are the rem(a)inder of man's connection to the dust of the earth from which he was born.

The Bible further captures the significance of naming throughout its text with multiple references to divine names, place names, and generational names. We only have to flip a few pages in Genesis to see the repeated catalogues of names. For example, we have the genealogy of Cain followed by the lines of his siblings:

> Cain knew his wife, and she conceived and bore Enoch. And then he founded a city, and named the city after his son Enoch. To Enoch was born Irad, and Irad begot Mehujahel, and Mehujael begot Methusael, and Methusael begot Lamech. Lamech took to himself two wives: the name of the one was Adah, and the name of the other was Zillah. Adah bore Jabal; he was the ancestor of those who dwell in tents and amidst herds. And the name of his brother was Jubal; he was the ancestor of all who play the lyre and pipe. As for Zillah, she bore Tubal-cain, who forged all implements of copper and iron. And the sister of Tubal-cain was Naameh. (Gen. 4:17–22)

Or, in Genesis 10, after the flood and after the death of Noah 350 years later, we have what is referred to as the Table of Nations, a listing of the genealogy of nations, long lines of descendants marching through the pages of the text—the branching out of the world from Noah's three sons:

> These are the lines of Shem, Ham, and Japheth, the sons of Noah: sons were born to them after the Flood. The descendants of Japheth: Gomer, Magog, Madai, Javan, Tubal, Mescech, and Tiras. The descendants of Gomer: Ashkenaz, Ripath, and Togarmah. The descendant of Javan: Elishah and Tarshish, the Kittim, and the Dodanim. From these the maritime nations branched out. These are the descendants of Japheth by their lands—each with its language—their clans and their nations. (Gen. 10:1–5)

And then there are the biblical names that mark the transition from a polytheistic to a monotheistic universe. Names of the patriarchs and matriarchs that recall the first families of a people roaming in the Land of Ur: Abraham, Isaac, and Jacob; Sarah, Rebecca, Rachel, and Leah. Names revered and blessed, hallowed and honored.

And from the line of Isaac/Israel we recall the twelve tribes: Reuben, Simeon, Levi, Dan, Naphtali, Gad, Asher, Judah, Issachar, Zebulun,

Joseph, and Benjamin. And from Judah descends beloved King David, son of Jesse. And from them, all of the descendants that follow.

In the New Testament, we find the following list:

> And when day came, he called his disciples and chose from them twelve, whom he named apostles: Simon, whom he named Peter, and Andrew his brother, and James and John, and Philip, and Bartholomew, and Matthew, and Thomas, and James the son of Alphaeus, and Simon who was called the Zealot, and Judas the son of James, and Judas Iscariot, who became a traitor. (Luke 6:13)

These universal names, the echoes of which are recounted in our stories and passed on to our children and grandchildren and our grandchildren's children, provide the backdrop against which Western civilization developed. Timeless names. Names without end that wrap themselves around us, entwine us with their power, their graven images and their divination. Names that infiltrate our worlds of letters, of music, and of visual representation. And following in the footsteps of God, historical man repeats this pattern of naming, obeying this dictum and casting his powers of nomination over a broad spectrum.

Man builds and names his buildings, his towers, his castles, and his industrial complexes: the John P. Robarts Research Library (Toronto), Parc Güell (Barcelona), the Eiffel Tower (Paris), the Dwight D. Eisenhower Memorial (Los Angeles), the Michael Lee-Chin Crystal (Toronto).

Man creates and names his sculptures, his paintings and sketches, his symphonies and concertos, his ballets, and his books: Rodin's Thinker, Beethoven's Fifth, Balanchine's Pas de Deux.

Man discovers and names his sea passages and inlets, his expeditions, and his islands: the Bering Strait, the Byng Inlet, the Franklin Expedition. Man invents and names his innovations, his technological advances, his diseases, his medicinal remedies and surgical developments: the Barr-Epstein virus, Tommy John surgery, the Salk vaccine, Asperger's syndrome.

Of course, in terms of the Jews, it was not just their sacred scriptures and the cultures around them that informed their naming practices; it was also their constant journeys from place to place, sometimes chosen by them, other times forced on them.

4

NAMES AND NOMADS

In the desert my dreams feature vast, open spaces, infinite stillness, boundless horizons. Sand sliding between my toes and light filtering through my closed eyes.

The sun burns my arms as I move through the desert heat. A trail of nomads, mere specks on the earth's surface. I stop and collapse, exhausted. I force myself to get up and move on. Where am I going? For what am I searching? All I know is that I am propelled by an insatiable urge to keep moving, as if by my movement I will find what I am seeking. Stillness thunders in my ears. Then the booming command: *Keep moving, do not stop* . . . I awaken. I am in my bed.

The magnificent Sinai wilderness is the only desert I cherish.

Sinai, the birthplace of the three desert religions: Judaism, Christianity, and Islam. The birthplace of the founding myth of a culture of Semitic peoples.

It was in this desert that the God of the Jews, the God of the Christians, and the God of the Muslims—a common God—revealed himself. In the shifting sands under the heat of the desert where human frailty and human limitations were most exposed, God first appeared to Abraham, the founding father of all three desert religions And it was in the desert where the Torah was given, first orally and then inscribed in tablets.

And it is here in Sinai that one group of Semitic people wandered for forty years while Moses, their leader, ascended Mount Sinai to speak to their God and receive the oral commandments. Angry, belligerent, truculent, frustrated, this small tribe refused the faith they had been asked to keep. Instead they turned to the worship of a golden mammal, the icon of a calf around which they danced and sang, refusing to believe their leader or to acknowledge the power of an invisible god. A band of men and women forced to explore, to endure, the mystery of the desert. And when their leader descended carrying the words of the Laws, which had been inscribed on stone tablets, he flung these on the windswept sand, smashing the precious words. And the people of the desert were given another chance to accept the word of their leader. And after this second journey up the mountain did their hero return to them, once again bearing the tablets with inscriptions of the Written Law, the Ten Commandments.

If my name is the home in which I reside, then Sinai with its rich history is my name's ancestral landscape, the place where the letters of those first words were inscribed. In this home sleep the ancestral memories of a forty-year trek through the desert, and the insinuation of my Hebrew name returns me there.

We were a few miles from Dahab, a Bedouin village on the Gulf of Aqaba, returning from an inland trip. The sun was hot between my shoulders; my skin was deep amber. I approached the desert with dry lips. Sand crept into my backpack, hid in my pockets and sleeping bag. I had become an Israelite roaming in the desert, returning to the landscape of my ancestors. Once again I had become that nomad searching in the sand for my ancestral inscriptions.

"Malkah, Malkah, we have arrived," says our guide. "Look over there. See those green palms? That's it, over there."

In this massive terrain of aridity, I had slid through copper-tinged canyon walls and scampered up mountain trails; I had awoken under a canopy of stars and watched a globe of fire paint red streaks across the sky; I had been tickled by the sands of a *chamsin* and purged of all desire to speak. I had rappelled down sheer cliffs and bathed in pools of mountain-fed water; I had walked miles by foot and been jostled and jiggled by the humps of a camel seat, my legs scratched by a rough woolen blanket. I had imbibed the golden radiance of a sunrise, and I had sipped tea from stained glasses in the tents of Bedouin.

Impermanence was the signature of this lunar landscape, with its parched soil and brooding rocks. My feet left prints, imprints, footprints, quickly erased by the shifting sands. But was there something of a trace? The outline of my footprints, my markings inscribed in their particularity? Perhaps the traces of my search had been added to all those who had gone before. After all, my ancestral history was tied to these fragments, these traces of a presence, these overblown marks in the desert sands.

"Lie down and listen to the sound of the desert," the guide had whispered. "Listen with your whole spirit, not just your ears. Listen to the sounds around you."

Jews. The wanderers, the tribesmen. The Twelve Tribes of Israel. The list of names of a people exiled from their land. Throughout their history it has always been a belief in words, the words of God, that carried this band of migrants across the desert sands. Trials and tribulations hindered their course of action, but they persisted in their journey.

Nomads. Gypsies. Names to describe groups of roving people without a home. Races of traces and footprints left behind. As the poet Jabès reminds us, born of exile and survival, the Jew carries the book in his head, memorizing the traces of the law.

Ancient Mesopotamia, this piece of land in the southern half of modern-day Iraq, was once home of the greatest civilization known to man in the Middle Bronze Age. The civilization, known today as Sumer, spilled over the headwaters of the Persian Gulf and consisted of a cluster of city-states that were sometimes united, or federated, and at other times antagonistic. A rich culture of barter, trade, and agriculture, these people produced generations of scribes, priests, soldiers, magicians, jewelers, and potters, among other professions. Clan loyalties and tribal rivalries precipitated intervention from neighboring Akkadians, Babylonians, Assyrians, and much later Persians, Greeks, and Romans. Their scribes were the precursors of modern-day script, replacing the earlier pictographs, whereby symbols were used to represent words, with wedge-shaped letters. Their religion dictated the erection of a pantheon of deities with towers honoring the gods of the air, earth, sky, and water.

In the heart of this rich region, bounded by the Persian Gulf and the mountains of Armenia, by the Iranian plateau and the Syrian desert, was Ur, the Sumerian capital. As the Jewish scholar Charles Raddock writes, "And here, then, within the shadow of a ziggurat tower that rose up from a moon-god temple dominating the city, the first Jew was born—physical and spiritual progenitor of the Jewish People, according to the ancient chronicles, which cite his birthplace as Ur Khasidim, in the valley of the Chaldees."[1]

This time, on a second trip, I was trekking farther south through the parched wilderness. I was returning to the exact place where the Book of Books had its beginning. A group of eight Israeli nomads, two Bedouin, one Canadian, and four camels exploring the desert landscape, a sandy wasteland that stretched out into infinity. I inhaled a timelessness that expanded into perpetuity.

It is the sixth day of my trek, which began at the mouth of a great wadi (dry riverbed) near Ain Hudera. Our band of travelers has been roaming through the sandy and stony wilderness of the plateau of Badiet el Tih, the "Wilderness of Wandering." In this area, south of a sandstone belt of turquoise and copper, miners of the Pharaonic period had once crossed paths with the pilgrims and monks attracted to the "heavenly Sinai." As I gain consciousness of the day, I rub my eyes in the still darkness. Each morning, until now, I have risen to face the east, where sunrise turns the variegated sandstone sculptures of this region into an array of gold and copper, reminding me of a palette of Jerusalem stone.

Our guide awakens us at 4:00 a.m. The frigid air seeps into my bones as I slip out of my sleeping bag and into my woolly sweater—from one warm cocoon into another. The tent is pitched several hundred meters away from the famous Saint Catherine's Monastery at the foot of Mount Moses.

This monastery was built under the order of the Byzantine emperor Justinian I in the sixth century CE to commemorate the site where Moses (Prophet Musa) talked to God in the miracle of the Burning Bush. Today monks continue to practice this heritage that extends from the giving of the Law, through the whole of the Old and New Testaments, to the multitude of saints whose memory has been enshrined at Sinai—above all, to the All-Holy Theotokos, the holy prophets Moses and Elias, and Saint Catherine.

It was in this region, then Upper Egypt, that Coptic monks traveled to the sandy and stony deserts of the southern Sinai Peninsula to lead a strictly ascetic life in extreme seclusion from the world, in line with the *consilia evangelica*. These counsels—absolute poverty, celibacy, and unconditional obedience—were taken seriously by those who wished to attain perfection in this life and the life thereafter as based on the Christian gospels.

Turning their back on the world, these hermits settled in the valleys and on the slopes of the inaccessible Sinai mountains in the south, founding small colonies of monks, living in little hand-built huts or caves fashioned out of the rock. In time, these scattered hermitages were joined by other monastic communities under the leadership of an abbot who kept vigilance and ensured strict adherence to the rules of monastic life.

This morning we are about to ascend Mount Sinai, the biblical Mount Horeb, known locally as Jebel Musa, where Moses is said to have received the Ten Commandments. We are eager to begin our ascent before the great solar disc paints the mountaintops in shades of red and orange. The climb is gradual until the final phase, where the necessity of doing nothing but put one foot in front of the other dictates our pace. Finally we arrive and settle on a rugged platform, like an audience in a high-altitude amphitheater awaiting the spectacle. We wait and we are not disappointed—the brilliance of sunrise on top of the world.

As we make our descent and retrieve our steps along the desert trail, I am reminded of Abraham's story, the story of a lone traveler making his way along the Euphrates River from Ur north to Haran, followed by a series of multiple wanderings. And it continues with another epic adventure of the region: the great Exodus from Egyptian bondage and slavery to freedom and liberation, the story of an entire nation of twelve Israelite tribes making their way to a new land.

In speaking with my guide, I learn that the words *Arab* and *Hebrew* are thought to share a similar root related to being nomadic. In the history of Arabic people in the pre-Islamic world, nomads roamed the Arabian desert under the guidance of those who knew the path. They understood the promise that awaited them at the next oasis and lived with the reality of that losing one's way meant aimless wandering. Men and women followed the lead of an elder of the family, the *shaykh*, who moved a herd from one oasis to the next. The unity of the family was necessary not only to avoid the possibility of getting lost, but also to protect the clan from inevitable raids, *ghazwa*, ubiquitous to Arabian society.

The shared nomadic origins of these two distinct but closely related peoples are easily forgotten in today's political climate.

❊ ❊ ❊

And so began my linguistic excursion into the world of nomads and nomadology, words and etymology. A journey that provided a compelling perspective for considering the origins of the term *name* that may add another dimension to the fixed designation of the proper name. First I wish to set the scene for this speculative journey that I call the shifting nomadic signifier. In fact, I owe these hypothetical comments to a friend and colleague, Claude Rabant, a psychoanalyst in Paris, who first introduced this notion as a sidebar at a presentation he was giving on the Unconscious.

Etymology is history's classroom. Etymological details, the documentation of word formations and development, provide clues and hints to the unfolding of the life history of word meanings. The original traces of a word's source lead to a primary wellspring of information about the growth of words, in particular the etymological history of the words *nomas* and *nomen*, both of which are related to the word "name," which in its Latin equivalent includes two possible chains—*nomen* and *nomos*—the former being the more typical.

Let us begin with nomadology. What do we know about nomadic life? Our ancestral predecessors, *Homo erectus* and, even later, *Homo sapiens*, were original naturalists. Living and subsisting by their aptitude and cunning, they foraged for wild food—eggs, nuts, fruits and vegetables, animal carcasses, and seafood—and uprooted themselves once supplies were depleted. Initially autonomous and self-sufficient, early man banded together and roamed the inhabitable lands of the earth's terrain in small groups. These hunter-gatherers, the itinerant wanderers of the Paleolithic era, were forever on the move wherever food and shelter beckoned. This pattern remained unchanged until ten thousand years ago.

The first human revolution, the Neolithic, so coined in 1920 by Vere Gordon Childe, an archaeologist and philologist, was a muted transformation in the evolution of man's development. It was not noisy or loud, obtrusive or brash, but nevertheless it radicalized man's relationship to the elements. The unprecedented development of emerging agricultural practices created a stir in the mode of survival in primitive man.

Embryonic agricultural practices were adopted and refined in an expanding network of communities.

Gradually the mappable landscape of early man spread into various areas, including parts of the Middle East, Asia, Mesoamerica, and the Andes, beginning as early as ten thousand years ago. Domesticated plants and animals were identified and named, while local culture incorporated the harvesting, breeding, and consumption of local species.

Today, thirty to forty million nomads redistribute and reposition themselves annually in small communities around the globe, preferring a lifestyle of movement rather than one of permanent settlement. Nomadic hunting and gathering, based on seasonal change and availability, is the grandfather of contemporary nomadic, subsistence living. Pastoralists confine themselves to certain areas but move through wet and dry seasons with their livestock as resources are depleted and replenished. These pastoral nomads trace their roots to the southern Levant, forebears of societies in the Sinai desert. Peripatetic nomads, on the other hand, typified by the Gitanes or other Roma clans, ply their trades and crafts for those with whom they come into contact through their travels, setting up camps within urban centers and industrialized countries.

So how do nomads figure into this labyrinth of word meanings? The word "nomad" is another cousin of the Latin word *nomos*. Etymology paints a convincing canvas for us. Nomads circulated in tribes and therefore were required to share territories with other tribes, which eventually led to the necessity of usage rights. This is my land, this is yours; this is the boundary between what is yours and what is mine. And so begins the establishment of a framework of law, or *nomos*.

In the beginning, I imagine tokens or traits of some kind to denominate space as mine and yours. I visualize bearded men on camels or donkeys approaching a gathering of tents. The elder male, hearing the sounds of rustling and movement by his own animals, emerges from the protection of his tent and with trepidation greets the newcomer. Words are exchanged; tea is offered or refused, granted or withdrawn. To avoid a constant degeneration into discord and conflict over boundaries and limits of land usage, these tribes needed the intercession of someone who knew the law and had a capacity to judge, a man (or woman) who knew the law (*nomos*), who could judge (*nomezo*), and who had knowledge (*gnosis*) to make decisions regarding land usages. This person, the judge, was then in a position to mete out decisions regarding property and land claims.

For this system to work, however, a name (*nomen*) was required. This name would be the mark, the signifier, that would identify mine from yours or his. This name would represent a certain cut or incision creating a division—a cut of identification as well as a cut that establishes a boundary. This land, named "A," belongs to me and is my land; that land, named "B," belongs to you and is your land. It has now been inscribed by a law that has been decided by a judge who knows about these things. This process of naming and inscribing into law established a legal order among the tribal groups. In fact, all of these terms share a common base root, *nem-*, which has to do with pastures (*nemein* means "put to pasture"), land allotment, and the dispensing of justice.

If we pull on the other etymological thread, we find that the English word "name" derives from the Old English *nama*, or *noma*, meaning "name" or "reputation," and is equivalent to the French *nom* from the Latin word *nomen* and the Greek word *onoma, onyma*. This family of words slides from the Greek word *gnomikos* back to *gnome* ("thought, opinion, maxim, or intelligence"), the root of which is *giginoskein*, "to come to know." By one's name or reputation, we come to know someone. From *nomen*, we derive nomenclature, nomination, and cognomen—all of which contain the seed word *nama* (or *nomen* in Latin). From *nomos*, Greek for "law" or "custom," we derive the concept of law developed in ancient Greek philosophy.

Similarly, the English word "nomad" slides backwards in time from its Middle French derivative *nomade*, to its Latin precursor *nomas, nomadis* ("wandering groups"), to its earliest source in the Greek word *nomas*, a sibling of the Latin *nomos*. So *nomos*, the human law of convention (to be distinguished from *physis*, the Greek term for the natural set of laws), shares with the root of *nomas*, the nomad, the common root *nem-*. This places it in proximity and contiguity with division and distribution, while *nomen*, with its rootedness in *gnome*, meaning "thought and knowledge," slips seamlessly from one to the other.

❋ ❋ ❋

I asked my friend Deborah about how Hebrew words might link to any of these terms. Our friendship goes back to our high school days. Different intellectual orientations and interests have separated our paths, but an appreciation of the power of speech and dialogue continues to unite us. She is a wise woman who holds mystery and a mystical sense of the divine close to her heart and her soul.

She responded with a smile of *sagesse*. "I speak something; I create something by my speaking. Too much speaking puts us in the desert since wisdom is also the silence within." The desert, this vast landscape, entails a journey into wilderness, a place of silence and stillness devoid of any-thing; yet to speak is to affirm or say some-thing. To speak is to create and to bring into existence.

The Hebrew language is based on a very structured system whereby each word contains a basic root structure of three consonants. A nomad is a *navad* who wanders (*noded*), with these two words sharing the same root *nun-aleph-daled*, or *nod* (migration). More interesting is the emergence of the word *midbar* (desert) from the verb *daber*, meaning to speak, closely related to *davar*, which means both "word" and "thing."

The Jews wandered in the desert. Idle chatter and the desert's silence was broken when they were "spoken to": Here are the commandments transmitted from God to Moses and then to the people. Here are the words of the Law, the inheritance which you shall carry forward from this place of wandering.

And the people responded and affirmed their connection to their God: Yes, we shall obey your commandments.

In a delightful book on Jewish journeys, Jeremy Leigh points out that, having left the vice of Egyptian stronghold and slavery "on their way to adopting a monotheistic and legal culture, the Jews needed to travel through a place of speaking in order to transform themselves."[2] The desert represents this transformative journey, and the trek through this no-man's-land of silence and speech is told and retold every year at the annual seder on the first night of the holiday of Passover.

We have names because we were nomads, suggests the poet Jabès, and because we have names, we will become nomads again. Paraphrasing these words, we can say: "The name continues the trek. Each name conveys the memories of those who went before and of those who will follow."

* * *

Oral tradition—that is, the recording and transmitting of oral history, oral law, oral literature, and other knowledge across generations—developed prior to the practice of the written word. Storytelling, its stepchild, is the combination of words and images, song and poetry, performed through improvisation, to communicate past events. We are familiar with this activity of passing on life stories and histories through fairy tales, the once-upon-a-time world of nowhere in particular, and the legends based on the transmission and embellishment of actual events; the stories based on the experiences of storytellers who have gone abroad and those who have stayed at home; tales of "the resident tiller of the soil" and "the trading seaman"; and, finally, the improvisational theater of stories that constitute the modern-day version of storytelling.

Family history is the birthplace of oral tradition and history. We all need and rely on a past and a memory to invoke the individual reminiscences of our own life. We carry our past in our pockets like nomads who carry with them the articles of their daily rituals. Narratives and folktales, family myths and secrets—these are the envelopes of legends we transmit to succeeding generations. Early man who lived in clans and tribes relied on an oral history that only later became documented. Only with the passage of time did the passing on of family and life histories become a written record through documentation and paperwork, a record that would be added to the treasure chest of family heirlooms and keepsakes.

5

CHOOSING NAMES

The proper name in most Western societies is composed of the given name, the middle name, and the surname (the reverse of the Eastern formulation of family name then given name). The given name is the *donato*, the gift or the given. This first, or given, name marks our singularity and particularity. Well before the newborn's arrival, parents along with friends and relatives will debate over the most fitting or desired name. Arguments ensue: Shall it be my mother's or your sister's middle name? Whom do we honor—Uncle Sammy or your cousin Theodore? I want to name my daughter Liza after Elizabeth Taylor or Ginny after Virginia Woolf. We will name our son after his uncle who is athletic and strong so that he may reflect these qualities; no, we will name our child after dear grandpa.

In many cases, tradition overrides personal choice. In certain cultures, names of the deceased are passed on to newborns; in others, words of title, such as Junior or Senior, are appended to mark the lineage. And in First Nations cultures, naming is selected by tribal elders who dream the names to be given to the newly born.

I met a woman who told me the story of her neighbor, a father-to-be who had been very concerned about the permanence of the name he was planning to give his child. Knowing it would be a son, he insisted there were three situations, each requiring the use of the name, that had to be considered in the selection process:

Can Zebedee come out and play?

Will we give the job to Theobald?

I want to marry Clothilde.

This man ended up naming his twin sons Robert and James. His sons, now in their thirties, have been blessed with good fortune, which he attributes to their "perfect" names. His questions point directly to the implicitly magical or prophetic associations we develop in relation to names and naming.

A recent radio broadcast discussed the pros and cons of naming children with double first names such as Jim James, Leslie Carroll, Bob Dylan, John Evan, Lyle Stewart, Susan Charmaine, or Peter Gabriel. The researchers concluded that this kind of naming created confusion and unnecessary and repeated questioning for the children.

Another study, carried out by an American Ivy League university and reported on the radio, mentioned the findings of university acceptance based on names. They determined that certain traditional-sounding North American names were more likely to lead to an admission over those that were either less conventional or sounded foreign.

Some parents—wittingly or not—have inflicted suffering on their children by giving them bizarre, unusual, or difficult-sounding names. As a colleague said to me, "Some parents do awful things to their children—imagine having to go through life with the name Honeysuckle, Lee Lee, Memphis, or Savion."

While the contemporary trend is to name children with more exotic or unique names than in the past, it can sometimes be too much for a young child to handle. A boy whose parents chose the name Arielle for him finally changed his name to John after constant teasing at school.

I remember the summer I worked at Expo '67 in Montreal selling postcards and tourist trinkets at an outdoor booth. All employees were required to wear nametags to help create an atmosphere of familiarity and informality. One day a gentleman, after staring curiously at my nametag, asked if Mavis was my given name or my surname, adding, "I wonder why your parents hated you." I laughed awkwardly but was startled by his comment. One friend later said, "Maybe he was staring at your chest and disliked what he saw!"

* * *

While we have moved away from certain older traditions that once imbued the name with a certain sanctity and power, the psychological resonances of the proper name inevitably linger within each of us. The close association we develop between our name and the person we are becomes inextricably intertwined over time. Seemingly innocuous when first given, the name takes on a life of its own once put into circulation from birth. Even seemingly frivolous names still carry a psychic weight and expand over time, for the sound of our name reverberates deep within us.

After all, our name, for better or worse, is our escort through life. No name, no history. The recording of human history is wrapped in a narrative that bears a collection of names. The name ensures each human being a place in life that extends beyond our pure biology and that travels forwards and backwards in our universal saga.

While the first name is more flexible and reflects personal, cultural, or religious practices, the surname is a fixed form, whether patrilineal or matrilineal. This is the name that guarantees each of us a place of honor in our family tree. It is a link to both a particular family and to a family within a larger community with roots that twist and turn backwards in time. Our ancestral name links us to our past and to the history of our family.

In the vast majority of cases, the surname or family name is also a geographical and/or ethnic marker. If we read a list of names, we can frequently yoke the names with their nationality, their geographical marker. For example: O'Reilly, O'Henry. MacLeod, McAlastair, Mac-Cutcheon. Van Deusen, Van der Meer, Vanderbilt, Van Brunt. Diamontopolous, Angelopoulous, Pappadakas. Manoukian, Atchabahian, Istamboulian. Wong, Chung, Yiang. Suyin, Shen, Suzuki. Takamura, Yamamoto. Rossi, De Lucca, Romano. Vasilyev, Romanov, Mikhailov.

Similarly, we can also identify ethnic origins by surname: Rabinovitch, Goldstein, Rothman. Abdullah, El-Gazzawy, Mohammed, Bannerjee, Pradapati, Singh.

Reflexively, we make assumptions about people's ethnic or religious attachment based on the sound of their names. Regrettably, our automatic reactions have led to discrimination and prejudice in the workplace, in educational institutions, and in the political sphere. The tradition of name change associated with marriage in our patrilineal society is an accepted cultural convention. In large urban centers, like New York or Toronto, where interracial marriages are more common, assumptions based on our associations of names leads to unanticipated encounters. We are surprised to encounter a Caucasian woman with the name Marilyn Wong or Susan Obasanjo or when we greet an Asian man with the name Jason Wong.

Unfortunately, some surnames carry undesirable meanings in a language, lending themselves nasty teasing: Shelley Gross, Jennifer Bland, Jeffrey Shmuckles, Jonathan Cox. All of us remember how cruel our classmates could be in verbal teasing and name-calling. *Mavis Heinz and Johnnie Weiner* is a phrase I recall; even writing it today makes me cringe.

A woman once told me there was no end to the name-calling she experienced in grade school with her surname, Lips: from Hot Lips and Wet Lips to Miss Kissy-Kissy and Miss Smoochy. She cried for a year trying to persuade her parents to change their name. Another friend told me he knew that in his grade school there was a boy of African descent who, whether affectionately or mean-spiritedly, was cajoled endlessly by children in all of his classes because of his surname, Blackman. He apparently would laugh along with the others as a way of shielding himself from pain. Recently, I met a woman whose surname Makelove made me wonder what kind of torment she endured in adolescence.

Middle names, a slightly later invention in the West, include one or more names. The North American tradition includes the option of either appending an additional first name or an additional surname (e.g., Edward Michael Winters or Charles Walker Humphreys). In some families, middle names are chosen to reflect a mother's maiden name or the name of a deceased family member (e.g., Margaret Darby Chatsworth).

The other term often heard in reference to names and naming is the patronym (or patronymic), a personal name based on the given name of one's father, grandfather, or even earlier male ancestor. In certain societies, this would be a matronym (or matronymic), based on the name of one's mother or a female ancestor. Today, patronyms have largely been replaced or transformed into patronymic surnames, although they are still used, even mandatorily, in many countries. For example, the prince of Saudi Arabia, Abdul Aziz bin Fahd bin Abdul Aziz Al Saud, is the son of the late King Fahd from the House of Saud and Al Jawhara bint Ibrahim Al Ibrahim, from the wealthy house of Al-Ibrahim. His wife's name is Al Anoud bint Faisal bin Mishaal Al Saud. In all these cases, the individual is clearly identified by both parents through the blending of patronyms and matronyms, a practice typical in many Muslim countries of the Middle East.

* * *

The name is so much part of ourselves, so much taken for granted, that it is only when our name is mispronounced or misspelt that we find a knee-jerk reactivity to such occurrences. We may be outraged or annoyed, amused or incensed, depending on the perceived ease of enunciation. But we always react and respond with the correction immediately at hand.

My colleague Ron Charach (pronounced sha-RACK) once wrote an article published in the *Toronto Star* about the typical errors he experienced as a child in the pronunciation and spelling of his name. Given the unusual combination of two identical diphthongs (*ch*) in his name, one at the beginning and one at the end, with each pronounced differently, he constantly had to correct his teachers and others who automatically spelled his name with a *Sh* instead of a *Ch*.

I was seated beside a woman at a social function once whose nametag read F-E-L-I-E-S. I must have looked perplexed, because she said, "It's pronounced Phyllis; my Hungarian parents invented this unique spelling of my name." She told me that people commonly pronounced it fe-LEESE or FEL-is. To this day, when asked for her name to be recorded on a form or document, she automatically sounds it out: F as in Fancy, E, L as in Lisa, I, E, S like in Sam. "This is the same phrase I have been using since grade school," she said. "It just rolls off my tongue."

For those with foreign-sounding or uncommon names, or names that challenge the dialect of the local population, mispronunciation becomes a common incident, a source of potential discomfort or even shame. The other day, I was noting the name of someone who spelled her name before I had a chance to even ask.

I just read in a newspaper about a man whose first name, Gintaras, was given him to honor his Lithuanian heritage. This birth name, frequently shortened to the nickname Gint, was inevitably mispronounced as Jintaras or Jint, with a soft *g*. And like Felies, he corrected people with the refrain, "It's Gint. Like *mint* with a *G*." He described the endless explanations required of him due to his name's unusual pronunciation until he switched to using his middle name, Paul. He said that polite Canadians who could not read his nametag at work either avoided calling him by any name or else referred to him as "you." While admitting that "Paul" seemed very un-Canadian in light of the country's encouragement of pride in one's homeland, he felt that his choice had simplified his life and made him a much happier Canadian.

My friend Anna tells me that her now-adult son, whose Polish name is difficult to both pronounce and read, had always insisted on retaining his birth name: Bogusz Kolodziejska. Teased by others as a school-age child (Bogusz is a bogus! Bogus money, Bogus honey!) and handicapped in his job searches as an adult—and encouraged by his mother to change his name—he nevertheless was adamant about this part of his identity. Anna, on the other hand, had shortened her own (maiden) surname to sound different, more interesting. "Why not? I wanted to reinvent myself," she says in her accented English. "New country, new neighborhood, new career, new name."

Another friend, this one from Croatia, tells me that she had named her younger son Veselko, which means "cheerful," and her older son Vladimir, which means "to rule with greatness." As far back as she can remember, Veselko hated his name and constantly threatened to change it to a more Canadian-sounding one. He hated standing out and did not want to be different. His mother confided to me that his name fit him so well, as he was such a sunny and cheerful child. She tried explaining to him that he could blend into his peer group in so many other ways—by his dress, through his activities—but that his name was unique and was his personal mark. Years later, he is still muttering about his name under his breath but is resigned to having a Croatian first name and surname.

✿ ✿ ✿

Today in North America, we are bombarded by new names. Originality and uniqueness characterize the current naming fashion. My friends' children who are now themselves having children consider such uncommon names as Spencer, Ebony, Nova, or Delyia. Yet in spite of the pursuit of originality, considerable attention and foresight is given in choosing names.

Parents often name their children after a person they admire in the hopes that their children will acquire those talents or rise to the stature of their namesakes. In certain cultures, young boys named after famous leaders are pressured to model themselves after those grand men for whom they were named, such as Alexander (the Great). The fickleness of names is a measure of changing times and circumstances. A hero in one decade may fall out of favor in the next. While Malvolio and Desdemona both mean "ill fated" and Mallory means "unlucky," today it is names that have become contaminated, like Judas or Damien, that remain stigmatized by superstitious beliefs.

A Frenchman I know named his newly born son Ambroise Luv. He told me that his son's name had come to him in a dream vision prior to the child's birth: Your son will be named Ambroise! Himself a writer, he said, "Ambroise, like the elixir of immortality of the gods of Olympus; Ambroise like the Norman chronicler of the third crusade, poet in the court of Richard the Lionhearted; like Ambroise Pare, father of modern surgery during the Renaissance; and like Ambroise Croizat, known as the Parisian 'minister of the workers.'" Then he added, "And his middle name will be Luv, like one of the twin sons of Lord Rama, an undefeatable warrior in the Ramayana; and of course, Luv like Love."

A Canadian patient of mine told me that her daughter and son-in-law, a Trinidadian of East Indian descent, had named their daughter Naiya Kalli. Naiya is a Lakota First Nations word for "breath," and Kalli is an orthographic variation of Kali, the mother goddess of Hinduism who brings death to the illusory forces of the ego and liberation to souls.

On the other hand, a friend whose daughter had just named her child Hunter, said, "What kind of name is that? Is it a surname, a girl's name, or a boy's name? I have to remind my daughter that her little girl will have to wear this name for life. And what will happen when she comes across the word *hunter* for the first time in a book? Will she become frightened and confused when she learns that a hunter is someone who shoots animals?"

Another friend of mine told me that her aunt and uncle had never agreed about the name given to her cousin. While the father preferred Nancy, the mother was enamored of the less-common name Meredith. The compromise was that she was named Nancy Meredith Smith. For most of her life, she was known as Nancy, her father's preference having prevailed. However, when he died, Nancy then being in her forties, her mother began calling her Meredith, never having quite given up on her own favorite. Today, Nancy has changed her name completely to Mary, a contraction of Mer-y; she could not tolerate the thought of using the fully contracted name Mer-cy.

One woman told me that there were five girls in her family. The first three were named Sharon, Sandra, and Sylvia. While she had been named Cynthia after a friend of her mother's who had died, her mother renamed her Shirley at six months. Her mother confessed that she felt it didn't sound right after all those S's. Then when she had another daughter, there was no question that it would be Sonya, as she was committed to the S names.

Given names since the 1950s have shown increasingly more variation with each decade than in previous generations. While Susan, Barbara, Linda, Michael, John, and David were popular in the mid-fifties and even sixties, Ashley, Jessica, Emily, Christopher, Tyler, and Brandon became the darling names of the nineties, only to be replaced by Ethan, Jayden, and Aiden for boys and Sophia, Abigail, and Chloe for girls currently. Sociological trends and socio-cultural movements insidiously work their way into naming practices. Sky, Autumn, Moonstruck, and Wind are names popular with certain individuals caught up in the heyday of the sixties hippie movement, while Justice and Charity signal a traditional preoccupation with Christian morality and ethics.

Fortunately, this uniqueness in the first given name is almost universally balanced by the consideration of a family relative for the second given, or middle, name. In some families, the name is cemented and strengthened by suffixes (e.g., Junior or Senior, the elder, the younger) replacing the more formal and regal numerals (e.g., Adam the Fifth, John the Second). Of course, the desire to be remembered or memorialized in history is a two-edged sword. Nazi officers who named a son Adolf in honor of their führer may have had second thoughts once the war was over.

The grace and sophistication of certain names make them truly memorable. When people are introduced to my husband, they inevitably comment on the elegance of his name: Lawlor Rochester. In fact, his full name is Bertram David Lawlor Rochester, a name with a resonance of distinction and merit.

On the other hand, we are repelled by the sound of certain names. Pollux is the name of the rapist in J. M. Coetzee's book *Disgrace*, a formidable novel about exploitation and violence in a time of transition in South Africa. While the protagonist makes an issue of the ugliness of the sound of this man's name, he refers to it often, as if intoning its disgraceful and reprehensible sound. Similarly, other names with harsh, guttural consonants—for example, Grammok or Pitka—are deemed unpleasant by their lack of musicality and softness.

Not only do names reflect generational and historical trends, they also tell a story about the local socio-political climate. Only fifty to sixty years ago, in certain geographical pockets of rural Quebec and Ontario where tension between the Anglophone and Francophone communities was high, certain French families insisted on names that could not be Anglicized in pronunciation or spelling: Leoni, Hector, Isidore, or Elmire instead of Michel, which could become Mike or Michael, and Guillaume, which could be changed to William. As a result, certain names became overused in those communities.

* * *

How did the modern usage of a given name followed by a family name come about? After all, for the ancient Greeks, a simple solitary name sufficed for both men and women (with no change for women after marriage). Not only the Olympian gods and goddesses—Apollo, Artemis, Athena, Zeus—and not only the heroes of ancient Greece—Heracles, Theseus, Medea, Perseus—but all mortals carried their reputations in a condensed name: Plato, Aristotle, Epicurus, Euripides, Cicero, Euclid, Virgil, Herodotus. However, to be distinguished from each other, these names might be appended with an indication of place of birth or a title. For example, Diogenes of Sinope (412–323 BC), better known as Diogenes the Cynic, was not to be confused with Diogenes of Apollonia or Diogenes Apolloniates (ca. 460 BC) or Diogenes of Babylon, better known as Diogenes the Stoic (ca. 230–ca. 150 BC). Many of these names recall a period when names were assigned on the basis of different criteria: the desire for complimentary associations or meaning and beloved characteristics (Megacles, "of great fame"; Theophilus, "the beloved of god"; or Demeter, "the giver of food like a mother"); the incorporation of the name of a god, such as Heracleitus, "glory of Hera"; the reflection of personal characteristics, such as Plato, meaning "broad-shouldered," or Simonides, meaning "type of flatnose"; or the circumstances of birth, such as Didymus, "a twin."

As we shall see in the next chapter, etymological meanings played a major role in many Greek names. Any list of popular ancient Greek names will include: Pericles, the fifty-century BC Athenian statesman and general whose name derives from *peri-* (around, in excess of) and *kleos* (glory); or Stephanos, meaning "crown," named after St. Stephen;

or Demetrius, the king of Macedon and the Seleucid kingdom, whose name is derived from the goddess Demeter.

Freely chosen names, those ancient names we still hear today in modified forms (Damion, Alexander, Rhoda, Sophia, Jason, Irene), alternated with names in respect of deceased or living paternal grandfathers. Lineage was never far from naming practices: A person's patronymic might be added to indicate *genos*, or clan. If further identification was necessary, a father's name might be added in the genitive case, such as Pericles, (son) of Xanthippus. On occasion, a person's *deme*, or parish/local community, might be also added. By contrast, the ancient Romans, inheriting a tradition from the Etruscans, announced themselves in full form: Marcus Tullius Cicero, Marcus Vipsanius Agrippa, or Gaius Albucius Silus—embellished names that commanded respect and admiration. *Tria nomina*: the praenomen, or personal given name; the nomen or gentilicium, or name of the clan, kinship, or gens; and the cognomen, a personal nickname or an inherited name indicating the branch within the clan. Over the centuries, notable people from this period have become renowned by a single name: Cicero, also known as Tully (Marcus Tullius Cicero), Pompey (Gnaeus Pompeius Magnus), Virgil (Publius Vergilius Maro), Nero (Nero Claudius Caesar Augustus Germanicus).

By the late Roman period, Christian names appeared, replacing Greek, Jewish, and Latin names that had been the tradition. Rituals of baptism ensured a religious significance to the assignment of names. Emerging in the lists of popularity were theophoric names, or those derived from names of divinities to ensure their protection (*deus-*, *theo-*); names derived from significant religious dates (Natalis, Epiphanius); names expressing Christian values (Felix, Victor); and biblical names and names of saints (Boniface, Liborius, Abraham).

Given names could be determined by birth circumstances (Deliverance, Thankful); by saints (Maria, Sophia, Teresa); or simply by the selection of classical names associated with each country, such as Edward, James, Samuel, Jane, and Elizabeth in English-speaking countries. Soon the pendulum swung back to single names, a trend that continued through the Middle Ages with the replacement of Latin names by Germanic names. Wider kinship was acknowledged by particular single names that then became associated with a single ancestral group.

Mononymous people, individuals known and addressed by a single name, have made an appearance throughout our collective history. When Christopher Columbus arrived in the Americas, the people he encountered had mononyms, a custom typical of First Nations people but a tradition that continued to survive until the nineteenth century: Geronimo, a prominent leader of the Bedonkohe Apache; Auoindaon, a Canadian First Nations chief; Pocahontas, a Virginia Powhatan Indian woman, born Matoaka, and later known as Rebecca Rolfe; and Moctezuma, or Montezuma, the fifth Aztec emperor.

In contemporary Western society, mononymity, used by the royals in conjunction with titles, has been primarily a privilege of famous persons such as prominent writers, artists, entertainers, musicians, and sportsmen: among numerous others, the artist Christo, the sculptor Chryssa, and the singer-songwriters Madonna and Enya. Masquerading behind stage names, some of these mononymns are the performer's actual given name (Cher, Shakira) and some are the performer's actual surname (Liberace, Mantovani, Morrissey), while others are invented names (Bono) or nicknames (Sting, Prince).

By the late 1500s, at the end of the medieval period, radical changes in the social and political context forced the need for the clarification and identification of individuals. The written documentation of land records and other civic transactions required an accounting of citizens. As the pool of single names became depleted and the inconvenience of identifying individuals by a single name became bureaucratically challenging in the records of municipal rulings, second names became obligatory. The managers of civic life soon began to demand a second name for the administrative convenience of tax collection, conscription, and bureaucratic decrees associated with the functions of public life.

Second (family) names had already been evolving from the eleventh century onwards, but it took another four centuries for them to become firmly established and transmitted from generation to generation. Europe was the advance guard of this unfolding development that began with aristocrats and royalty. Early family names reflected birthplaces (Warsaw, Mannheim, Pollack); topographical features (Cranbrook, Bergson); occupations (Goldschmit, or goldsmith; Fischer, or fisherman; Stein, or stoneware, beer mug); or names embellished with patronymic prefixes or suffixes. Originality mixed with practicality gave many names a distinctive flourish: Schmuckler (jeweler), Grossbard (big beard) versus Gelbart (yellow beard), Shein (good-looking), and Kirschenblatt (cherry-colored paper).

Paralleling the growing shifts and transformations within the political and socio-economic spheres were modifications in family structure and dynamics. With the demand for a second (family) name, family extraction was more easily recorded. Dynasties became linked through males and the rights of primogeniture (special privileges accorded the first-born male child) developed in families of nobility and royalty. The patronymic became an important mode of naming by a translation of the simple term "son of" through the use of suffixes or prefixes, such as Mark*son* or Jens*sen* (English), *Fitz*patrick (Anglo-Norman), Leon*ov* (Russian), *Mac*pherson (Scottish), and Fernand*ez* (Spanish). This was especially true of smaller and less established families.

From the sixteenth century onwards, in Europe and Britain, naming practices once again shifted. While the second or family name clearly rendered legitimacy to a child and the transmission of lineage from father to son/daughter, first names were also considered a symbolic patrimony to be passed down according to strict rules. Names were both a link in a chain of dead ancestors and a program for the future, designating a particular role and perhaps even an inheritance.

A woman I met by chance recently told me the meandering transformations of her surname, Toogood, over time. The name derives from the English meaning "do good," starting as Togood around 1200, to Tougod from 1297, to Togoud from 1332, to Toogood and Twogood from 1763, to Tigwood from 1770.

✽ ✽ ✽

I am speaking to my friend Penny, whose surname, Lawler, is the same as my husband's given name, Lawlor, which was also his mother's maiden name. They tease and argue over the correct spelling of this Irish surname. Penny, an ardent feminist, raises the question of how her married daughters, who retained their hyphenated maiden names, will name their own children.

"Do you think they will drop their double surname made up of mine and Peter's family names and simply choose to adopt their husbands' surname? Will they create a new compound name with Peter's or my surname and then their father's name? And how would they choose which name to drop?"

Penny is a pragmatic woman. In the end, she takes a deep sigh and jokes, "I guess they'll just have to work that one out on their own. But it would have been easier if they were Spanish. You know, the Spanish have hyphenated surnames of their mother and father, too. But when they marry, the women simply drop their father's name and keep their mother's surname. Of course, this only applies to the upper class and the nobility so they can trace the matrilineal line. Not for folks like you and me, of course—only the blue bloods." She adds, "You'd better check this out before you quote me."

My research told me that each person born into a Spanish-speaking family is given a first name followed by two surnames, the first being the father's family name (or, more precisely, the surname he gained from his father) and the second being the mother's family name (or, again more precisely, the surname she gained from her father).

Take, for example, the name of Teresa García Ramírez. Teresa is the name given at birth, García is the family name from her father, and Ramírez is the family name from her mother. This custom of a double surname apparently was influenced by earlier Arabic traditions.

In the generational transmission of surnames, the paternal surname's precedence eventually eliminates the maternal surnames from the family lineage. So when Maria Blanco Cortez marries Rafael Lopez Santiago, their children will be named José Lopez Blanco or Adelina Lopez Blanco. While contemporary law allows the maternal surname to be given precedence, most people observe the traditional paternal-maternal surname order. Regardless of the surname order, all children's surnames must be in the same order when recorded in the Registro Civil.

I see that Penny was partly correct in her information when I also discover that patrilineal surname transmission was not always the norm in Spanish-speaking societies. Prior to the mid-eighteenth century, when the current paternal-maternal surname combination norm came into existence, Hispanophone societies often practiced matrilineal surname transmission, giving children the maternal surname and, occasionally, even a grandparent's surname (born by neither parent). The deceptive motive was based on pride and cachet. It was hoped that the young woman so named would be perceived as gentry, and therefore a profitable catch.

In contemporary society, naming practices continue to vary across cultures. In North America, the feminist movement has modified what was once a traditional patrilineal naming pattern. Young women today deliberate on the decision of adopting their husband's name, and I know young men who have chosen to adopt the surname of their wives. My parents certainly never would have considered such an option. To this day, my mother continues to receive mail addressed to Mrs. Louis Himes even though my father has been dead for several decades.

The socio-political and socio-cultural landscapes inevitably shift over time with a predictable ebb and flow of trends, actions, and reactions—as is well documented in this editorial in Toronto's *Globe and Mail* on January 4, 2013, which I quote in full:

> The tiny Nordic nation obliges parents to pick their children's first names from a government-approved list that does not include Ble Ivy, Pilot Inspektor or Audio Science, all of which are the real names of the real children of famous people who don't come from Iceland. Now a young girl is challenging the state for her right to use her off-list given name. Sometimes it's hard to know which side to come down on. The 15-year-old girl in question was baptized Blaer by a priest who thought the name, which after all means "light breeze" in Icelandic, was an approved one. However, it's not on the list of 1,712 male names and 1,853 female names on the country's Personal Names Register: consequently, Blaer is referred to on all official documents as "Stulka" which means "girl." A panel that oversees the register has rejected the name on grounds the noun it comes from takes a masculine article. It issued this decision in spite of the fact Blaer is the name of a female character in a novel by one of Iceland's most revered authors.
>
> The ruling was made by the same panel that has approved Elvis as a girl's name in Iceland. The girl and her mother are prepared to go to the country's supreme court in their fight. "It seems like a basic human right to be able to name your child what you want, especially if it doesn't harm your child in any way," the mother is reported to have told the local media. That's all that needs to be said in this case. Blaer should be Blaer. Meanwhile young Pilot Inspektor can take heart in the fact that, in countries that don't enforce government-approved monikers, changing one's name is a relatively simple matter.[1]

✳ ✳ ✳

Thomas Carlyle, the Scottish writer and satirist, once wrote, "Giving a name, indeed, is a poetic art; all poetry if we go to that with it, is but a giving of names."[2] In this quote, Carlyle reminds us not only of the functional significance of name-giving but also of its poetic qualities— the assonance of sounds, the rhythmic composition, and the aesthetic spirit. In this sense, the inscription of a name is a precious art form akin to a poetic act.

Indeed, consider the name Abu al-'Abbas Muhammed ibn Ya'qub ibn Yusus al-Asamm al-Naysaburi. Arabic-speaking people devote considerable time and deliberation to the practice of child naming. The bestowal of a name for a new life must be appropriate; but more significantly, it must sound right. "Do the syllables flow well? Do the various parts of the name roll mellifluously from the tongue? Is the name poetry? Do all the various elements fit well with each other?" After all, "the language of angels"[3] demands a poetic name. The constituent elements—ism, kunya, nasab, laqab, and nisba—must all sing in harmony, for the prophet Muhammad says: "On the day of Judgment, you will be called by your names and by your fathers' names; therefore keep you good names." Perhaps the Muslim philosophy, with its emphasis on words bringing man closer to God, has become woven into the tapestry of naming rituals.

Siyi, a colleague of mine, explained to me that Chinese proper names are constructed individually from blended calligraphic characters with multiple meanings resembling verses of poetry. For example, her name is a compound Chinese name that means "If I am thinking, I feel joyful" and derives from the combination of Si (thinking or thought) and Yi (joyful). Siyi and her husband gave much thought to the name of their recent newborn. In the end, they agreed on the name Yuxin (pronounced hu-shyn). This is a compound of the Chinese characters yu ("language" as a noun and "talking and discussing" as a verb"), which itself is made up of two Chinese figures, the first meaning "word" or "talk" and the second meaning "I" or "me," and xin, which can mean "strong and pervasive fragrance" and "reputation," and is formed by another two figures, the first meaning "sound, tone, voice, reputation" and the second meaning "fragrant incense."

From Siyi's explanation, I understand this to imply: "May her name (the sound of her voice) be so fragrant that she will be well-known far

and wide." As a psychotherapist also interested in Lacanian psychoanalysis, Siyi elaborates, "I believe that as humans we live in language and
look for ourselves through language; life is the process for people to
speak about themselves, and in speaking about themselves, they can
find themselves. Once my daughter speaks, I hope that what she says
will be fragrant and spread far and wide, so that her reputation will also
spread. If you could read Chinese, you would also see that her name
looks like a beautiful picture with many Chinese characters."

Names in Japan are also selected with care, hope, and blessings. The
Japanese believe that "a name becomes a man" and that to give a name
is to truly offer a person something. For example, the word for "business card" in Japanese is "a thin slice of a man"—hence the care with
which it is offered: a ritual attached to this exchange by the extension
and positioning of the hand. In Peter Oliva's novel *City of Yes*, an
American who has moved to Saitama to teach English is informed by his
Japanese counterpart that "to say a man's name is to bring him close,
close enough to see with the eyes or with the mind."[4]

By contrast, we can compare these Eastern traditions with the more
purposeful and functional approach of name-giving in Western cultures. For example, Marie-Joseph-Paul-Yves-Roch Gilbert du Motier,
or the Marquis de Lafayette, or simply Lafayette. Status: French aristo-
crat and military officer, major general in the Continental Army under
George Washington. Like other Europeans of the mid-eighteenth century, Lafayette's full name announced his kinship as well as the lands
owned by his family. His full name announces prosperity; his surname
the practicality of brevity. Like the names of the royalty, nobility, and
gentry of Northern Europe, feudal names were abbreviated into bare
place names, as the inheritance of a name necessarily included the
inheritance of land and property.

6

CELEBRATING NAMES

As if to honor the sanctity of life, the symbolic act of name-giving was once marked by elaborate ceremony. Such is still the case in cultures in which ritual is still tied to the rhythms of daily life. Today in North America and much of the West, baby naming is typically celebrated within the privacy of our homes. For the most part, private family festivities have replaced the solemn formal receptions once associated with communal name-granting.

I am told that my naming occurred without fanfare. A simple inscription on a birth certificate recording my name, date, and place of birth. In Judaism, no formal law requires a naming ceremony for girls. Within the religious community, the naming of a baby girl typically was announced by the father in synagogue on the first Shabbat, a day when the Torah is read, following the birth.

By contrast, had I been born male, there would have been the ritual circumcision ceremony (*Brit Milah*) on the eighth day of life. This fundamental tenet of Judaism, the covenant of circumcision, follows a direct commandment to Abraham, the first patriarch, and, in turn, to all his descendants: "This is My covenant, which ye shall keep, between Me and you and thy seed after thee: every male among you shall be circumcised. And ye shall be circumcised in the flesh of your foreskin; and it shall be a token of a covenant betwixt Me and you" (Gen. 17:10).

In a typical ceremony, the honor of handing the baby from the mother to the father, who in turn carries him to the *mohel* (the man who performs the circumcision), is given the title of *kvater* (male) or *kvaterin* (female). A childless couple is usually chosen for this honor, with the hope of *segula* (or efficacious remedy); that is, of having children of their own. Another example of superstitious thinking steeped within Jewish tradition.

As women in the past few decades have demanded more equality within the institution of Judaism and its ritual practices, the *Simchat Bat* ("celebration of the daughter") or *Brit Bat* ("welcoming/covenant of the daughter") has now become a popular naming ceremony for girls. Families gather at the child's home for a communal welcoming, with naming over a cup of wine, quotations from the Bible, and the chanting of traditional blessings, all against a backdrop of chatter, laughter, and joyous song. In an attempt to maintain egalitarian status with their male counterparts, new rituals are now performed either singly or in varied combinations, such as the lighting of seven candles (symbolizing the seven days of creation) with the newborn held towards them, enfolding the newborn within the four corners of a tallit, and the lifting and touching of the baby's hands to a Torah scroll.

My friends have described the Christian equivalent: the baptismal christening that ushers in the new life of a baby boy or girl. Dressed in an embroidered white christening gown, a keepsake handed down for generations, or decked out in a special pair of white rompers designed for the event, the infant, cradled in the arms of his parents or godparents, is sprinkled with water by the minister or priest as blessings are recited.

An alternative to a baptism, for those who have no church affiliation or who do not wish a formal baptismal service, is the Dedication (or Thanksgiving) for the Gift of a Child ceremony. This ceremony is also a celebration with prayers and promises. It is believed to symbolize the act of Jesus, who blessed the future of each newborn: "He took the children in his arms, put his hands on them and blessed them" (Mark 10:13–16). Performed by a minister in any suitable setting desired by the family, such as a home or community center, it is a more contemporary ritual of the welcoming and naming of new life.

In Hinduism, baby naming is always a sacred occasion that demands an elaborate ceremony known as Namakarana Sanskar, typically occurring ten days following a birth. Hindu parents are obliged to perform this social and legal ceremony. The naming process creates a bond between the child and the rest of the family, and is therefore considered to be a highly auspicious occasion. On the eleventh or twelfth day, the parents of the newborn, the paternal and maternal grandparents, and few close relatives and friends gather together with a priest. Rituals vary within different communities; in some, the sacred fire is lit and the priest chants sacred hymns. He offers prayers to all the gods and to the Agni, the elements, and the spirits of the forefathers, entreating them to bless and protect the child. In other traditions, there is a sprinkling of water for purification, with the blessings focused on the hopes that the child develop and become a great person like his renowned forefathers.

According to the date and time of the child's birth, a particular letter of the Sanskrit alphabet associated with the child's lunar birth sign (*chandra rashi*) and believed to be particularly lucky is chosen. The child's horoscope, if written, may also be placed in front of the image of the deity for blessings. The baby is then given a name starting with that letter. Usually the father or paternal aunt whispers the Hindu name four times in the right ear of the baby by using a betel leaf or its silver imprint, or a few leaves of kusa grass, to direct the words into his ear. After the customary blessings received by the priest and all guests, an elaborate feast is organized as a closing festivity where friends and relatives have an opportunity to bless the child by touching honey or sugar to his or her lips.

❊ ❊ ❊

Membership in all tribal and ethnic groups, in all religious and dynastic communities, demands ceremony; ceremonial traditions sustain continuity. Naming and its inaugural act ensure the ongoing chain of identity and affiliation. Ritualistic festivities punctuate and strengthen the bonds that link together like-minded peoples. Participating in an emotionally significant rite of passage forges ongoing connection.

People have shared unique experiences associated with their naming with me as I researched this book, some of which I describe in what follows.

Rakgwedi is a twenty-one-year-old man. He is the son of a colleague; I met him at a social function where he was working as photographer. Tall, slender, and upright in his posture, he has high cheekbones and long fingers. His voice does not match his height as he speaks in a quiet voice.

My name is a gift from my Ancestors. When my mother was pregnant, my Nkgono (paternal grandmother) had a vision in which she was visited by the Ancestors. They came to her in the form of the original Rakgwedi and his wife, Mokhotswane, who were pastoralists. Had I been born a girl, I would have been named after the wife, but as a boy, I was given the name Rakgwedi; the closest meaning in English is *ra* (man) and *kgwedi* (moon). My African heritage on my father's side dictated that this spirit reside within me. For it is said, "You have a strong spirit on you. May you live up to this gift with the help of the ancestors, whom you must appease." I am the last-born son.

My ethnic group is Sotho; my people are Basotho, and my language is Sesotho. My name is spelled differently in the northern and southern dialectics of Sesotho. Not only have I inherited the name from my paternal ancestors, but my body, long, lean, and angular, and my height also remind me of my Basotho heritage. People think that my brother and I do not resemble each other. I'm not so sure; I think that people are distracted by skin color. I am light-complected like my father, Ramohnametsi.

My brother's skin is darker, not unlike our Nkgono, who is Tswana. My first-born brother's name is Molifi; in English it would translate "the one who is prayed for." Coincidentally, his surname, Motau (pronounced like mo-da-oo), means "the one who comes from the lion" or "son of lion," Tau being the clan totem for the Ramphore family, our father's clan. As my Ngkono would say, "The Ancestors know how to work these things out."

When I was born, my father introduced me to the Ancestors. All the elders were called to attend this ritual. At six days, they all gathered in the village of my birth. My father cut off my hair and wrapped it in a small cloth sack, made of traditional material with beads and a medallion, the totems my father chose to represent my culture. My father then took me to the ocean, where the Big Spirits live. From a cliff overlooking the waters, he lifted me up and held me high in the air. Calling on the Ancestors, he introduced me to them. Then he took the totem of hair and bead and traditional material and tossed it into the waters.

Now as a young adult, I had to be reintroduced to the Ancestors as a man. Once again, I returned to South Africa for this thirty-six-hour introduction with specific ritualistic components. My brother and I both shared in this reintroduction. Two sheep were slaughtered as sacrifice, and this had to be done ritually by our father; in order to make it right with the Ancestors, the place of slaughter and the location of the fire-pits were very significant. One pot contained the traditional sorghum-based beer to be used and served in a calabash. There was a huge fire pot used to cook the meat. The blood from the beasts was drained and buried in a secret place in the earth. My brother and I were wrapped in colorful Basotho traditional blankets. Molifi's was brown and African sky blue; mine was gold with black-outlined maize and small shields of red; both color combinations are totems of the Basotho. Feasting, praying, and singing lasted over a day with no sleep. Now that I have been reintroduced to my Ancestors, my brother Molifi and I are Sotho men. To be a Sotho man is to take on the responsibilities of the culture. We are communal in all things and believe in Ancestral alignment.

The young man who recently completed a web design project for me had an unusual-sounding name. I could not help but question him about his name, as it was such a challenge for me to pronounce.

My name is Ngqabutho Zondo. My maternal family is from Zimbabwe, and my paternal family is from South Africa. My paternal grandfather named me Ngqabutho because he thought I would be an important person in my community, as this name is given to either a first-born or a leader of a group. I could have become an elder—that is what my grandfather wanted for me. But instead, I have moved away from Africa and followed another path and career. Who knows? One day I may return to South Africa and follow the path ordained by my name.

Ngqabutho. An impossible name for Westerners to pronounce, as it has a click in the first three letters. In Canada, I am called N-g-q Click, Butho, Zee (short for Zondo), or Nabutho (without the pronunciation of the click). Some people, like you, try to pronounce my full name. I respond to all of these; and no, I have never thought of changing my name to make it easier for others. It is a name of which I am very proud. My surname Zondo is a name that originates from southern Africa. It is used in specific clans, namely, Ndebele, Mthiyane, Sokhulu, and Luvuno, which are all based on the "Zulu" clan from South Africa. I am Ndebele, a clan constituting approximately 50 percent of the population within Zimbabwe.

Names are significant. Their meanings are usually well thought out by parents to reflect the type of future you would like your child to embody. Today, this type of process is not as common within

southern Africa, as newer generations have begun to change cultural-
ly. An interesting fact is that after Zimbabwe's independence of
1980, there was a huge boom in naming newborns with traditional
names as a revolutionary assertion of a right and a statement of a
return to autonomous rule. This arose as a reaction to the period
before independence, where black citizens were forced to name
their children with English names due to colonization by the British.
This effectively halted naming according to tradition with the blessings of the Ancestors. The names of my parents are Jerry and Margaret. My mother's maiden name was Chitambo, a Zimbabwe name,
but she adopted my father's surname of Zondo, as is typically done in
the West.

The North American Ojibway tribe traditionally bases its system of
kinship on patrilineal clans, or *dodems*, that are passed on from generation to generation. As a result of European contact followed by the
gradual colonization in the early seventeenth century, there was a
breakdown in tradition and, consequently, considerable damage to the
society of First Nations people. Ensuing legislation resulted in prohibitions and decrees, and censures on land ownership, spiritual practices,
cultural traditions and rituals, and language. Many fundamental aspects
of life were decimated, and residential schools created a tremendously
negative impact on most families, an impact that persists to the present.

My friend Anne, a member of the Anishnaabe, has agreed to speak
with me about names and naming practices among First Nations. As I
wait in the coffee shop where we are to meet, I look up from my book
and see the silhouette of a woman with long hair and curvaceous figure
approach. I know it is she. We embrace warmly. She is excited about
the topic and eager to share her knowledge.

"Colonization in Canada," she explains, "moved in waves from east
to west so that the impact would be felt differently in central Canada
versus the west coast. In all cases, the federal government, the provinces, and the church decimated the integrity of tribal life as it was
known." Anne tells me that through her own research she has discovered her *dodem* to be "caribou," which, she explains, is a clan signifying
the "protector of aspects of social living." Other clans might relate to
medicine or other aspects of the society.

Anne told me how she had found out about this clan. She made an
appointment with a professor of history at the University of Toronto

who had done her doctorate on *dodems* and showed her the document of a treaty signed at Rama (the Narrows) in Ontario on June 17, 1852, which contained two written markings: the signature of James Bigwind, who was a family relative, and the drawing of a clan symbol. Anne thought the symbol resembled a deer hoofprint, but the professor explained that the single cleft in the hoof was characteristic of caribou tracks. The professor also explained that it was typical of signatures in treaties to contain these animal paw markings, distinguished by various claw patterns: Caribou tracks, being circular, typically show two half-moons with a dewclaw, whereas deer hooves are cloven with sharp arches that are not round.

Anne was surprised by the reference to caribou in southeastern Ontario but was told that caribou followed the available supplies of lichen that grew freely on the rocky granite outcrops of the Canadian shield in that region, which accounted for their presence so far south. So the unusual paw print was, in fact, a mark of her caribou *dodem*.

Her husband, also Ojibway, grew up on a reserve with a traditional lifestyle of hunting, gathering, and fishing and attained an extensive knowledge of Native language, culture, and traditions. He does not know his clan name, however. Anne says that this is an example of a generational breakdown that had occurred in earlier generations. Anne told me her story.

> My family name is Bigwin, an Anglicized name and likely a modified translation of Bigwind, which would have been *che* (big) and *nodin* (wind) in Ojibway. Someone must have thought Bigwind sounded funny and so they dropped the *d*. One family member is married to a man whose surname is Starblanket, a direct translation from the Cree. My Ojibway brother-in-law, a man who grew up on a reserve, has the surname Jamieson. And my husband's surname is Meawasige, an Ojibway word that means "beautiful light."
>
> So there you go: Bigwin, Starblanket, Jamieson, Meawasige. Four names, four different manifestations of naming. We are all First Nations and our names tell the story of my people in Canada, the First Nation experience in this country—the modification, the English translation, the English name, and the First Nation name without change or translation. I find it incredible that this phenomenon is represented in one family.

Anne and I continued to speak about ongoing disappointments with the Canadian government and its rulings. While the federal government apologized in 2008 for the excesses and ongoing impact of sexual and physical abuse in residential schools, Anne clearly was still disturbed by the chronic psycho-social repercussions at both the individual and the collective level.

I ask Anne to tell me about naming ceremonies. She says that she can only speak for the Ojibway people, her people, who are part of the Anishinaabeg, known as the woodland people and identified by the Algonquin linguistic group.

When a parent or parents want to give their name to a child, they approach the Medicine People to give them an Indian name. The child may already have a Canadian name, but the Indian name is to be used at the person's discretion and always with utmost respect. Again, due to generational breakdown, today an Elder would be approached for this task. The Indian name would always come through a vision, a dream, or through the spirit of the person to be named. It would never be a random selection or a request by the parents, and it would always contain a reference to nature in respect of the importance of interconnectedness and balance in nature.

The naming ceremony is very elaborate, with very explicit rituals that must be observed. First a fire is lit, as smoke connects Mother Earth with the Creator. The tobacco, considered a sacred plant used in all traditional rituals, would be first offered to the Elder who is conducting the ceremony and a prayer on the name would be said. The person to be named would then be walked around the feast by the Elder, who would be talking to him at the same time. This walk-around signifies the circle of life. Then he would be taken outside for the sunrise ceremony and the Elder would lift him up in the four directions—north, south, east, west—four being significant in terms of the four directions, the four winds, the four seasons. At that point, he would be given his name, and more tobacco would be put on the fire. There would then be an elaborate feast with traditional food that would take all night to prepare. The feast would then be consumed and the occasion celebrated with great joy and happiness.

My son's name, which was given to him at three months, was the name of his paternal great grandfather, and actually the name of the father of the Elder performing the ritual. This name is Meshkeeg-wun.

In response to my question about medicine men, Anne was very succinct. "They are the carriers and transmitters of ancestral knowledge, a knowledge that is always oral, never written. They are the intermediaries between Mother Earth and Father Sky—the Great Spirit, or the Creator."

❖ ❖ ❖

After returning from a trip to Russia, I read the memoir *The Chukchi Bible* by Yuri Rytkheu, a Russian (Siberian) writer. Tucked away on the northern shores of the Bering Sea, the Chukchi people, resilient survivors living in the vast Arctic tundra of Siberia, still struggle to maintain their cultural heritage and mythology. To this day, elaborate rituals associated with naming may still be performed in this remote community. Shortly before his murder by a Soviet official, Mletkin, one of the last remaining shamans of the Chukchi, officiated at the naming ceremony of Yuri's grandson. Mletkin himself had been named at the time of his birth in 1868 by Kalyantagrau, the unspoken leader and shaman of the village Uelen.

According to tribal tradition, each newborn, especially if it is a boy, is endowed and invested with all the aspirations and hopes of the parents, dreams they had for themselves but were unable to fulfill. Mletkin's own parents had told Kalyantagrau that they wished their son's name to contain the meaning of all the past family names within it. As the ceremony began, the shaman began chanting the history of the family names, beginning with the words: "Each of us, the people of Uelen, shares a common ancestor—the whale Reu, whose descendant Ermen led our people to the shingled spit . . ." The shaman recounted a short summary of the family names. Then,

> plucking an ember from the fire, he drew a thick black line on the wailing infant's forehead and intoned: "I name you Mletkin. I hope that you will acquire the deep meaning of your name with honor as you bring it with you into the future, and that you will serve your people well . . . Mletkin!"

> Outstretched Wings [a sacred amulet hung suspended by a thin leather strap from the smokehole of the tent] visibly dipped in the child's direction.

The child abruptly fell silent, as though listening carefully for the echoes of his name.[1]

The chosen name Mletkin meant the crux of time and was intended to signify something of the infant's relationship to his past and future. According to Chukchi tradition, it is believed that the name chosen endows the child with something of the knowledge of the ancestors who bore him before, and will symbolically return him to the tribe.

On the Day of Naming of his own grandson, Mletkin pulled out Outstretched Wings, the same amulet of carved walrus tusk incised with shamanic symbols that had been used at his own naming ceremony, and suspended it from the ceiling of the ceremonial lodge. He knew that various names would be chanted, invoked, and if the correct name was announced, the circling talisman would magically incline towards the newborn.

However, Mletkin's children were now full-fledged Soviet citizens indoctrinated into the culture of their surroundings. Instead of the more traditional name chosen by their grandfather, they wished to name their child Lenin, a strong revolutionary name. Mletkin believed that a name's root meaning had the power of ancestral transmission from previous descendants, be it unconscious or deliberate, and so he refused this secular Soviet name. Instead he called out various traditional names, but as each name was invoked, the amulet rotated in an unchanging circle, as if the gods had deserted the shaman. In despair, the old wise man spoke deliberately to his grandson, "Since the gods will not hear my pleas, from now on you shall be called Rytkheu—a name which means the Unknown!"[2]

* * *

In the Mohawk language, Kaha:wi means "she carries." It is the name the Mohawk dancer Santee Smith chose for her modern dance company, which performs traditional First Nations dance. Smith, the artistic director, explained this choice of name in the program notes of a performance I once attended:

It is significant because it was the ancient traditional name of my family. It is thousands of years old: it was the name of my maternal grandmother and it is the name of my daughter, and it will be passed on to other individuals in my family for generations to come. My name is timeless . . . it spans past, present, future. "I am carrying" the history of my family, or that is how I feel it, and I will transmit this to my children and it will be carried on to their children.

❊ ❊ ❊

Ibrahim al-Koni, a Libyan Tuareg, writes about the desert and the naming practices of his tribe. A Berber people with a nomadic lifestyle and a long history of inhabitance in the middle and western Sahara and the north-central Sahel, the Tuareg continue to sustain themselves mainly by settled agriculture and nomadic cattle breeding. Unlike in other North African cultures, Tuareg women traditionally do not wear a veil, whereas men typically wear the *alasho*, an indigo-blue veil. The men's facial covering likely originates from a belief that the action wards off evil spirits, although it also serves to protect them from the harsh desert sands. Like the wearing of amulets containing sacred objects and, more recently, verses from the Qur'an, taking on the veil is associated with a rite of passage to manhood. Animistic beliefs infused with Muslim practices are interwoven with the spiritual fabric of this pastoral people.

In his book *Anubis: A Desert Novel*, writer Ibrahim al-Koni speaks about the quintessential name that must be discovered by each Tuareg. This particular folk tale describes a Tuareg youth venturing into the desert on a quest to find his father, a figure he remembers only as a shadow. A profound encounter with a priestess and an apparition confound the youth in his tent on the first day of his solo journey. Unable to speak, he emits a cry, "Iyla! Iyla!"

> Encircling my body with her arms, my lady replied, "He spoke the prophecy!"
>
> The apparition squatting beside the tent post remained quiet for a long time before marveling, "The prophecy!"
>
> My compassionate lady rocked me and hugged me to her bosom. I felt such deep warmth. I can compare it only to the feeling that overwhelmed me the moment the sky's heart opened to disclose the sky's secret and that of her consort the earth. Eventually my lady responded, "He spoke in the Name."
>
> "The Name? But what name?"
>
> I detected a note of respect in the lady's tone: "The Name that cannot be preceded or followed by falsehood."
>
> "But is prophecy of the Name a good or bad omen?" The lady did not reply.

She did not reply, because she had decided to take on the mission of compassion: she began to teach me the names. She called in my ear as loudly as she could, "Rau . . . Rau . . . Rau . . . Rau . . . From today on your name is Wa."[3] Next she struck her chest with her hand and howled into my ear, "My name is Ma."[4] Turning toward the ghostly figure squatting beside the post, she shouted the name in my ear: "This fellow is Ba."[5] Then she took two steps towards the entrance of the tent and carried me outside to bathe me in a flood of the light emanating from the amazing golden disk. Finally she shouted as loudly as she could, "This one is nameless, for he is master of all the names. He is the one you called Iyla. You shall call him Ragh once your speech clears and you regain an ability to make the 'r' sound."[6]

In this parable, the Tuareg youth discovers the names of the elders, those significant beings who inhabit his universe and who eventually will find space in his inner world. At the same time, he must search for and discover his own name. The quest for his father and his father's name becomes entwined with the quest for his own name.

And, as the second part of this book shows, our names are proxies for all of the good and bad that we can cause and that can happen to us.

Part II

Burden or Blessing

7

THE STRANGE FATE OF NAMES

My field of study as an undergraduate was psychology. While many of my friends were immersed in great literature, I was holed up in a laboratory working with mice and rats, performing experiments to further the cause of science. It was only later that I entered the clinical domain of psychology and, after that, the field of psychoanalysis. And it was when I was engaged in my latest studies that I returned once more to my literary interests.

The Life and Opinions of Tristram Shandy, Gentleman, a novel by Laurence Sterne published in the mid-eighteenth century, often is compulsory reading for university English literature students. It is the abridged version, a mere single book greatly reduced from the nine-volume original, that students study, struggling with the English style of its time. As a satirical work, it spans a history of the comings and goings, the musings and ruminations, of a gentleman named Tristram.

The first section relates the philosophical viewpoints of Walter Shandy, his father, a man obsessed with the influence of names on a person's character, to the point of potentially prejudicing a person's nature and fortunes. In fact, the word *shandy* carries the meaning of "half-crazy." To safeguard his son from misfortune, he decreed that the boy would receive an especially auspicious name, Trismegistus, but, as luck would have it, or not, the name was distorted when given to the curate, and so the boy was named Tristram. According to his father's theory, this name, being a conflation of Trismegistus, after the esoteric mystic Hermes Trismegistus, and Tristan, associated with the Latin *tristis* (or sorrowful), doomed him to a life of woe with the curse that he would never discover the causes of his misfortune.

Neither Tristram nor his father had the benefit of psychoanalysis, a field still to be developed. However, as astute observers of life, they understood how names could become imbued with personal meaning and semantic determination. As his father says, "There was a strange kind of magick bias, which good or bad names irresistibly impressed upon our character and conduct."[1]

Centuries after Cratylus, in Plato's dialogue of that name, declared that names had an inherent, essential quality that made them fitting for each person, Tristram took this a step further. He implied that names took on a life of their own when attached to a person and could in some way direct their future.

* * *

While we tend to chuckle at the seeming coincidence of names—such as the artisan named Ms. Weaver, the dentist Dr. Molar, the carpenter Mr. Woodman, the engineer Mr. Steel, the neurosurgeon Dr. Brain, the oncologist Dr. Hope, or the poet Robert Frost, who wrote about winter scenes—we are still perplexed by this apparent coincidence. Why are we amused or even startled at such phenomena? Why does it seem both humorous and presumptuous when we hear a name connected to a person's profession, personality, or conduct? Why do we laugh nervously, as if to belie a certain credence in such apparently preposterous ideas of a fate bound up with a name? Can there be some semantic coincidence that makes the name of an individual the one into which we develop and grow?

Determinism is the philosophical concept that all events that occur in life, including human actions, could not have happened otherwise, given certain conditions. We can speak of biological and genetic determinism, cultural and social determinism, or even technological determinism. Semantic determinism refers to the notion that semantics, or the meaning of words (and in this case proper names), have a determining value on a person's life trajectory and can directly influence mental life. The slang use of "weiner" as a reference to "penis" turned congressman Anthony Weiner's sexual adventures on his computer into a theater of the absurd and left him prey to wave upon wave of sarcastic comments about his name. An example of semantic determinism!

Just as early man's predecessors placed a significant value on the power of names, psychoanalysts also assign a premium to the function of the name and its significance in our lives. For us analysts, coincidences are never simply coincidences. In the same way that a common noun describes a referent, so can a proper name take on a predictive quality, insinuating itself into the life of its bearer in a very real way.

Already in the early 1900s, psychoanalysts were writing about the "hidden relations between names and occupations as well as between names and neuroses,"[2] according to Karl Abraham, one of Freud's contemporaries and colleagues. He also noted that some, instead of repetition of certain names, characterized by certain qualities, imposed a duty on subsequent family members when they too have been named in memory of the first ancestor bearing such a name. As an example, Abraham cites one of the characters in Goethe's novel *Elective Affinities*, a former priest named Mittler, who took on a role of resolving disputes—*mittler* being German for "go-between" or "middleman."

In my own practice, a patient whose middle name was the same as a major figure in German history found herself drawn to writing a dissertation on this individual's parents. It was only during her personal analysis that the resemblance of this person's name to her own was what had propelled her to study his story.

Psychoanalysts from the time of Freud have claimed that *man is not master in his own home.* Our conscious ego, that pompous and stubborn "I" we parade around with, is not directing the show. Instead, it is this elusive thing we call the unconscious that is pulling the strings, making us servant to its directives and commands, even sometimes inciting us to perform in irrational and unwanted ways.

For Freud, the unconscious is dominated by impulses and drives. We are all servants to our wishes or drives, caught between the warring factions of an *id*, a *superego*, and an *ego*. As a result, we are in perpetual struggle to maintain a balance between our true wishes and our obedience to well-established parental and social demands. Thanks to that little ego's role as conductor, we usually live with a comfortable degree of inner truce. In a reformulated version, Lacan would say we must try to maintain that balance between our desires (what we want) and the law (what we are permitted and not permitted to do), a tension that forever places a limit on our total satisfaction and pleasure.

The seizing, or "taking hold," of our proper name that is assigned or given from outside ourselves (from our parents) creates the conditions for its potential to instill a certain deterministic quality, or *nomen est omen*, a phrase referring to the commonly held belief in the ancient world that a person's name indicated or predicted his destiny. It literally means "the name is an omen," "the name is destiny," or "fate in the name of."

* * *

How does this happen? How does the proper name acquire this power? To understand the valence, or impact, of certain words, we can consider the distinction between words and signs, signifiers and signifieds. In linguistic theory, a signifier is a word's physical form, a linguistic unit or pattern, such as a succession of speech sounds that conveys meaning. A signified is the collection of word meanings associated with a certain phonological unit of sound. For example, the conceptual element of a tree (the signified) is directly related to the phonological element t-r-e-e (the signifier). In everyday speech, we mostly employ words as signs: The signifier of the image tree is directly related to the word "tree." The signifier and the signified are permanent lovers, glued together in an initially arbitrary but ultimately fixed bond. Interdependence breeds reciprocity and durability. Signs are the immutable, universal word meanings we share with each other in common discourse.

In psychoanalytic theory, however, we say that there is a distinction between signs and signifiers. Instead of a fixed relationship, the meaning of a signifier is not glued to a word in the same way that the word "table" and the letters spelling t-a-b-l-e implicitly conjure up an image of a surface with legs on which one may write or eat. Signifiers move and shift; like autonomous buoys, they float in detached form from any specific referent and are defined independently of any permanent reference in an initial or inaugural moment. Sovereign in status, signifiers are characterized by their differences from other signifiers and by their personalized nature. Signifiers are forever infused with private meanings: My association to the desert is necessarily different from that of yours. My association to the word "peacock" may be laced with a particular memory or memories and imbued with an emotional charge that may be conscious and unconscious.

What all this means is that, as master signifier, the proper name is particularly prone to all the interpretations and meanings that one can ascribe to it. Each of us will read our history and the meaning of our name in a unique way, interiorizing and ascribing to it our own personal renderings of meaning. For example, we only have to ask siblings from the same family to speak about their surname to see the multiple interpretations that can be attributed to it.

* * *

A given name is rarely given randomly. In the present context, what is most significant and relevant is the connection between our name and our parents' desire in naming us. Our unique name, be it Samantha Ellen Chatsworth or Thomas Brandon Duckworth Junior, carries with it a psychological impact, one that evolves from the one we have been given to the one we carry and create for ourselves. Either consciously or unconsciously, explicitly or implicitly, as we develop and mature, we are forced to reckon with that part of our identity over which we had no choice. The inherited surname carries a valence associated with lineage (and not parental desire), a fact that does not preclude it from also becoming bound up with the potential for semantic determinism.

As the example of my patient illustrates, some people become obsessed with the background of a person after whom they have been named without realizing the connection to their own name. This is different from the cases of those who research their family tree. My patient had no inkling of the connection between the names she was researching and her own name.

In the choice of partners, the determining influence of names can also be apparent. Some people are suspicious about marrying people with names they deem to be inauspicious. Others end up marrying people with names that remind them of their parents, ex-lovers, or heroes. Some people are suspicious of names that are either the same or too close in spelling, seeing the names as ominous or ill-omened and therefore to be avoided at all costs. In these cases, it is never the name but the meaning imputed to the name that is at stake.

A friend of mine told me of a woman she knew who had fallen in love with a man she had met serendipitously at a concert. They both were attending alone due to recent spousal deaths. What started as a conversation while they stood in line at the refreshment counter at intermission continued over drinks after the concert and into the wee hours of the morning. This romance continued in storybook fashion until a few weeks later when the woman discovered that the name her boyfriend was known by was in fact his middle name, and that his first name was the name of her deceased husband. Unable to move beyond this unfortunate coincidence of names, she abruptly terminated the relationship. My friend's comment: "You would think she wouldn't have to worry about calling her husband's name in a moment of abandon!"

Salvador Dalí, the eccentric Spanish surrealistic painter, "scanDAL-Ized" the world with his artwork and multiple acts of provocation. He frequently made reference to the meanings of both his names: He interpreted his first name as savior, by which he insisted on his predestination to save painting, and his surname as desire, an etymological stretch perhaps connected to *delir*, the Catalan term for ardent desire. A desire to save painting. A savior of modern art.

The significance of his name was overdetermined even further. Dalí had a complex relationship with the surrealist French "pope" and founder of Surrealism, André Breton. Breton and the other surrealists, irritated by Dalí's independence and self-appointed autonomy, felt that his art ran counter to the traditional surrealist methods of automatic writing and dream associations. In the end, Dalí was excommunicated from the group as a result of a political statement in which he appeared to be on the "wrong side" of the art cognoscenti—that is, the rich and famous.

For many of Dalí's friends and admirers, the break with Breton, who had been such a mentor and father figure, was the repetition of a pattern of parental rejection that Dalí had experienced with his own father. Dalí's father had initially disowned him for living with a divor-cée, the former wife of the French poet Paul Éluard (né Eugène Émile Paul Grindel). Having settled accounts with his father for this misde-meanor, a second and final breach with his father came when Dalí scrawled across a picture depicting the Sacred Heart, "Sometimes I spit on the portrait of my mother for the fun of it."

Dalí was known by his friends as Divine Dalí, and derogatorily named Avida Dollars by Breton. Catherine Millet, a student of Dalí's writings, writes that this second rejection by an adoptive father may have been instrumental in pushing Dalí to reconstruct his life as a work of art. As Dalí himself wrote: "The anagram 'avida dollars' was a talis-man for me. It rendered the rain of dollars fluid, sweet and monoto-nous. Someday I shall tell the whole truth about the way in which this blessed disorder of Danae was garnered. It will be a chapter of a new book, probably my masterpiece: 'On the Life of Salvador Dalí Considered as a Work of Art.'"[3]

As Millet notes, the book was never written, but his life as a work of art definitely was realized. It did become "a life's work," as Dalí himself further describes it: "Before, less aware of what was inside me, I felt no responsibility at all. Today, I pay more attention to my actions and my thoughts. I measure my ideas against those of the greatest living men. In my everyday life every action becomes ritual. The anchovy I chew is in some way a part of the fire that lights me. I am the dwelling of a genius."[4]

On a recent trip to Barcelona, I was introduced to the work of Antoni Tàpies (1923–2012), a Catalan painter, sculptor, and art theorist who became one of the most famous European artists of his generation. Initially influenced by the surrealistic works of Miró and Klee, Tàpies eventually evolved his own style of painting in which he incorporated nonartistic materials such as clay and marble dust, paper, string, and rags into huge wall canvases. Visiting the Fundació Antoni Tàpies, I was struck by the artist's comment, "I have come to appreciate the strange fate of my name"—for *tapia* means "wall," the bearer of his huge works. The genuine unconscious impact of the name was only discovered after the fact, when the artist could reflect on the coincidence between his name and his artwork.

※ ※ ※

While my name Mavis has the dictionary meaning of a bird, it was my surname Himes, derived from the Hebrew word *chaim* ("life"), that I find myself considering. Those of my close friends who spent their twenties and thirties living in Israel continue to write my name with the Hebrew spelling and I am always surprised to see it written that way, as it reminds me of my name's literal meaning.

Life. I have been fortunate to enjoy all that life can offer: health, education, family, work. I am engaged in activities and explore my interests that are creative, stimulating, and life affirming. My adventurous spirit has brought me into contact with people and places around the globe. I share my life with people I love and cherish. Because of my history of work with cancer patients, I treasure each day, knowing my time on this earth is limited. I value life-enhancing causes; I respect the life of others. *L'chaim* is the blessing we Jews say over food and wine. Yes, to life. The name's potential to determine the fate of an individual and to direct his or her history in a particular direction is certainly a curious phenomenon. And yet it is this quality, this power of the name to direct our life, that gives this word a unique standing in our life's narrative. The Italian philosopher Adriana Cavarero notes in a book on narratives and storytelling about oneself that our name, in the absence of any preordained or known qualities, somehow becomes "the phonetic glue of our identity, sealing our biographical and autobiographical stories."[5]

8

TRANSMISSION AND INHERITANCE

Transmission and inheritance: a duo of terms. What can we say about the difference between these terms? We tend to think of inheritance on the side of passivity: We receive, we are given a history and a genetic foundation; we choose neither. An early fifteenth-century term, which means the receiving by hereditary succession, inheritance descends from the old French term *enheriter* ("make heir, appoint as heir"), which descends from the late Latin term *inheriditare* (also "to appoint as heir"). Our inheritance, like our name, is prescribed to us and predetermined for us by someone else, for better or for worse.

As for transmission, we view it as active: We transmit a lesson, a skill, a value, or a belief, although it may also be a silent, invisible initiative.

As family members, we all partake in this complementary dynamic of receiving an inheritance and transmitting a legacy: As children we inherit, and as parents we transmit. By definition, at least two individuals are required: the one receiving and the one sending. Mentoring relationships, such as between student and teacher or apprentice and master, can be viewed in the same way.

* * *

Most of us consider our inheritance in terms of the genetic makeup we carry from our biological parents. My birthmark and skin texture, my freckles, and my coloring are genetic, the transmission of a biological blueprint encoded in my body.

The lines on my forehead and at the sides of my eyes are now engraved on my face. Between my brows, an increasingly deep set of furrows. These fissures record the expressions of my life's escapades. Creases punctuate my eyes like the smile lines of my father. The faint trace of a vertical line down my back from between my shoulder blades to three inches above my tailbone documents the faded scar of a surgery for scoliosis, a condition that I inherited from my father (at least according to family lore). The thin skin and raised veins on my hands are the genetic gifts I received from my mother and maternal grandfather. I wear my history on my body: They represent the tattoos of a life not only acquired through a life lived, but also inherited from birth.

I see in my niece the smile of my sister, the raised eyebrow of my brother-in-law, and the big feet of my uncle. I discover in my friends traces of their siblings and parents. Our bodies do not lie; without surgery, we cannot bury the physically inscribed traces of our immediate family and distant relatives.

Sometimes, genetic history operates on a hidden level, concealing a particular divergence of cellular anomalies or a perfect storm of microscopic DNA: the unexpected emergence of a rogue gene, a grandmother's high blood pressure, an as yet undiagnosed hereditary heart condition, a pelvic bone malformation.

Families do not always know or share their genetic legacy with children. Sometimes a family history is revealed only after the diagnosis of a medical illness. One of my patients was diagnosed with lymphoma at the age of forty-three; it was only after his diagnosis that he learned of his father's treatment for the same disease at the age of twenty. A family secret exposed. Genetic inheritance has no respect for personal privacy. The unwanted inheritance, the disfigurement, the willfully banished inevitably return.

If we are so blessed or favored, we may inherit property and worldly goods, the material inheritance that typically follows a family death. Or we may be fortunate enough to inherit a family treasure or heirloom, a memento infused with nostalgia and memory. These remnants sometimes become amulets that link us to a departed loved one. Who does not know someone who has traveled halfway across the globe to find the navy and burgundy scarf that warmed the neck of a loved one or the whereabouts of a particular family treasure?

We inherit the olive-colored sweater, the silver earrings with the amber stones, the Murano glass vase bought on a Venetian escapade, the photographs from Bucharest and Barcelona, the butane lighter em-

bossed with an engraving of the family name. When my own father died, I inherited his gold watch, a hand-woven silk tie, a pair of his cufflinks, his caramel-colored sweater, and three passport photographs.

We also inherit the family archive, a storage box of memories that connect one generation to the next: the stories, the legends, the family secrets, the misconstrued gossip, the revered lies—what is talked about and what is whispered; what is concealed and what is revealed. The rituals of family gatherings and holidays are key opportunities for the transmission of family memory and genealogical knowledge. These rituals offer a symbolic structure for a family to situate itself in its past and to construct a representation of its own history, past, present, and future.

"Remember the time Grandma argued with Mom over the color of the shirt Dad wore to that Christmas party?

"A war of colors. What was the big deal?"

"Must have been the principle of it. You know Grandma always had to have the last word."

"Right. Stubbornness is an inherited trait. It's called the MacIntosh gene."

We also inherit certain patterns of behavior and rituals, idiosyncratic traits and subtle preferences that are passed seamlessly from generation to generation. These marks of family identification are insidious and tacit and are always beyond our conscious awareness. These are the breeding grounds of prejudice and racism, rivalry and family feuds, that become linked to family name and honor. To carry a certain name can also be to acquire a readymade and particular code of ethics.

* * *

The Old World was saturated with the names of nobility and dynastic families stretching back centuries to a time when church and state were twins questing for power—sometimes in concert, sometimes as rivals. A certain deference to those endowed with wealth through inheritance was given to the kings and queens, dukes and duchesses, who ruled the lands. Not only were nobility identified by their family name, but they were also distinguished by their lands and possessions. The feudal world was like a large village with certain names that dominated the landscape, ruling over those marked by a single name. Long-dead ancestors retained a living authority over successive offspring.

During the medieval period, the impact of ancestry on one's character and behavior was continuously reinforced. Consider the Crusades of the twelfth century in which recruits were expected not only to remember but also to pay homage to the achievements of their ancestors through battle. In the review of a recent publication on the Crusades and family memory, Nicholas Paul points out that Pope Eugenius reminded young men to salute and pay tribute to their ancestors who had conquered the Holy Land half a century earlier: "God forbid the bravery of the fathers will prove diminished in the sons."[1]

Explicit appeals and demands by clergy and state were typical of this period, when the aristocratic cultures of Western Europe conditioned the choices of offspring, and, in particular, sons. Paul mentions that deference to dead elders satisfied two important factors in the determination of elite status: "the obligations of inherited nobility and the need to demonstrate personal prowess, or *probitas*."[2] In this plea for the maintenance of tradition, sons were expected to honor their ancestors by joining the ongoing battlefields of their fathers and grandfathers. In this way, their actions would strengthen that linked chain of family valor. These times demanded compliance of filial devotion and piety, and no exceptions would be tolerated.

In the Old World, distant ancestry was also the basis for establishing title and property rights, status and privilege. Castles and manors, heraldic badges and pennants, were all the symbols of prominent family names. Relatives were commemorated for their virtues or vices and occupied the family's collective memories in narratives of honor, bravery, and duty. As a result, ancestry was prescriptive, determining the actions of offspring. Not only were wealth and power to be sustained during one's lifetime, but, as dictated by custom, they were also to be transferred in one's old age.

❊ ❊ ❊

Shakespeare's King Lear struggles to determine which of his three daughters will inherit his wealth. Misguided, seduced, and betrayed by the alluring words of Regan and Goneril, he misinterprets the silence of his favored Cordelia and misdirects his anger at what he perceives as this most beloved one's rejection. As Shakespearean scholar Stephen Greenblatt points out in *Will in the World*:

> In the culture of Tudor and Stuart England where the old demanded the public deference of the young, retirement was the focus of particular anxiety. It put a severe strain on the politics and psychology of deference by driving a wedge between status—what Lear at society's pinnacle calls "the name, and all the additions to a king" (1.1.136)—and power. In both the state and the family, the strain could somewhat be eased by transferring power to the eldest legitimate male successor . . .[3]

The dilemma for Lear, who could not rely on a son or male heir, was the question of family transmission. Which of his three daughters could he trust and rely on to bestow his family property in return for the provision of food, shelter, and clothing?

The importance of status was not unfamiliar to William Shakespeare and his father. In order to increase the honor of his own name and the social ranking for his children and grandchildren, John Shakespeare applied to the College of Heralds for a coat of arms. While blood determined one's entitlement to the elite status of a gentleman, it was always possible to acquire, indirectly, the necessary qualifications. After an initial failure, John's application was subsequently reviewed and approved, due to the intervention of his son. By helping his father, Will also benefited, raising himself and his children to a gentleman's status.

Will had by this time no doubt played gentlemen onstage, and he could carry off the part outside the playhouse as well, but he and others would always know he was impersonating someone he was not. Now he had the means to acquire legitimately, through the offices his father once held, a role he had only played. Now he could legally wear, outside the theater, the kinds of clothes he had donned for the stage. For a man singularly alert to the social hierarchy—after all, he spent most of his professional life imagining the lives of kings, aristocracy, and gentry—the prospect of this privilege must have seemed sweet. He would sign his last will and testament "William Shakespeare, of Stratford-upon-Avon in the county of Warwick, gentleman." "In Elizabethan times, this transformational step of social identity was paramount. Even more significant is the motto chosen by Will to accompany the shield and crest: *Non sanz droict*, 'Not without right.'"[4]

* * *

The New World did not share the same history of names associated with a long lineage of pedigree, class, and status. However, as described by François Weil, in *Family Trees: A History of Genealogy in America*, many Americans in the first half of the nineteenth century became obsessed with pedigree, seeking an individual and collective connection to England or other "civilized" nations in Europe. Lacking a distinct national character in the New World, New Englanders spoke of their "Puritan stock," New Yorkers of their descent from distinguished Dutch families, and Virginians of their Cavalier associations, even if it took fraudulent claims to do so.

Weil also points out how this search for pedigree took a nasty turn in the direction of eugenics, or the science of "better breeding." While Anglo-Saxons were considered to be at the peak of the racial scale, scholars began noting, with favor, Aryan and Teutonic influences on American culture. Prominent scientists soon began urging genealogists to consider their work from the perspective of genetics rather than lineage, with clear supremacist and racial implications. Eventually, genealogical research began to focus on family identity rather than pedigree. However, social ranking and status still seem to make their appearance in the media.

The family history of the prominent, award-winning Canadian artist Michael Snow, according to a magazine article, includes these words: "He has a prestigious lineage: his father, Gerald Bradley Snow, was a civil engineer and the grandson of former Toronto mayor James Beaty; his mother, the haughtily mannered and fabulously named Marie-Antoinette Françoise Carmen Lévesque, was the daughter of a former Chicoutimi mayor named Elzear Lévesque."[5]

✿ ✿ ✿

Today the rivalry over status and class structure, once the domain of royalty alone, continues to make its appearance around the globe. While fewer monarchies continue to exist, their popularity swells with media events, such as the weddings of royal couples or the death of a popular icon like Princess Diana. Today, competition and rivalry over social status and power in the current climate are not played out as in Elizabethan England, when the public image and status of a particular family name were embellished by emblems and insignia, emblazoned flags, coat of arms, shields, and other personal items, but in the acquisition of consumer items.

Well-known haute couture designers, expanding beyond the walls of their fashion houses, have begun to lend their name to other fields, notably awards of achievement in the arts. Recently, the Ralph Lauren Corporation became one of the national sponsors of the PBS Masterpiece series, lending the name Ralph Lauren to such popular period dramas as *Downton Abbey*, *Silk*, and *Sherlock*.

In Toronto a growing list of urban buildings reads like a bulletin of financial success stories. In today's global economy, financial institutions have replaced the names of individuals whose hard-won financial achievements were rewarded with the privilege of naming rights. In the landmark days of Toronto's development, the iconic names Sam Schneiderman (Sam the Record Man), John Lyle, and Bluma Appel were associated with many of the arts buildings of the downtown core.

In the late forties, Edwin (Ed) Mirvish, a financial wholesaler, philanthropist, and theatrical impresario, began his adventures in the Toronto real estate market, eventually purchasing many buildings that he converted into theaters that line King Street in the entertainment district, as well as Mirvish Village, the Markham Street block of restaurants and boutiques. The son of Ukrainian (paternal) and Austrian (maternal) parents, he had been given the name Yehuda, but at his cousin's insistence, he changed it to the more Anglo-sounding name of Edwin. His famous bargain department store, Honest Ed's, his first major purchase, once straddled an entire city block, welcoming immigrants and students, the young and the old, through its glass doors.

Until recently, the CIBC and TD Bank buildings and the Scotia Plaza and Olympia York buildings all vied to be the tallest in Toronto, yet today major hotels, such as the Shangri-La, are competing for this measure of greatness.

Name-changing on several buildings in the financial district, such as Brookfield Place, attest to the growing competition for immortality through naming. In 1960 Toronto opened the doors of the first art centers funded by the generous philanthropist E. P. Taylor, then head of the O'Keefe Brewing Company and Argus Corporation. One of them, the O'Keefe Centre, became the Hummingbird Centre thirty years later, in 1996, when Hummingbird Communications Limited donated $5 million to undertake a number of improvements and renovations. Then again in 2007, Sony bought the naming rights for the building; today, Toronto's cultural elite are welcomed into the interior of the Sony Centre for the Performing Arts for their entertainment needs.

✧ ✧ ✧

While the naming privileges of corporations vie today for pride of place on the boulevards of the downtown core and its expanding centers, there was a time in the history of this relatively young country when the inhabited world grew through the daring and hard-won efforts of its early pioneers and explorers. Place names in this New World, in particular the remote northern regions of the Yukon and the Northwest Territories, derived from the leaders of expeditions cutting across great land masses and waterways: Graham, Vanier, Bathurst, Cornwall, and Brock all have islands to memorialize their efforts. Separating and indenting the islands are a labyrinth of channels, straits, and bays that also bear the names of those men—admirals, commanders, and patrons—who arrived on wooden ships from far afield to probe an inhospitable landscape.

In an attempt to parade success, wealth, and status, today's most successful personalities in the entertainment, sports, and fashion worlds frequently brand paraphernalia with their own names. In the scent industry, we can find Seduction in Black by Antonio Banderas, Love and Glamour by Jennifer Lopez, Heiress by Paris Hilton, White Diamonds by Elizabeth Taylor, Midnight Fantasy by Britney Spears.

After all, we all know that naming privileges, as a universal form of transmission, are intended to guarantee eternal remembrance. We recognize certain philanthropic trust funds and foundations, such as the Rockefeller Foundation, the Laidlaw Foundation, the Molson Foundation. Not only do they provide much-needed monetary support, but they also ensure permanent testimonial and tribute to their donors. Similarly, names assigned to museums, art galleries, hospital wings, and public auditoriums are all contemporary means of establishing perpetual acknowledgment and homage by those with financial resources.

✳ ✳ ✳

Yet what is the impact on society of this trend in name-changing from the personal to the collective? Are there social implications or ramifications of this sliding chain of names? Does this trend in some way reflect a devaluation of the individual swallowed by corporate interests? Will future generations have a different perception of their city if the names of its founding fathers and mothers have been erased from the architectural landscape? We can only speculate as to the impact of this trend. We will undoubtedly have to wait for future generations to examine these questions.

In spite of the newer styles of social status, social ranking, and naming privileges today, the significance of family loyalty has never faded. We have seen how, in the distant past, transmission of a family or clan name demanded honoring and obeying the laws and customs associated with that name, and how, over time, on a collective level, this loyalty was transferred to the state and its rulers. And it is in the name of those titled individuals that battles over land and territory haunt the history of society.

In *The Tiger's Wife*, a novel set in a mythic, unnamed Balkan country, the protagonist, a young doctor, reflects on war and territory:

> When the fight is about unravelling—when it is about your name, the places to which your blood is anchored, the attachment of your name to some landmark or event—there is nothing but hate, and the long, slow progression of people who feed on it and are fed it, meticulously, by the ones who went before them. The fight is endless, and comes in waves and waves, but always retains its capacity to surprise those who hope against it.[6]

Téa Obreht, the young American author of this novel, was born in war-torn Belgrade. In her book she reminds us that hate and rage, fomenting into battle, always develop when the conflict centers on names and the places in which one's blood has been spilt. The attachment between name and landmark, name and territory, is a powder keg of bloody dissension and strife that we see around the globe, both in man's collective past history and continuing to the present.

Regimes that rule through intolerance and autocracy demonstrate a perversion of the power of the name. Territorial wars, which have tarnished and haunted human history from time immemorial, are all battles over title and name. This belongs to me, my family, my tribe, my history. Nationalism over homeland is a vestige of clan loyalty and honor. Xenophobia, the step-maiden of familial and social inclusivity and exclusivity, relies on the inheritance of bloodlines to maintain national purity.

In this context, we can retrieve and insert the notions of *nomen* and *nomos*, those etymological carriers of the name and the law, whose twinning may provide an explanation. After all, it is the division of property, the physical attachment to this named land won and lost by bloodshed, that foment and incite these interminable battles.

9

WHO WE ARE IS ALWAYS THERE

I remember the repeated times in my childhood that my mother grabbed my little hand and dashed across the street and the words that accompanied the maneuver: "Mavis, never cross in the middle of a street; always look both ways. Listen to my words, Mavis; now you don't copy my behavior." As an adult, I whiz through empty intersections paying no heed to the traffic lights; I jaywalk in foreign cities; I impatiently edge forward in crowded queues. "You are your mother's daughter," she chides me today. According to her, I have inherited her bad behavior.

Transmission occurs in the convictions and principles, the ethics and significance, of our moral faith and the body of knowledge we each acquire through a lifetime of living. This transmission happens within families seamlessly and in silence. It is born in the daily ritual, the nonverbal gestures, the spoken as well as the unspoken word. This silent transmission is a powerful force in our early experiences, creating powerful identifications. These are the words and ideas that enter through the porous surface of our minds and penetrate into our darkest recesses.

The obligation we feel to live up to our name, be it a name of fame or obscurity, bespeaks the ongoing nature of social ideals and convention, the realm of the shoulds and should nots that we all espouse. For better or for worse, we are all subjects of identification; we all conform to certain social expectations, certain belief systems and values imparted to us by those significant others who have been part of our formation.

Standards of social convention, like fashion, are ever evolving. Just as pants were not to be worn by women downtown during my childhood years but pantsuits became de rigueur as a work uniform in my adolescence, so do family mores modify over time.

We expect a decorum and demeanor of public personalities; we make assumptions about how a Rothschild, Trudeau, Kennedy, or Roosevelt should behave in social situations, which is why the paparazzi strive to put them in a compromised light. In the sphere of child rearing, far from the camera's glare, parents are prey to the pressure and expectations of social etiquette. After all, a well-behaved child reflects on a parent's success.

"You can't do that, Susie; after all, you're a Watson." It is important to most families that its members be seen as well behaved, well-turned out, and well-spoken, however different what this means may be from family to family. "We must always be on our best behavior."

Or, with unabashed affectation, I have heard parents say, "We don't do that in our family. We are the Smiths."

"We don't eat like that!"

"Now don't forget who you are—you are a Robertson. So you go out and show them!"

"You know that that is totally unacceptable in this family. After all, we have to keep up our family name—I can't have you traipsing around downtown looking like that!"

The humor slips through in the pretentiousness of these statements. And yet pedigree is of utmost importance to many families. Expectations, values, and beliefs are inevitably handed down and revisited on the children. In the narcissistic fantasies of parents, their children are a reflection of their achievement and accomplishment. Even in the Mafia family so well documented by the television series *The Sopranos*, we see a particular code of ethics being enacted by the family.

Our inheritance also includes the mythical and powerful claims of another type of behavior: those personality traits that we wish to fob off onto some other family member. I remind my patients that there are no genetic markers for character traits. But still they insist: "I swear my husband inherited his explosive temper from his father."

"I know my sister got her stubborn streak from our mother."

"My grandfather was always scared of airplanes. I'm sure that's why my uncle won't travel."

While my father stressed our family name as a link to my distant ancestral history with its cultural and historical roots, it was my mother who brought my sister and me back to the present. It was she who reminded us of certain day-to-day social conventions and behaviors, the canon of implicit and explicit dos and don'ts we were expected to follow.

* * *

In my family, what it was to be a Jew was not passed on wordlessly, and yet it was without sets of injunctions, threats, or decrees. It was communicated through certain rituals marked with a regularity that made them special: holiday celebrations, Shabbat meals, rituals of food preparation, my mother's Hadassah meetings. The year was punctuated, in a cyclical manner, by the agricultural festivals—the Feast of Unleavened Bread, the Feast of the Harvest (Shavuot), and the Feast of Ingathering (Sukkot)—and the three reverential holidays of Rosh Hashanah, Yom Kippur, and Pesach.

The patronymic Himes, in spite of its diminutive spelling, also contained within it a shorthand of behavior, a particular code of ethics with no need for elaboration. In this way, what distinguished us from them was already inscribed in our surname.

I was made aware of my difference from other children and adults who did not share in our religious and cultural tradition: These differences were always pointed out and prefaced by such statements as "We don't do that" or "That is what they do," referring, for example, to the celebration of Christmas or the eating of certain foods. This other world straddled my own as I played with all the children in the schoolyard; entertained my friends with lemonade, ice cream, and cookies; and shared intimate games of show-and-tell. Yet I was aware of a difference that I could not articulate but which entered my being; I learned by osmosis of a great divide that separated my world from that of certain others, a separation that could not be easily crossed in those formative years.

On the other hand, I had always known that my father's family had been Orthodox and that my father had resisted the tight reins of my grandfather's demands. There had been the stories of how he and his brothers had to trudge through the snow-covered streets of downtown

Montreal at dawn to attend the early services of a local synagogue. And there had been the hushed silence around the restrictions, rigidity, and harsh discipline of that household. Perhaps as a result of the enforced reverence of the Mosaic code, my father did not maintain a religious outlook or insist on regular synagogue attendance. I remember his mutters of vitriol as we strolled through Clanranald Park against the ultraorthodox Jews for parading their religion in "outlandish dress." The disquietude and conflict that I sensed in him bewildered me—and settled within me.

On my maternal side, it was my grandmother's presence and subsequent residence in our house that reinscribed the rituals of kashruth (dietary laws) and Yiddishkeit (sense of Jewishness) within the home. Friday nights were infused with ritualistic splendor. The smell of chicken rubbed tenderly with a paste of oil, garlic, paprika, and salt roasting in the oven; a cake plate adorned with the deep amber of honey cake; my grandmother's embroidered tablecloth inherited from her mother, who had hidden it in the folds of a suitcase she carried from Bukovina. Holidays were moments of family reunion.

What was passed on, aside from these rituals, and aside from the basic moral ethos, was a message about the way I conducted myself. And all the ways of imparting knowledge and attitudes—through a shrug, a word, a gesture, through touch and the body, in words spoken in the living moment—were communicated by my parents in a form that was fleeting and evanescent.

And it was through this unwritten code, more powerful than any written text about how to live or what to believe in, that I learned what it meant to be a Himes and a Jew. These fleeting words and gestures became written into my life, into my body, and into how I lived out the script of my life. My outer life in no way reflected this inner text. My assimilated life in an urban center hid these earliest influences. They lay dormant under a blanket of my intellectual acquisitions, to be challenged and analyzed as I became an adult.

＊ ＊ ＊

While we all carry a desire to speak our own voice and create our own signature, consciously or unconsciously acknowledging a debt to our family history, we sometimes cling to a wish for parental answers and a quick and easy solution to life's challenges.

I am reminded of a patient, a young woman who had always struggled with her relationship with her mother, who died during the course of our work together. Alternating between poise and frustration, calm and anxiety, one day she reminisced about the days just before her mother had given way in her brief battle with cancer:

> When my mother died, I had wanted her to pass on some teachings, some words of wisdom, something that would be the opposite of all the demands she made on me, all the insignificant lessons with which she tried to brainwash me. I suppose I wanted her blessings on my life. And I wanted an answer, a truth that she could pass on to me. But instead, my mother looked at me on her deathbed, frail and forlorn like a pixie under a mountain of blankets, and all she did was shrug her shoulders. Imagine—a shrug of her shoulders—that was what I was left with. All of her life, so much advice and warning and teaching, and then a lousy shrug. A shrug open to interpretation.
>
> At first I thought, it's like she's saying to me, "What's it all about?" like the song from the sixties film *Alfie*. But then I thought, no, she's admitting something she could never admit to me before: "I don't have the answer, I don't have any answers. I simply made it up as I went along." I interpreted this as her failure. My mother, a woman who always dictated what, when, where, and how. And at the last moment, nothing. I am left with nothing, a shoulder shrug. This is my inheritance—her failure. Now what do I do?

✿ ✿ ✿

In a remarkable book, *The Hare with Amber Eyes*, a memoir by a British ceramicist, we learn not only what has been revealed, but also what remains to be discovered or uncovered about one's inheritance. The spoken and the unspoken, the revealed and the concealed. Edmund Arthur Lowndes de Waal inherited a family collection of 264 wood and ivory Japanese carvings called netsuke. With the weighted gift of this inheritance, he began a search to uncover the significance of these objects for different family members over the years. In doing so, he also discovered the rich story of his family. His search begins in Berdichev, a city in one of the provinces of northern Ukraine, and lands him in the Paris of the late 1880s, fin-de-siècle Vienna and beyond, and eventually to Tokyo, where he encounters the legends of his great-uncle Ignace, familiarly referred to as Iggie.

Edmund's father, the Reverend Dr. Victor de Waal, who was married to Esther Moir, eventually became Dean of Canterbury Cathedral. It was Edmund's grandmother Elisabeth, a member of the wealthy and established Ephrussi family, who broke the family's Jewish tradition by marrying Hendrik de Waal, a Dutch businessman who moved to England and from whom Edmund received his distinctly Dutch family name.

In an interview with Eleanor Wachtel, the host of the CBC Radio show *Writers & Company*, Edmund acknowledged the reticence he had felt at the outset of his writing regarding his family quest. He did not know what secret or surprise, mishaps or skeletons, he might come across. In fact, as he admits, he discovered an array of characters he had never known, a history of financial success and artistic opulence, a community of trustworthy friends and emerging twentieth-century artists, a legacy of remarks and silences, some hidden encounters, and other public facts.

In that radio interview, I discovered an interesting detail that had been deliberately omitted from the book. As Dean of Canterbury, his father had been required to sit for a picture to hang along with the other portraits in the collection of the deanery. A Viennese cousin who had known Victor, Edmund's father, since childhood, requested to be the one to paint his picture on the condition that Victor not see the portrait until its completion. Edmund's father agreed. When the portrait was finally unveiled, there must have been a gasp among those assembled, as the Jewish Viennese cousin's rendering of the Reverend de Waal revealed the dean as a rabbi. In the interview, Edmund chuckled and said: "Who you are is always there." An inheritance of the name that hid the truth as the truth was hidden in the name. The truth of one's family story is waiting to be revealed.

The inheritance of the name can be modified and changed but never forgotten. It always lies waiting for its truth to be revealed by a family member at some point. As I placed the book on my bookshelf, I saw the subtitle I had not noticed: *A Hidden Inheritance*.

10

THE FAMILY TREE OF LIFE

Acer saccharinum. A magnificent silver maple tree stands outside the window of my home office. It would take four adults with outstretched arms to encircle its trunk. At least five hundred people could be protected from the sun's rays by the scope of its crown. I try to imagine the root structure buried beneath the surface—an underground network of canals thrusting downwards and outwards.

My neighbor refers to this imposing tree as the Tree of Life. My husband calls it The Nine Sisters because of its nine major trunk offshoots and because the cemetery in which it stands is the burial ground for an order of Catholic nuns. This grand maple stands near the eastern side of St. Michael's Catholic Cemetery, well-hidden in the center of Toronto. Inaugurated in 1855, it is now the resting place for over 29,000 individuals, many of them immigrants who had fled the Irish potato famine and fell victim to the 1918–1919 Toronto flu epidemic. The tombstones form an irregular pattern of tall Celtic crosses and spires alternating with marble, slate, and limestone gravestones. A cluster of small cross markers commemorate an entire order of nuns. On the eastern side, a mortuary vault interrupts the horizon with its domed top, a temporary resting place where dead bodies were stored in the snowy winter months. An inactive cemetery, this silent park of the dead is one of many graveyards telling a story of local history.

In *A Thousand Plateaus*, a massive treatise on capitalist society, Gilles Deleuze and Félix Guattari, two radical twentieth-century thinkers who devoted their lives to developing subversive ideas, write, "The

Western world has an arborescent structure . . . It is odd how the tree
has dominated Western reality and all of Western thought from botany
to biology and anatomy, but also gnosiology, theology, ontology, all of
philosophy . . . : the root-foundation, *Grund, racine, fondement*." [1]

Yes, the maple outside my office symbolizes our relationship to
knowledge and to one another. An ever-expanding layer on top with its
outer beauty that sheds foliage in the fall but returns each spring: a
sturdy trunk that acts as a conduit between the upper and lower, the
visible and the invisible, the inside and the outside; and a vast underground of support, an anchor to support the weight of its crown. I could
go further and say that the tree represents man with its head, arms, and
legs.

For Antoni Plàcid Guillem Gaudí i Cornet, more popularly known as
Gaudí, the renowned Catalan architect and patron saint of Barcelona,
the cypress tree with its permanent foliage and straight form pointing
upwards to the celestial bodies represents the tree of life. And so he
crowned the Sagrada Família, his magnificent yet uncompleted masterpiece, with a cypress, aimed towards the heavens and filled with doves
like angels, fluttering in its foliage. Gaudí, with his deep respect and
reverence for the lessons of nature, once remarked, "The tree near my
workshop is my teacher."

As I look out the window at my stalwart muse, I realize that in my
imaginary painting of the Garden of Eden, the Tree of Life reigns
supreme, center stage in the canvas. What better universal icon of life's
interconnectedness, of the cosmic symbol of immortality and a metaphor of humankind's common descent? Is it the acacia tree of Iusaaset
from which the Egyptians believed that Isis and Osiris emerged? Or is it
the Christian tree of life "bearing twelve crops of fruit, yielding its fruit
every month" (Rev. 22:1–2) and whose leaves are said to be used for the
healing of all nations? Or is it the mystical symbol of Kabbalistic Judaism with its ten outspread branches directing us towards the path to
God? Unlike the rendition in Genesis, I would paint the Tree of Knowledge of Good and Evil off to a side. Hidden from immediate view, this
tree with its bountiful fruit beckons and calls. It tempts and attempts to
be seen, to be touched, to be tasted. The tree of knowledge promises
the secrets of all knowledge.

* * *

Trees are a lifeline in the history of man's civilization: the first rub-
bings of twigs and stems for warmth and fire, the nourishment for our
food supply, the source of products for private and commercial usage.
From birth to death, we are sustained by the generosity of our leafy
companions. It is the tree's trunk that provides us with life's materials:
the planks of rocking cradles; the parchment of Lucretius's *De Rerum
Natura* and Shakespeare's *Hamlet*, *Macbeth*, and *Othello*; the paper of
the *Toronto Star* and the *Manchester Guardian*, the *New York Times*
and the *Washington Post*, the *Encyclopedia Britannica* and the col-
lected works of Freud and Lacan; hardwood floors and baseball bats;
violins and pianos; and the envelope of wood coffins that accompany us
in death.

In the cemetery where my father is buried, in a French-dominated
quartier of Montreal, there are few trees and no bushes; only grasses
and rows of tombstone markers crowd the land. Sometimes when I visit
his gravestone, I see a line of pebbles sitting on the black granite and
know that my father has been visited by an anonymous guest. My
father's body lies buried in a coffin of mahogany, wood that will deteri-
orate with time so that he will return to the earth. When I am there, I
sometimes read the names of the men and women who are my father's
burial neighbors and imagine that they have become friends in some
otherworldly universe.

"The family tree is like a family romance," says one of my patients.
"It always begins a question: Who am I? Where did I inherit these big
feet? Who was my grandfather's twin that we can never speak about?"

Questions about our family tree may also be a search for an exotic
past: the discovery of a royal lineage, an encounter with a family secret,
the unearthing of a distant relative. For those engaged in family research, each additional detail uncovered has the potential for an opening into an exciting labyrinth of blind alleys, dead ends, and chance
meetings. We search for a connection, a surprise, a discovery of an
unknown fact. *Oh my god, my sister really was adopted!* We search for
an explanation, a causal connection. *Oh, so he had pointy ears and a
Roman nose. I really am my father's daughter.*

We search for a reality check on the fiction we have constructed. *I
think I am really the bastard child of an affair my mother had before
she was married.* We search with a sense of fascination and curiosity,
with a hope of possible intrigue and a frisson of mystery. Like reading a

detective novel, we follow the clues and cues to a city across an ocean that was once behind the Iron Curtain, to a foreign village or hamlet, to a seaside town on the Mediterranean. We are hoping to be surprised, maybe shocked. Yet we are never prepared for the tragedy of the unforeseen: illness, premature death, wars.

We search out our history in spite of the cost, effort, and unpredictability—or perhaps because of it. For some, it becomes a lifelong project; for others, it is a rather peculiar piece of history. But there it is: a piece of paper with a diagram fanning out in all directions with names in little boxes floating above the ground in the shape of a tree or botanical graph, with names hanging off vertical and horizontal lines as on a clothesline.

❊ ❊ ❊

I met a woman who had been trying to find out about her family line. She soon was stymied by the number of times the spelling of her name had been changed. As she was about to abort her project, she was contacted by a man who identified himself as her deceased mother's great-uncle. It turned out that he had been in hiding during the Second World War and lost all contact with his family. After he contacted her, they met and the reunion led to an album of shared information on her deceased relatives and his missing siblings.

While researching her family history, my friend discovered a child out of wedlock to an aunt who remained overseas. This child had been the product of an intriguing affair with a paternal uncle. She also unearthed the fact that her mother previously had been partnered to another man with whom she had two children, both of whom died shortly after birth. My friend had always been curious and perplexed by her mother's advanced age when she was born, but her mother always slipped behind a veil of silence whenever she asked her about it.

This fascination with memory and history is part of the human condition. Psychoanalysts spend a considerable part of their time in the caves of reminiscence. Artifacts and relics of a past intermingle with souvenirs from the present. The factual and the fictional weave themselves into a personal and familial tapestry. One of my patients showed me a book about Maritime Canada; she was proud of the prominence of her family story recorded in print, with a Post-it at each of five cherished entries.

With their names well disguised, I will let you eavesdrop on some comments by my patients:

> You know, there are three names that keep repeating themselves through my family history: Raimonde, Philippe, and François. They are like shadows that keep appearing and disappearing. I know that my mother's side landed in Canada in 1666 from the Loire valley in France and my father's family arrived thirty years later from Normandy. I am the archivist in my family, and so I have the official documents safeguarded in my home office. This work is making me want to go back and do some family research. These names—I wonder what these recurring names were all about. To this day, I do not know.

✿ ✿ ✿

> I don't know very much about my family history. I do know that my grandmother came from Istanbul, a very aristocratic lady, and my grandfather was Persian. What a mix—no wonder it didn't last. But then there were all these aunties and uncles with children of ages from my own to thirty years my senior. Maybe it's time to put it down on paper. With the Internet, I have been contacted by people from around the world who are my cousins, and I want to know who they are, what they look like, what the stories are.

✿ ✿ ✿

> My mother's people were Scottish-Irish. It was all mixed up at some point. But my father's people were French Canadian. The spelling of our surname has been modified and Anglicized in its pronunciation, but the Tonnerres are a proud family. My great-great-great-grandfather owned land and that land was passed down to my father, as he was the eldest son. If you go anywhere in rural New Brunswick, people will recognize my father's name, the name I no longer carry.

✿ ✿ ✿

My own family tree is a hybrid of Russian and Austro-Hungarian branches. All four of my grandparents spent their childhoods imbibing the Yiddish language and culture in shtetlach, or towns, in the Pale of Settlement, that region of western Imperial Russia beyond which Jews were prohibited. They made their way from Radauti, Romania; from Minsk, Belarus; from Raskol, Russia; and from Czernowitz, Bukovina.

In my desk lies a file of family memorabilia, for I am the keeper of the embarkation certificates and documents of my family's history. I have always wondered what my grandparents carried on their long voyage beginning in the east and across the Atlantic, but none of them are alive today, and my mother is a poor archivist. I have tried to re-create the scenes of departure but do so in vain: a fourteen-year-old girl traveling with her parents, a nineteen-year-old man traveling alone to meet a brother, a sixteen-year-old girl traveling alone to join up with a sister and brother-in-law.

Unlike family searches from other nationalities, the Jews are at a certain disadvantage in their search for tribal origins. Constant movement and exile, especially in countries behind the former Iron Curtain, multiple linguistic families and dialects, and the obliteration of records, synagogues, and cemeteries during the Second World War—all create obstacles to the search. On the positive side, in the more distant past, the rabbis of the medieval period considered recordkeeping a sacred and pious duty. They mandated for recording genealogical information about the authors of Talmudic commentary and responsa of rabbinical students. Genealogical information is now pooled in several distinct sources. With the population of Jews worldwide being a finite number, it is possible to perform a reasonable search.

Equipped with a treasury chest of paraphernalia and documentation, my cousin Mel is engaged in the pursuit of our family ancestry. Records of birth, death certificates, medical records, passports, photographs, federal census records, newspaper clippings, telephone directories, immigration and naturalization records, city directories, ships' passenger lists, and probate records—all populate his desk in neatly arranged piles. He has contacted various living relatives, consulted books on Jewish geographical history, searched the Internet, and pursued correspondence with source contacts in Russia to enlarge his search.

My husband has recently discovered that his cousin has been researching the family genealogy on his maternal side. He has discovered, through his cousin's investigations, that his lineage places him in the same bloodlines as several royal figures in the Netherlands, France, and Britain. In his family tree are Counts of Holland, Dukes of Friesland, Kings of Alsace, and even a link to Charlemagne and Pepin III. Appar-

ently, the family lines have yielded productive results due to the colli-
sion of the family's genealogies with well-documented lines of historical
significance.

"You must begin to treat me with respect," my husband says. "There
is a family line that goes right back to Roman emperor Flavius Valentin-
inus the First!"

A similar search of family history is narrated by the Chilean author
Cynthia Rimsky, but her family narrative sinks into a tribulation of
uncertainty and doubt. In her autobiographical novel, *Poste Restante*
(Unclaimed Mail), she sets out on a search to uncover details of her
family's unknown past, which until then had been revealed only in
fragments and scraps. A second-generation Chilean, Rimsky becomes
obsessed with her discovery, at a flea market in her hometown of Santiago, of a photograph album with the inscription of her surname spelt
with an *i* instead of a *y*. She convinces herself of her connection to this
photograph through a family link based on the fact that many immigrants' names had been modified by customs officers who transcribed
and registered "the Cohens as Kohen, the Levys as Levi, in a way that
Rimsky could well have been Rimski."[2]

And so the fragility of her identity is transferred to this name and
becomes the catalyst of a journey through twelve countries, culminating
in her final destination, Odessa in the Ukraine, the birthplace of her
parents. Six months into her trip, she is informed that the name "Rimski" is a referent for Rimski Vrelec, the location of a Slovenian thermal
bath, which explains the dress of the family in the album from the flea
market. However, when she removes one of the album photos and
discovers the date 1940 on the back, she realizes that, since this area
had been evacuated of its Jews in this time period, the album's contents
could not possibly be of her family's relatives. Several months after her
return to Santiago, she receives a letter from Israel; it is from a woman
claiming to be a relative on the maternal side of her family. And so
another journey of discovery begins.

* * *

Genealogy is the writing of history on a personal scale. From its root
gen(e), we derive the Greek *gignesthai*, "to become, to happen," and
the Latin *gignere*, "to beget," and *gnasci*, "to be born." From these
derivatives flow the words *genius, ingenium, generic, genotype, misceg-
enation, degenerate, general, generous,* and *gender.*

Genealogy draws on our desire to carve a place for ourselves and our family out of the larger historical context, to eliminate the fear that one day we will be buried along with the family photos in some bottom drawer of a basement dresser. It is the insurance that we will be commemorated in a chain linking generations that both precede and succeed us. The preservation and sanctity of the family line is momentous.

American antiquarians were already stowed away in library archives recording local history when John Farmer, considered the founder of genealogical research in America, decided to commemorate the founding fathers and the heroes of the Revolutionary War. By so doing, he established, in 1839, the first genealogical society of its kind: the New England Historic Genealogical Society.

Today, the Genealogical Society of Utah is home to the largest microfilm database of genealogical value, with over two million microfiche and microfilm documents. Founded in 1894, it is currently the primary hub for genealogical research and a stopping place for millions of people engaged in personal family research. Similarly, the National Genealogical Society in Washington, DC, founded in 1903, had grown from 395 members in 1948 to over 4,000 by 1974 and today has over 4,600 local family history centers around the world. Due to the growing interest in genealogy, Library and Archives Canada created a website in 2002 to supplement existing resources and provide assistance to Canadians.

And so, in the arborescent system of Western man, we scramble up and down those limbs of transmission that precede our birth, trying to place ourselves on those preestablished branches. We design trees with multiple roots and place our names in little boxes below the ground. Or we draw photos of named faces floating in the tree's crown. Trees with boxlike leaves, trees with green leafy branches; sticklike trees, human trees with legs for the trunk and arms for the branches—all of the creative forms in which we honor our family history.

As Deleuze and Guattari, mentioned above, write: "The tree imposes the word 'to be.'"[3] A fixed stickiness is associated with this signifier. We can try to eliminate the power of our rootedness in a family, yet we are permanently glued to some part of its structure. We are a part of the seed from which we have been born.

✳ ✳ ✳

Social history is also a story of bloodlines, but rather than the individual family tree, its branches depict the recounting of a community on a collective level. This branch of history identifies families and clans grouped together by genetic inheritance or racial traces.

Bloodlines are blueprints for genealogical research, the physical basis on which genealogical trees are built. They are the physical carriers that trace population genetics. Genomes, the genetic code of chromosomes inherited from our parents, can never lie. They detail the specific history of shared genetic markers through genetic mapping.

The English Monarchs. The Plantagenets. The United Kingdom Monarchs. The House of Stuart, the House of Hanover, the House of Saxe-Coburg and Gotha, the House of Windsor. The family tree of today's British Royal Family is a history of Europe with marriages and suitors, spouses and lovers, rampaging across national boundaries. In 1917 George V changed the name of the royal house from Saxe-Coburg and Gotha to Windsor to enhance the family's public image with a more British house name. At that time the British Empire, the French Republic, and the Russian Empire were allies at war with Italy and Germany.

On November 30, 1917, King George V issued letters patent defining who could be defined as members of the Royal Family. The text of the notice from the *London Gazette* on December 14, 1917, reads as follows:

> Whitehall, 11th December, 1917. The KING has been pleased by Letters Patent under the Great Seal of the United Kingdom of Great Britain and Ireland, bearing date the 30th ultimo, to define the styles and titles to be borne henceforth by members of the Royal Family. It is declared by the Letters Patent that the children of any Sovereign of the United Kingdom and the children of the sons of any such Sovereign and the eldest living son of the eldest son of the Prince of Wales shall have and at all times hold and enjoy the style, title or attribute of Royal Highness with their titular dignity of Prince or Princess prefixed to their respective Christian names or with their other titles of honour; that save as aforesaid the titles of Royal Highness, Highness or Serene Highness, and the titular dignity of Prince and Princess shall cease except those titles already granted and remaining unrevoked; and that the grandchildren of the sons of any such Sovereign in the direct male line (save only the eldest living son

of the eldest son of the Prince of Wales) shall have the style and title enjoyed by the children of Dukes.[4]

In 1996 Her Majesty the Queen modified these letters patent with a notice in the *London Gazette*. It is likely that these further restrictions were intended to limit access and to protect the wealth and power of the Royals. The formal change in law ensures that wives of the royal family are curtailed in their access to money and title. Curiously, this notice appeared a year before the death of Diana, Princess of Wales:

> The QUEEN has been pleased by Letters Patent under the Great Seal of the Realm dated 21st August 1996, to declare that a former wife (other than a widow until she shall remarry) of a son of a Sovereign of these Realms, of a son of a son of a Sovereign and of the eldest living son of the eldest son of The Prince of Wales shall not be entitled to hold and enjoy the style, title or attribute of Royal Highness.[5]

As with every empire, we can enumerate the emperors and rulers, the princes and princesses, and the assortment of related men and women who constitute each of the royal assemblies. The Xia Dynasty. The Shang Dynasty. The Zhou Dynasty. The Qin Dynasty. Indian dynasties, Japanese dynasties, Egyptian dynasties.

* * *

While bloodlines trace a history of the collective, they can also be a pretext for the desire for genetic purity. Bloodlines can be a ruse for national perfection, the sinister underbelly of inbreeding for perfection.

The Nazis are the most recent and infamous example of those who have defended racial integrity and ethnic cleansing. In the name of Aryan purity, they sacrificed millions of people, notably Jews and gypsies, whom they considered inferior breeds. Unfortunately, in too many countries today, individuals with particular ethnic or foreign-sounding names automatically become the victims of racial abuse and even "purging."

The notion of genetic purity has filtered down through the generations. Joseph Jacobs was a leading physical anthropologist in fin-de-siècle Europe. As a Jewish polymath, he was interested in literature, philosophy, history, and mathematics. Deeply affected by George Eliot's book *Daniel Deronda*, in which an English gentleman develops an affinity for the Jewish community, Jacobs discovered his own Jewish heritage, embraced his roots, and married Mirah, a Jewish singer. Like Daniel's transformative self-discovery, Jacobs subsequently turned his attention to Jewish history and texts. Studying with Francis Galton, the cousin of Charles Darwin, he became convinced that certain races and nations were unique, and that these racial differences, which revealed themselves in the intellectual output of a race, could be decisive. Jacobs felt that a study of Jewish history, when combined with an analysis of Jewish racial characteristics, would provide him with a powerful arsenal in the battle against anti-Semites and therefore with a possible resolution to the Jewish question.

Today, with advances in technology, the field of genetic research has blossomed around the word in internationally shared research paradigms. In his informative book *Legacy: A Genetic History of the Jewish People*, Harry Ostrer suggests that the exploration of physical ancestry through genetic testing makes it possible to examine certain lineages. Through the testing of particular chromosomal DNA and other genetic markers, the field of population genetics has opened the door to detailed studies of population evolution and migration patterns.

The genetic analysis of contemporary Jewish populations scattered around the globe has suggested certain trends in the movement of people who may have originated from the same place. Ostrer points out that, by studying certain biological markers, we can deepen our understanding of the deep ancestry of all major human populations. Consequently, teams of scientists around the world are now tracking population shifts and genetic migrations.

But let us beware. For many people, the study of genetic ancestry arouses a curiosity about those primal tribal connections and roots and a biological basis for ethnic singularity. And from ethnic purity there are only a few steps to national purity, xenophobia, and racism. Extreme caution must be taken to ensure that genetic research does not backfire. Ostrer notes that the American Society of Human Genetics has "issued an advisory against using genetic tests as a basis for predicting personal ancestry."[6]

11

IN THE NAME OF THE FATHER

While my birth was celebrated with great joy and ceremony, or so goes the family legend, I have always been convinced that my parents anticipated, and perhaps even wanted, a son. My mother had been an only child, but my father's large family, with two sisters eclipsed by seven brothers, made me think my parents had expected to have at least one male child. In a moment of weakness, my father once confessed that, yes, he had wanted a son, but, no, seconds after my birth, it had all been forgotten. "You were just so adorable. I melted when I saw you," he said. But then there were his repeated quips, "I am overruled in a household of females. It's only me and the dog." Or, the more quasi-serious one familiar to many women, "And what will happen to the Himes name when you girls get married?" Of course, that was before the trend of women maintaining their maiden name. Do women not also hope that their family line will not be extinguished by the absence of children?

Several strongly patriarchal cultures still place a premium on the birth of boys. For example, the celebration of a son's birth often out-weighs that of a daughter's, or, as noted in chapter 5 in reference to Muslim names, both boys and girls are named with a patronymic (son of . . .).

Until recently, with more stringent birth quotas in place, baby girls in China were either killed or "exported" for adoption. That country, and other nations such as Pakistan and India, are known to have practiced female infanticide, resulting in the current imbalance of the male-to-female population.

While naming rights suggest the potency and ascendancy of men over women, we must not forget that there was a time in the early history of mankind when the female element was considered the primal and divine source of all nature. Among the ancient religions, female deities were worshipped as a maternal wellspring of creation invested with sacred powers. It took a long struggle before the male, conceived as a father, replaced female deities—in this process female deities were repressed and transformed into demons, and the place of women came to be devalued.

Traces of this struggle still linger in certain scriptures and textual elaborations. For example, in Judaism, the female presence of God, referred to as the Shekinah, or "divine wisdom," suggests an ongoing respect for the sensitivity and wisdom of women.

* * *

And the tensions persist to this day. Today, we women continue to challenge the remnants of male overvaluation. We continue to ask: What is it about the extra chromosome that makes him so valuable? Why is it the name of the father and not the mother that confers status on the next generation even in matrilineal societies?

I escaped to a retreat center recently to write in silence for a few days. At suppertime, a small group of women sat around the table, doing what we do naturally, sharing food and sharing conversation. Having struggled that day with a complicated issue, I decided to mention my writing project. Curiosity led to many questions and, to my benefit, a fruitful discussion.

One young woman told me about the process that she and her husband had undergone in naming their two children, now aged seven and two years:

> My name is Rosita Pollock, Pollock being of Scottish origin, and my common law partner's name is Jason Hunter. We were together for four years before having children. When it came to naming our first-born, we had many heated discussions about our child's surname. We did not want to go the route of a double surname because that gets so confusing, and if our child wanted to get married, there would be all the complications of three or even four surnames and how to manage that. I was sure that I did not want to give up my

surname, as I am very proud of my name. Besides, I was opposed to the notion that women have to automatically forfeit their name for the sake of some tradition that says all children must assume their father's surname. My name is just as important!

Eventually, we decided that if the firstborn child was a boy, he would assume his father's surname, and if it was a girl, she would take my name. Then, the second child would automatically take the name of the other parent irrespective of the gender. As it turned out, our firstborn was a girl and so she took my name, and our second is a boy and he took my partner's name. It was a very hard decision for my partner to agree on this, but thankfully he did.

But the story doesn't stop there, because then we had to decide on the first name, which also became a weighty selection process. I wanted my child's name to be different and unique—it had to be a name I had never heard before, and since I am in the event planning industry, I have seen thousands of names on registration lists over the years. You can imagine how frustrating it was for my partner and me when he would suggest a name and I would say I had already heard it before. He then suggested that we walk through cemeteries and read all the headstones for ideas. Eventually I came across a name I liked but we modified the spelling, so instead of Emeline, we gave her the name Emeleen. As for her middle name, we gave her the name Sonja, which is an anagram of Jason, her father's first name. This way he could feel like she was named after him as well.

There were other issues that made the naming process difficult. We had considered giving our first child the gender-free name Hunter, my partner's surname, as a kind of compromise, but as I read through the four pages of Quebec laws on the Registration of a Birth, with all the rules and regulations related to name-giving, I understood that you were not allowed to use a parent's surname as a given name. It made sense to me that Quebec would not want a child to have a double name such as Hunter Hunter. With the uncertainty of whether it would be allowed or not, we ruled out Hunter Pollack. We also learned that the government has the right to deny parents a chosen name and that every name is vetted before it is registered on a birth certificate. Apparently, in the history of this law, there has only been one name where this ruling was exercised and a name denied. I think this is so people do not name their child something like "Teacup" or "Spoon."

As for our son, he was three when we adopted him, so we kept the first name he had been given by his birth mother: Tyler. We did change his middle name from Joe to Jonas so we would have an anagram of Jason's name, just like his sister. We tried doing an anagram of Rosita, but we did not like any of the combinations. And, as per the original agreement between my partner and I, Tyler was given Jason's surname, Hunter.

The sharing of this anecdote led another woman, five months pregnant, to comment on the names and naming in her family. Her mother, sitting to her side, rolled her eyes and said with a laugh, "You will need a whole chapter to cover the names in our family." Her daughter spoke to me after I retrieved a paper and pencil:

My first name is Shiva and my surname is Barbosa Khorramshahi. My mother is Brazilian, but one-eighth Italian (somewhere on her father's side, ergo Barbosa), and my father is Persian. My mother's full name is Ana Rita (pronounced Ana Hita in Portuguese) de Mattos Barbosa, but she usually goes by Ana. As it turns out, Anarita is also a name used in Iran. My father's name is Shahram Khorramshahi.

My maternal grandmother had difficulty carrying a child to full term and had several miscarriages. During the time in which she tried to have another child, she made a vow to St. Ana that every female child born would carry her name, and that the first one would carry the name Ana Rita. After five years, she had my mother, and in tribute to the success of her pregnancy and delivery, she gave that name to my mother, Ana being the saint of pregnancy and childbirth. When she had my mother's sister a few years later, her name also included the patron saint Ana; her name is Ana Carla. My siblings' names are Andre, which is Brazilian, and Bruna, which is Brazilian and Italian. My name, Shiva, is clearly Persian.

The father of my baby is Argentinean, and he also carries a complex name. I very much want this baby to carry my mother's name, and double names are typical in both our cultures. So we agree to a double family name, but we cannot agree on the name order. He says, jokingly, that he wants to know whether the first or second of the family names is more "important" or more "official" in Canadian culture. I guess we will have to see what happens when the time comes to make that decision. The jury is still out on that one.

I asked another woman at the table about her name.

My name is Neeraja, but I am called Neera here. My name is a Sanskrit name that means "lotus." My surname is Shukla, which means "white" or "purity." My father's generation was the first to take on a surname in the Western tradition, and like many others who took the name Shukla, it is a name adopted from the Hindu caste system. My mother did not have a surname, so when she got married, she took my father's surname. She explained to me that the naming convention in Southern India at that time was the father's place of birth followed by the father's name and then the given name.

*　*　*

In spite of the changing patterns of naming, the paternal structure continues to be a source of friction for feminists and academics alike. While the challenge may remain for each couple to determine their own solution, it does not answer the more general question of paternal domination. Why the father? Why all the fuss about him?

For many men and women, patriarchy, or the rule of the father, is interpreted as a desire for control and possession. Man seeks to dominate and control. Therefore, man assumes authority and power of the woman and her baby by the granting of his name. By this name, I have rights over you and this baby; and in return, I will protect and care for the both of you. Conversely, the woman accepts her husband's name for her child on the condition that he will provide and look after both of them.

Let us consider one possible explanation of this notion. The status and definition of a mother is an unquestionable and unquestioned reality. Nine months of an expanding belly that provides the first temporary domicile of a developing fetus attests to the absolute certainty of a newborn's biological mother. No additional proof or testing is required. After all, we have watched the baby's development, felt its feet and fists pound the walls of a smoothly rounded abdomen, seen its heartbeat on an ultrasound monitor, and witnessed its delivery.

By contrast, the father's identity slides into the realm of faith. Strict, positive identification of a newborn's father is never an act of irrefutable and categorical truth, as it is based on an implicit assumption endorsed by the declaration of the mother. And yet we all know that she could be lying. Women from early history on have falsified a father's identity, withholding the truth to save a relationship or to ensure a child's future stability. Fact and fiction lie closer than we think regarding paternity and the creative potency of a man's sexual prowess. It is this doubt and uncertainty that makes the father's status unreliable and suspect. Even today, recurrent jokes about paternity are told: "Maybe she's the post-man's kid." "He kinda looks like the car salesman." "Are you sure this one is mine?"

Could it be that in the act of naming (and here I am referring specifically to the granting of the surname), the father lends his name, by this gesture ensuring that he will be authorized as the father? Does the man, by bestowing his surname, symbolically legalize a claim on his status and right as father? After all, we know that when a child is adopted, he or she takes on the surname of his or her adoptive father as a means of establishing "ownership." It would appear that by assigning his name to the newborn, the father simultaneously names (the child) and is named himself; he is named father of this child.

Shortly after I wrote this, a young mother told me about a hospital scene the day after she had given birth.

> My friends said to my husband, "She looks just like you, she really looks just like you. Just look at those eyes." "Do you really think so?" he responded. "Really?" Quite frankly, I thought she looked like an alien or a wrinkled-up prune, but I let him believe what he wanted to.
>
> He later admitted to me that in some strange way he had felt reassured, for he said, "I found myself thinking, I guess it really is my child and no one else's. And then I began to wonder if people always say that a newborn looks like the father so that the father feels a greater connection. After all, you were the one who carried the baby around for months within you and so you have already established that close bond. Whereas I didn't have that experience. But when our friends said she looked like me, I felt a real connection. Like, hey, this little baby girl really is mine."

Is it possible that man also needs reassurance to feel a powerful bond with his newborn? Does the act of naming a child with the father's surname create a bond and commitment that might otherwise be lacking? Can it be that this act satisfies or fulfills a certain absence of bonding that is automatic for the mother but nonexistent or unavailable to the father?

In today's society, many fathers are more involved in child-rearing, assuming a larger role in co-parenting. Shut out from the arena of breast-feeding, are men seeking a way of remaining connected to their newborn and becoming involved not only in name? While a current of male-female tension and mother-father friction still underlies family dynamics, today's parents at least discuss the positives of mutual respect and job-sharing within the family unit.

* * *

The Haida totem pole staring down at me from my bookshelf reminds me of a trip to western Canada and my own journey of discovery, before then and since, regarding the deep history of totemism that underlies naming. It was the summer of 1997, and my husband and I were on a week of kayak paddling with six others, off the northern coast of Vancouver Island. We were in search of the orcas, infamously known as killer whales but in fact only predatory and dangerous when swimming in nonresidential waters. It was a week of dampness and rain that penetrated my limbs, a week of eating dried food with lots of trail mix and campfire marshmallows, a week with a lot of laughs with strangers, and, yes, one that was punctuated by two close encounters with pods of whales performing acrobatics alongside our boats.

On the last day of this adventure, we disembarked and walked along a beach of shale and colored glass, remnants of a deserted community. As we ascended onto the flat land, we saw three gigantic totems lying like dead warriors. We walked around the vestiges of a longhouse to arrive at a shack in which two men were working. The younger of the two stood behind a long table on which lay several ornamental objects: a shaman's rattle, a dance rattle, and an impressive number of traditional masks. Our small group surrounded him and he explained that he was preparing these pieces for an upcoming celebration—a throwback to a traditional potlatch.

The word *potlatch*, he told us, comes from the Chinook language and means "to give away" or "gift." He said it derived from an older word meaning "to make a ceremonial gift in a potlatch." His voice was low as he continued. He mumbled about the olden days when the purpose of the potlatch was tied to a redistribution and reciprocity of wealth, a showing of one's prosperity, with the wealthy members hosting elaborate potlatches in longhouses built specifically for the occasion. Celebration of births, rites of passages, weddings, funerals, namings, and honoring of the deceased—all could be occasions for a potlatch celebration. As he spoke, his hands adeptly moved a carving instrument back and forth along a piece of wood shaping the mask.

There was something shy or self-effacing about this soft-spoken man. He did not wish to share too much with our group of inquisitive members. He did not tell us that the potlatch would usually involve a feast, with music, dance, and theatrical events. He did not show any enthusiasm or zeal. I think maybe he had been caught unawares by our group. He remained reticent, and we left respectfully without asking too many questions.

When we returned to our kayaks, our guides told us that in the mid-1800s, 90 percent of the indigenous population had been decimated by a smallpox outbreak brought to the Queen Charlotte Islands, the home base of the Haida. We were told that in 1894 the Canadian government outlawed the potlatch. With the collapse of this tradition, all ceremonial items associated with potlatches, such as bowls, ladles, masks, head-dresses, and all dance regalia, became defunct.

The unforgiving wording of the decree, now available on the Internet, is harsh:

> Every Indian or other person who engages in or assists in celebrating the Indian festival known as the "Potlatch" or the Indian dance known as the "Tamanawas" is guilty of a misdemeanor, and shall be liable to imprisonment for a term not more than six nor less than two months in any gaol or other place of confinement; and, any Indian or other person who encourages, either directly or indirectly, an Indian or Indians to get up such a festival or dance, or to celebrate the same, or who shall assist in the celebration of same is guilty of a like offence, and shall be liable to the same punishment.[1]

When I returned to Toronto, I followed up with some more research and discovered that many artists died without passing on their knowledge of the traditional style of carving to the next generation. However, in the mid-twentieth century, after a strenuous and lengthy struggle, the ban was repealed. Elders, recognizing the importance of their history, tried to remember what they could to help the next generation rebuild their rich heritage. However, just when the people were regaining their identities, the missionaries moved in and convinced the people to give up their old beliefs and traditions. Totem poles were burned for firewood, and children were placed in boarding schools, without their families. They were prevented from speaking their language and forced to speak English, with severe punishment for noncompliance.

It is the rich history of early man—the traces of which we can see in the culture of Native peoples—that helps us get a glimpse of how nomination came about. What do we know about its origin? What is the early relationship between man and his name? Earlier we discussed that pair of linguistic terms, *nomen* and *nomas*, the interweaving of the name, patriarchy, and the law. Now let us begin another journey, this time with anthropology, not etymology, as our guide.

Before the God of Abraham and the three desert religions created the birth of the universe and fashioned man from the dust of the earth by blowing the breath of life into his nostrils . . .

And before the birth of Athens and the war of Troy, before the rape of Europa and the marriage of Cadmus to Harmony, before the Olympian gods and the heroes cajoled man into a cosmos beyond their reach . . .

And before the Greeks sat on the steps of the Coliseum discussing the nature of the universe and the importance of self-inquiry and free reasoning . . .

And before the birth of Logos, the divine word of God, represented by the wisdom of Jesus; and before the kiss and the betrayal by Judas Iscariot, whose name Judas (Ioudas) is the Greek form of Judah (Hebrew for "praised"); and before Christ's crucifixion and resurrection . . .

Before all of that, primitive man, according to the sciences of anthropology and ethnology, traversed the earth's mountains and valleys and set up habitations in roaming bands. Eventually these bands formed into group collectives: tribes, clans, moieties, or phratries. Man, the social animal, discovered his natural world and lived off the land in harmony, respecting the forces that dominated his universe. In terms of the brotherhood of man, it was a time of both mutual generosity and fierce competition for the earth's bounty: a time of the forming of early social bonds.

Nineteenth-century anthropologists working in field studies around the world discovered that group totemism circumscribed the lifestyle of early man who lived off the land through hunting and gathering. Extending from African pygmies through Oceania to Australian aboriginals, from Native North American peoples through South America Indians, and from the hunters and reindeer breeders of Siberian steppes to the herdsmen in North and Central Asia, totemism was a social and religious or spiritual form of collective organization.

The term *totem* is derived from the Ojibway word *ototeman*, meaning "one's brother-sister kin," while the grammatical root, *ote*, signifies a blood relationship between brothers and sisters who have the same mother and may not marry each other. This word was introduced into the English language in 1791 by a British merchant and translator who gave it a false meaning in the belief that it designated the guardian spirit of an individual who appeared in the form of an animal.

Totemism involves a system of beliefs that marries man to nature. Like the animal spirits carved on my totem pole, totemism insists that each human being has a spiritual connection or kinship with another physical being, either plant or animal. Each clan or tribe, sharing common blood ancestry, distinguishes and differentiates itself on the basis of its group totem.

Like the vows we implicitly and explicitly make within our nuclear family, clan behaviors were dictated on the basis of relationships between man and his particular spirit-being. Elaborate rituals and ceremonial rites—our Mother's Day and Father's Day celebrations perhaps being a muted equivalent—were carried out to reinforce identifications with the group totem.

Clan members considered themselves brothers and sisters, bound to help and protect one another. If a member of one clan was killed by an outsider, the whole clan of the aggressor would be responsible for the deed, and conversely, the whole clan of the murdered man would be at one in demanding satisfaction for the blood-shedding. Stronger than our current family bond, clan relationships commanded total commitment.

From the inception of this practice, two striking prohibitions were imposed among all clan members: no marriage between men and women of the same clan, and no killing of a tribal ancestor (that is, no killing of a totemic animal and no eating or killing of a totemic plant). The prohibition against marriage and sexual intercourse between clan members, the precursor of both exogamy (the proscription of marrying outside the clan) and the incest taboo, remain two of the most fundamental tenets of our civilization, inscribed by law in all human commandments.

Anthropological studies also describe a strong link between nomenclature and totemism. Early man named his clan after animals, plants, and other inanimate objects. Clans, needing to distinguish themselves as separate individuals and families, used these heraldic badges and objects as forms of clan identification. Just as we saw in the linguistic division between *nomen* and *nomos*, history shows that early man living in community always required a permanent mark, which then could be fixed in a form of writing or documentation. In this way, collective man could distinguish himself from others.

It has been argued that this primitive form of classification predated naming as a mark of tribal identification, just as communal living predated the establishment of the nuclear family with its more personal naming rituals. According to one theory, proper names were derived from totems and based on sacred and esoteric knowledge, as well as certain personality traits. The origin of these names was subsequently forgotten, with the clan totem surviving as a trace memory. Another possible explanation is that totems, borrowed from animals and plants, arose from practical needs, and that the original core of totemism, nomenclature, was the result of this primitive technique of writing.

Through the preexisting bonds between man and totem as well as name and totem, individual kinship ties could be linked to ancestral history of the clan. Max Müller, an English philologist, expressed it succinctly when he wrote, "A totem is a clan mark which then becomes a clan name, then the ancestor of a clan and finally an object of worship by the clan."[2] A clan and its name, totemism and ancestry, were clearly well forged in this early period of history.

Anthropologists disagree over how different cultures constructed and developed their myths, rites, and customs, and what they valued as sacred and profane. Cultural determinists believe man's knowledge of his external world to be relative, not fixed by cross-cultural conventions. Each culture or community creates its own worldview of reality to which all group members must comply. We are not "born" into like-minded families and marked with a common name to cement our bond; rather, we freely create family or kinship bonds on the basis of our system of knowledge. Anyone with the same name or from the same village may be viewed as a kinsman. For example, one may be kin to another by being born on the same day (Inuit), by following the same tribe (Araweté), or by surviving a trial at sea (Truk) or on the ice (Inuit).

By contrast, the rival defenders and proponents of biological, or genetic, determinism argue that all human behaviors and characteristics are encoded in a form of genetic mapping that is universally inscribed. Kinship ties and bonds are necessarily biological and fixed, and names are assigned on the basis of blood ties.

❊ ❊ ❊

I would like to offer another perspective that stands in radical opposition to both these anthropological theories. Many people associate the name of Sigmund Freud with his concepts of the superego, the ego, and the id; conscious, preconscious, unconscious; libido and childhood sexuality; the pleasure principle; or perhaps even his theories on dream interpretation. Yet he is probably best known for his elaboration of the Oedipus complex and thereby radicalizing our thinking about man's psychological development.

Freud referred to the unfolding of each family drama as the dynamics of the Oedipal complex; on the basis of Sophocles' Athenian tragedy, *Oedipus Rex*, he insisted on this triangle—mother, father, child—as the structuring of man's psychic constitution. Throughout his lifetime, he never wavered from this belief that every human child, at an early stage of his life, was forced to encounter these primal passions: a sexual desire for the parent of the opposite sex and a desire for death of the rival parent.

Indeed, who has not witnessed the powerful outbreak of emotions in the young child? The powerful want, the full bodily rejection of no, the tender embrace of yes? Rivalries and jealousies, powerful impulses of love and hate, all mix to create an emotional alchemy underlying man's earliest relationships and forming the template for all future ones. Persisting in the universality of this complex across cultures, Freud writes that every new arrival on this planet is faced with the task of mastering the Oedipus complex.

Now, the father of psychoanalysis was very much a Renaissance man, widely read and with broad interests. His lifelong passion to understand the source of neurotic suffering and the causes of psychic conflict led him to pursue all avenues of academic pursuit. In his middle years, he turned his gaze to the past in the search for man's origins, which resulted in his seminal text *Totem and Taboo* of 1912–1913. In this controversial piece of writing, Freud walked back into that phylogenetic history, or prehistory, to continue the journey of his search for man's psychic beginnings. He hoped to uncover, in this mythic past, a relationship between the underlying psychology of primitive peoples, as explored by social anthropologists, and the psychology of neurotics, as uncovered by psychoanalysis. By entering a time when men lived in clans and tribes, the vestiges of which we see in some surviving indigenous communities, Freud would also push man's origins from an individual to a collective level in a more archaic past, describing his hypothetical theory as the myth of the Primal Horde.

Here is my rendition of this myth: In the beginning was the Archaic Father and the Primal Horde who traversed the earth's landscape, living off the bounty that nature provided. The Father, a dominant male undoubtedly tall, handsome, and muscular (or whatever shape you imagine him to have been), had access to all the women. The young men (undoubtedly even taller, more virile, and better looking) resented this alpha man who thwarted their *jouissance* by forbidding them access to these women. And so these robust and vigorous men blended together, rebelled, and killed the father, thereby releasing them to have full access to all of the women.

Unfortunately, all acts of such magnitude come at a price, with unforeseen and unanticipated consequences. While the brothers rejoiced with bacchanalian fervor, the dead father, in spite of their deed, rose up from the ashes and inserted his presence over the sons and daughters. As we might imagine, without his law there would have been chaos and disorder: fraternal rivalry, fratricide, homicide, incest, rape. And so, the silhouette of the dead father darkens the lives of his progeny. The father is killed to ensure order; as we analysts say, the dead father rules from the grave.

Freud never suggested that this mythic complex was ever enacted; rather, he intended it as symbolic of the inevitability of man's encounter with his own Oedipus-in-the-making. For Freud, the proposed hypothesis of the killing of the primal father became the quintessential first moment in the genesis of mankind. By adopting this hypothesis, he placed the father at the core of civilization.

Like the anthropologists, Freud considered the totem animal a primal father, a common ancestor personified in the figure of the father or father substitute: a kinship unit, a totem, a name. With the fracturing of clans into the evolution of the nuclear family, naming rituals would have changed over time. Family units initially would have carried the clan name or a variation on it, which would then have been passed down to the sons and daughters of each family unit. In time, these would be transformed into the names with which we are all familiar today.

The power of patriarchy lives on in the traces of those prohibitions and injunctions of certain cultures and ethnic groups. Ongoing practices regarding naming provide some proof: Have you ever wondered why there is a prohibition against naming someone after a parent or relative who is still alive? Or what about tribes who prohibit naming the dead? The repressed traces of the incest taboo bans certain naming practices that are considered too close or too threatening to the underlying fabric of the family.

✿ ✿ ✿

Now let us return to the present for a moment with the sketch of a very early time in our lives, a time that can only be reimagined and retold, but never relived. A blissful cocoon of love and tenderness, an illusory bond of unity—the image of Madonna and Child. A time of mutual pleasure and satisfaction.

Helpless in the cradle of attention, an infant finds himself at the complete mercy of a woman who comes and goes at will. Our little one becomes increasingly attentive to his mother's presence and absence, fascinated by her behavior, and tries to figure out her movements and desires. What does she want? Where does she go? Who or what is more important than I am? He begins to realize that there are other people and situations that also demand her attention and take her away from him. He begins to wonder about these things—about what she wants and how he can satisfy her. He creates a fantasy of what she possibly desires from him and his role in it. *Do I need to smile for her? Eat all my food? Poo in the potty every time on command?* Eventually, his attempts and strategies will form a blueprint for his later interactions with significant others.

Gradually, our little one becomes aware of others in his environment and begins recognizing the music of their speech, the interludes of comings and goings, the pauses and flow of conversation. The father, while also present from the beginning, begins to assume a position of greater significance. He arrives as a permanent fixture in the child's consciousness, breaking up this primary duet and forcing it into a party of three or more. The father shatters the cozy cocoon of mutual satisfaction and dual fascination between him and his mother.

This intervention ushers in another period of psychic maturity. Deprived of the exclusive love and attention of his mother, the child, male or female, is forced to look for love and satisfaction elsewhere. It is as though the father draws a line in the sand between his wife and child, forcing his child's evacuation from the clutches of its mother's embrace.

While the blissful union of Madonna and Child may be paradigmatic, it is an exclusivity and inclusivity that also threatens to engulf the child in a possible psychic death. As the analyst Lacan noted, the child is already in the mouth of the crocodile (of the mother), but without the intervention of the father, who knows when the child will be devoured by the closing of that crocodile's mouth?

In this way, the father ensures that the child learns to find his own playthings and his own friends. After all, we are all ultimately compelled to become adult human beings in our own right, seeking out our own partners and struggling with the multiple complexities of human relationships.

In his rewriting of Freud's Oedipus complex, Lacan labels the father's intervention between the mother and child the paternal metaphor, or the name-of-the-father (*le nom du père*), a short step beyond the path already laid down by Freud. (In English, we miss the homophonic equivalence between *non* and *nom*, the no of the father and the name of the father.) In psychic terms, the father, as a representative of the law, forces the child to move beyond the dualistic, imaginary relationship with his mother. By this intervention, he introduces the child to what is called the symbolic dimension of life; that is, the world of universally shared language and socio-cultural mores.

Note that it is not the person of the father that is significant but the function of the father (or surrogate), for it is just as possible for the paternal function to be fulfilled in the case of a child whose father is absent, and, conversely, the presence of a father is no guarantee that this function will not be distorted or unfulfilled. Perhaps we can understand this distinction by considering the difference between the *person* of the father as an individual (the man who gets up every morning, gets dressed, goes to work, and returns every night) and the *function* he upholds (the task or purpose of his symbolic role).

The mother also supports the name-of-the-father as it occurs in daily activities. Every time she says, "Now, we all have to listen to what Daddy says about touching everything in the store. We all have to be quiet in the movie theaters, for even Mommy and Daddy must not speak too loudly inside," she too is demonstrating her compliance with a symbolic order that goes beyond herself. In fact, both parents are called on to educate children regarding the transcending, all-encompassing laws with which they too as parents must comply.

This symbolic father, or his substitute (family relatives, the community at large), not only ensures that each child will be introduced to this order of language, social norms, and cultural history, but also requires each of us to recognize and preserve the tenets of a law to which we are all accountable. One interpretation is that the first ruling, the vestige of that archaic law that we have seen described by anthropologists—the ban of incest, or the forced separation of the child from the mother and vice versa—repeats itself every generation and in every family.

* * *

The universal structure of the paternal metaphor, therefore, serves as a shorthand for the necessity of our compliance with the law, be it the individual laws of the family or the collective laws of society. Which brings us back to our original question about patriarchy, names, and the father: How did it happen that the father became the one who typically carried the surname with which the child is named?

According to some psychoanalysts, to uphold the name-of-the-father, a process that occurs automatically without conscious deliberation, is to put the father in a position of authority, a status linked to the primordial law against incest but one that includes all rituals of naming. By placing the father in the position of lawgiver and upholder of certain traditions, the child assumes his name and can then enter the chronology of history, which in turn will place him or her in the position of successor. By saying, "You are my child and you shall carry my family name, Smith," and giving the child his surname, the father (in a patrilineal culture) inscribes in him a destiny that will allow him to be named-to or named-in the succession of generations. And equally in a matrilineal culture, the succession will occur through the mother's name yet still in conformity with the laws of that culture (or, in the present context, in conformity with the symbolic order upheld by the paternal metaphor).

In this way, we can see how the proper name takes on the function of a transmission, a passing-on or insurance that the father's name will sustain a continuity; it ensures a place of affiliation or belonging and filiation for each child. Yet, in order to pass on the family name, the father is defined as the upholder of this law. The father is the one identified by the totem/clan or by the name inscribed on his burial. We honor his name and in so doing show respect for the continuation of our ancestry transmitted by our surname.

We can see a parallel in the realm of religion. Monotheism confers a particular status on the law of the father. In the ancient world, the Israelites perceived their god primarily as a law-giver. It was God the law-giver who enunciated the Ten Commandments, inaugurating a binding law that would become a universal code of ethics. Perhaps it was necessary for a figure of law to insert himself in the everyday affairs of men and women. After all, the Decalogue is the expression of a code ensuring an ethics based on the universals of family dynamics with which we are all too familiar: sibling rivalry and the vying competition for parental favoritism, the problems of transmission and inheritance, and the definition of ourselves in relation to the values of our family and society. In spite of all the complexities of human nature, we manage (or struggle), for better or for worse, to overcome these basic conflicts and to honor our responsibilities as citizens and as family members.

And so we can say *le nom du père*, the name/no of the father, a concept borrowed from religion, yokes together the father and the name. As a foundational concept, it confers identity on a subject by naming him and positioning him within the symbolic order (*le nom*), while simultaneously introducing the oedipal prohibition of the incest taboo and its corollaries (*le non*).

❋ ❋ ❋

And thus it largely continues. While our ancestors may have stood in closer proximity to the gods in their daily lives, today we continue to practice the inherited rituals of our forefathers in certain religious traditions. For example, to call upon or to invoke the authority of the father in a religious context is to endow that figure with a certain power. We accept and recognize that authority of a figure when he derives legitimacy from a community of believers.

From the past—an epithet in prayer: *Ashur god of my father; Illaprat the god of your father*; an oath: *By the name of the god of my father*; an appeal to a king: *By the name of the god Adad, lord of Aleppo and the god of your father.*

To the present: *In the name of the Father, the Son, and the Holy Ghost*; *By the power invested in me . . .*; *I am the Lord your God*; *Our Father, who art in heaven . . .* In the name of, we justify our behavior, we plead, we cry, we seek forgiveness. We call on and summon a force "beyond" for witness, for inspiration, and for help, placing our faith in a named figure of authority.

12

VOLUNTARY NAME-CHANGING

Our name is like an elongated shadow attached at our heels. A tenacious sign of identification, it is intimately connected to our being. My proper name, Mavis Carole Himes, shares with me a long and (at least to me) captivating history. After all, we were born at almost the same time. While I have not always liked my first name and at times have even wanted to change it, there is an immutability to its presence. While my surname has been abridged from the original, it remains the name connected to my intergenerational past. Mavis Carole Himes is the name I inhabit for better or for worse. We make assumptions about names: one name for life, inscribed with my essence and my journey. A name that I take for granted.

However . . .

There are voluntary name-changes for popularity and commercial motivations: pen names, nicknames, mononyms, and pseudonyms that many people choose to match a fantasized future of success and status.

There are name-changes in response to persecution and oppression: new immigrants forced or willingly choosing another name to mark a new chapter and to avoid further harassment and prejudice.

There are name-changes due to adoption in which the birth name is effaced and rewritten.

There are the name-changes of marriage, in societies where women adopt the surname of their husbands.

There are name-changes associated with a religious conversion or spiritual transformation or upon admission to a religious order.

And there are the explicit and insistent name-changes motivated by a desire to remove oneself from a family lineage or to extract oneself from the unbearable weight of a name in one's history.

If the name is a gift and a symbol of lineage from another, we can ask the questions: What does it mean to change or modify one's name voluntarily? Is it seen as a rejection of the name-givers? Can it be modified without impact? Is it like changing a certain feature of one's body, like the plastic surgery to alter or disguise one's identity? What are the consequences of a name changed involuntarily? Perhaps even forced or coerced?

* * *

From 2006 to 2009, Jane Siberry, the Canadian singer-songwriter famous for such tunes as "Calling All Angels," "One More Colour," and "When I Was a Man," decided to change her name to Issa. In fact, this was not her first name-change. Born Jane Stewart in 1979, she had become Jane Siberry by adopting the surname of her maternal aunt and uncle, who she admired for their strong bond of mutual love, hoping it would be a reference point, a touchstone in her life.

She enjoyed many years of national and international success, but then, following a professional failure, she dispossessed herself of material life and went into seclusion. Following this period of brief invisibility, she reemerged with the new name Issa, the feminine equivalent of the eighth-century prophet Isaiah. Curiously, this name also means "salvation" and "protection" in African cultures.

In describing this process of disappearance and name-change, Siberry said, "I had to do something, I had to let go of Jane. I was silent for twenty-four hours and Issa appeared at that point."

However, after three years, Jane reverted to her former name. She told reporters: "I felt the need to make some strong changes in my life. It seemed important to change my name, so I did. I changed it to a name that I thought was simple, an empty cup. I had never heard the name Issa before, and it turns out to have some wonderful meanings, including a haiku poet in Japan, and the name that Jesus had in India. But two weeks ago I officially changed my name back to Jane Siberry. I felt with the name-change, I had gotten in my own way, in terms of devoting myself to my career, making my work available to people. So, Jane Siberry is my name again until further notice, but I feel richer from having been Issa for three years."[1]

* * *

Voluntary name-change can be temporary, a trial run at being another character in a theater of one's own making. I, too, tried to relaunch myself with another name, a temporary change although one that was not completely foreign to me.

When I lived in Israel for a couple of years in the late seventies, I became Malkah. As my Hebrew name, it was not really a name-change per se, but I had never been called that before and no one knew me as Malkah. I retained this name in Israel even though I was repeatedly told that it was considered an old-fashioned, biblical name. Today female children in Israel are named after flowers and trees inspired by the beauty of nature: Aviva, Dahlia, Shoshana.

Malkah emerged as a different woman than Mavis. Malkah became *sabarit* (Israeli): strong, painted burnt caramel by the sun, made sweet like the fruit of the land. I was camouflaged in the landscape, anonymous to those around me. I moved about the country in my spare time, climbing mountains, swimming in caves, trekking through the desert sands, inhaling the aroma of orange blossoms and *za'atar*, imbibing the Mediterranean sea air. Israel brought me closer to a center that did not exist in my Canadian-born soul.

While working as child psychologist in a children's mental health's clinic, I maintained a certain distance. My female colleagues were all married, brooded over their children, and hovered around me like anxious mother hens. My status as a divorced woman made me an object of concern, for it was important that I find a partner and build a family. "Life is too short, too lonely as a single woman."

"Life here in Eretz is difficult. You need someone to help you."

"A woman without children is like a plant without water."

"You need a husband, someone who can negotiate on your behalf."

In contrast to my well-intended peers, I relished my freedom, my ability to choose how, where, when, and what. Being almost thirty, nearly everyone I met was married. And in a country so tied to tradition and celebration, it was often isolating to be in attendance as a single woman. But there was Zvi and Yigdal, Ben and Chaim. There were brief encounters intermingled with relatively longer relationships. There was the excitement of a novel caress and the easy exit from rancor and friction.

On the other hand, I felt myself to be in perpetual conflict or tension. Here was this country of my people, of my ancestors. A tiny strip of land over which so many millions of people had died and whose death count had not yet stopped. The first *intifada* in Lebanon was about to erupt; I would leave shortly before its outbreak.

Here was a country inhabited by peoples from Yemen, Iran, Morocco, Turkey, Tunisia, and Georgia whose faces and mannerisms were foreign yet whose practices of certain rituals were familiar. Pushy, aggressive, arrogant—all the stereotypes of Israeli transplants that I had encountered in my own city in Canada I reencountered in Israel. Yet alongside those with whom I felt no outward connection was an unspoken bond of recognition.

Here was this country of a desert people representing a particular faith, a race of Semites, a nomadic people whose history I shared and whose language I spoke. It was not the Hebrew words, it was not the Yiddishisms interspersed in the conversations with my friends; it was not the oriental accent but a familiarity of presence, a glance, a smile of recognition. Malkah had returned: Exodus revisited. I made aliyah, "gone up," ascended to the House of Israel, the house of my ancestors.

I lived in a *maon* for new immigrants. Turks and Argentineans, Russians and Persians, French and Mexicans. We shared a utopian vision, a dream of something as yet ill-defined, the challenge of deconstruction amid reconstruction, the syntax of a new life. We shared a common language of broken Hebrew, which we studied five hours every day (except Shabbat, holiest of the holy). We shared pita and hummus and *laban* and *gil*, *eschel* and *gveenah lavanah* and *lachmaniot*, at the wooden tables in the cafeteria while we awaited the next chapter of our new life.

* * *

I dreamed about Morris (Moshe) Heimovitch. My grandfather is walking down a deserted street. It is pitch black and he cannot see where he is going. He stumbles on a sharp object and falls. There is no one there to help him up. When I awake, my eyes are moist. I search in the darkness for a tissue.

After months of personal disorientation and adjustments, I thought I might write a book on immigration, a how-to manual for *olim chadashim* entitled "Surviving the First Year in the Homeland." It would be devoted to a theory of change: the climate, the chemicals in the air, the food, the routines, the water, the foreign language; and it would be dedicated to the memories of Moishe Heimovitch and Hymie Rabinovitch, the first pilgrims of my family. The pages of an empty notebook may still lie in a drawer in a *maon* (residence for new immigrants) in Ramat Aviv.

Malkah continued to emerge, grow, and expand. A woman unconstrained by city fences, unencumbered by stale relationships. I explored the body of this homeland with the attention and care of a woman in love. I studied its landscape . . . the water sites, the hills, the deserts, the seashores, and the plains. I explored its mountains and valleys, riverbeds and deserts. I took in the cliffs at Nahal Darga; I stood under the waterfall at Ein Qilt; I toured the oasis at Ein Gedi. I hiked along Nahal Zohar and Nahal Perazim; I climbed Har Sedom and descended to the springs at Ein Yorque'am. And when I was ready, I "went up" to Jerusalem, the heart and soul of this enchanted landscape.

✵ ✵ ✵

One morning in early July, after two years of work and travel, I decided to leave Israel. I remained silent about my decision for a week. I did not tell my colleagues, my friends, my lover. Instead, I made the necessary arrangements in secret, and when I had confirmed a date for departure, I began the process of separation and detachment.

At a farewell party, my boss, Shoshana, put her arms around me and whispered her best wishes into my hair. My friend Leon insisted we agree to meet in the *merkaz* in Rechovot in five years. "It will be like a reunion, the same place we first bumped into each other over a heap of persimmons." Leah, Tal, Dahlia, and Yosefa took me out to dinner in old Jaffa, to the fishermen's restaurant by the sea. There they presented me with a pair of silver candlesticks, and the wrapping tissue turned damp from the sea air and the emotion of farewells. Chaim did not ask questions; he did not ask for an address in Canada.

I took a taxi to Ben Gurion Airport, working my way through the channels of bureaucracy. I could afford to be patient with the El Al ticket agent who talked too loudly, demanding my papers of identification, my luggage, my old immigration forms. With amused sarcasm, I asked her, "What's the rush?" raising my shoulders in mock imitation of an Israeli standard. My boldness offended her. She thrust my passport across the counter so that it slid onto the floor. "Gate seven. Straight ahead!" she shouted.

Malkah did not board the plane; she remained somewhere on the tarmac, waving shalom as Mavis mounted the metal staircase and entered it.

* * *

It is not uncommon for celebrities and people in the arts to change their name. For some, a certain flair, a quirkiness, a memorable rhythm, a sexy innuendo communicated in a name invites fame, commercial success. For others, a name-change is an attempt to conceal an ethnic-sounding name that may be considered too difficult to pronounce or remember.

In many cases, especially after the Second World War, when the world was still fraught with the slander of anti-Semitism and deep-seated prejudice, name-changing was considered a concession, a facilitation for access to certain professional or environmental settings. Think of such celebrities as Robert Allen Zimmerman, aka Bob Dylan; Benjamin Kubelsky, aka Jack Benny; Simone-Henriette Kaminker, aka Simone Signoret. The number of Jewish men and women who adopted Christian names is endless. Is it surprising that Walter Matasschanskay would change his name to Walter Matthau or that Allen Konigsberg would choose to become Woody Allen?

In the field of literature, some pen names are fairly well-known. Many know that Mark Twain was the alias of Samuel Langhorne Clemens, George Eliot of Mary Ann Evans, Ayn Rand of Alisa Zinov'yevna Rosenbaum, and C. S. Forester of Cecil Smith.

Charles Lutwidge Dodgson adopted his pen name Lewis Carroll in 1856 because, according to the Lewis Carroll Society of North America, he was modest and wanted to maintain his privacy. When letters addressed to Carroll arrived at Dodgson's offices at Oxford, he would refuse them to maintain anonymity. Dodgson came up with the alias by Latinizing Charles Lutwidge into Carolus Ludovicus, then loosely Anglicizing that into Carroll Lewis, and then changing their order. It was chosen by his publisher from a list he offered of several possible pen names.

Józef Teodor Konrad Korzeniowski is a bit of a mouthful. When the Polish novelist began publishing his writings in the late 1800s, he used an Anglicized version of his name: Joseph Conrad. He was reprimanded for this by Polish intellectuals who thought he was disrespecting his homeland and heritage; they thought so all the more when he subsequently became a British citizen and published his books in English. As Korzeniowski explained:

> It is widely known that I am a Pole and that Józef Konrad are my two Christian names, the latter being used by me as a surname so that foreign mouths should not distort my real surname . . . It does not seem to me that I have been unfaithful to my country by having proved to the English that a gentleman from the Ukraine (Korzeniowski was an ethnic Pole born in formerly Polish territory that was controlled by Ukraine, and later the Russian Empire) can be as good a sailor as they, and has something to tell them in their own language.[2]

Ricardo Eliecer Neftalí Reyes Basoalto (another mouthful) had an interest in literature from a young age, but his father disapproved. When Basoalto began publishing his own poetry, he needed a byline that wouldn't tip off his father, and so chose Pablo Neruda in homage to the Czech poet Jan Neruda. Basoalto later adopted his pen name as his legal name.

When Eric Arthur Blair was getting ready to publish his first book, *Down and Out in Paris and London*, he decided to use a pen name so his family wouldn't be embarrassed by his time in poverty. He chose the name George Orwell to reflect his love of English tradition and landscape. George is the patron saint of England, and the River Orwell is a popular sailing spot that he loved to visit.

In a recent review of Salman Rushdie's new memoir, in which he reinvents himself as Joseph Anton, I learned that Rushdie's father, "a non-practicing Muslim, changed his 'fine old Delhi name' to Rushdie in homage to Ibn Rushd, the twelfth-century Spanish polymath who wrote commentaries on the work of Aristotle"[3] and who coincidentally wrote convincingly of rationalism over Islamic literalism, eight hundred years before the tumult over *The Satanic Verses*.

And only recently did I read in a glossy tabletop book that the master designer of the Guggenheim Museum (Bilbao), Disney Village (France), the Olympic Fish (Barcelona), the Serpentine Gallery (London), and the Art Gallery of Ontario (Toronto) was born Owen Goldberg in Toronto. In 1954, at the age of twenty-five, he dropped his Jewish-Polish name and became Frank Gehry, but it was not until years later that he became the "demiurge" of the architectural world.

While some artists struggle with the traumatic impact of mental illness and premature deaths, family chaos, and dysfunction (e.g., Henrik Ibsen, Tennessee Williams, Sylvia Plath, David Foster Wallace, Truman Capote, and Graham Greene), others feel choked, stifled, and thwarted in their creative potential by the coils of their family identification. They require and desire a new name in order to begin from an anonymous start. With the name-change comes a burst of productivity. For these men and women, the refusal of their family heritage induces and inspires their creativity.

When François-Marie Arouet was imprisoned in the Bastille in the early 1700s, he wrote a play. To signify a rupture with his past, especially his family, he signed the work with the alias Voltaire. The name, the Voltaire Foundation explains, was derived from "Arouet, the younger." He took his family name and the initial letters of *le jeune*—"Arouet l(e) j(eune)"—and reformulated them into an anagram. (In Voltaire's day, *i* and *j* and *u* and *v* were typographically interchangeable.)

Some artists are unable to put their name to their creations, their signature being infused with too many disturbed and disturbing memories and associations. Their work allows them to forge a new name. Sometimes the invention of a pseudonym coincides with the invention of a new work. The creation of oneself and the creation of art.

For Vincent van Gogh, whose history of illness, both mental and physical (temporal lobe epilepsy, severe depression and anxiety, and lead poisoning, among others), is well-documented, a forfeiture of his name was necessary. It is possible to speculate about the meaning of the absence of his signature. Vincent's older brother, also named Vincent van Gogh, had died at birth shortly before his birth. Vincent felt his name had already been "taken" and therefore could not be used again by the surviving sibling. His suicide at the young age of thirty-seven was the culmination of a painfully challenging life. He produced over nine hundred paintings, along with many volumes of letters, but only one painting had sold during his lifetime. It was only after his death that he became famous, thanks to the dedication of his sister-in-law, Theo's wife, Johanna.

Fanny Mendelssohn, later Fanny Cäcilie Mendelssohn Bartholdy, and then, after her marriage, Fanny Hensel, was the sister of the composer Felix Mendelssohn. Fanny was a talented German composer in her own right; however, due to the prevailing attitudes towards women in the 1800s, she was prohibited from publishing her material, as is so explicitly noted in a letter written by her father in 1820: "Music will perhaps become his [i.e., Felix's] profession, while for you it can and must be only an ornament."[4] Instead, her brother agreed to publish some of her compositions under his name, a practice that was not uncommon for many women artists of that period.

Sojourner Truth was the self-given name, from 1843 onward, of Isabella Baumfree, an African-American abolitionist and women's rights activist. Truth was born into slavery in Ulster County, New York, but escaped with her infant daughter to freedom in 1826. After going to court to recover her son, she became the first black woman to win such a case against a white man. Hers is the familiar but tragic story of an early life indentured to multiple slave owners. Truth was one of the ten or twelve children born to James and Elizabeth Baumfree. Her father was an African captured in modern-day Ghana, and her mother, also called Mau-Mau Bett or Betsy by the children who knew her, was the daughter of enslaved Africans from the coast of Guinea. In 1806 nine-year-old Truth (known as Belle) was sold at an auction with a flock of sheep for $100. Truth's name-change was a shorthand for her life's mission.

✳ ✳ ✳

Deliberate name-changing can also be an attempt to efface any traits of a previous social standing. The endeavor to rise to a new-found fame has been repeated throughout history: Ioseb Besarionis dze Dzhu-ghashvili, aka Joseph Vissarionovich Stalin; Lev Davidovich Bronstein, aka Leon Trotsky. These names were chosen for their linguistic and semantic appeal.

Sophie Friederike Auguste von Anhalt-Zerbst-Dornburg was the birth name of the German-born Russian empress Catherine II, also known as Catherine the Great. After her conversion to Eastern Orthodoxy, having immigrated to Russia, she received the name Catherine (Yekaterina or Ekaterina) and the artificial patronymic Alexeevna (Alekseyevna, daughter of Aleksey). Like her male counterparts, her name-change permitted a certain repositioning of social status and position.

And like the politicians and leaders who wish to embellish their social standing with an impressive honorific or mononym, so too do those who wish to rise above a corrupt past. An article in the *New York Times* exposed an impostor and confidence man, Christopher Chichester, aka Christian Gerhartsreiter, who had adopted the name Clark Rockefeller. Through his role-playing with this new name, doors had been opened and a new identity had been conferred on the soon-to-be convicted criminal.

❊ ❊ ❊

Voluntary name-changing frequently occurs when men and women remove themselves from the tumult of everyday life or follow a religious calling. When a woman enters a convent or a man a monastery, choosing to enter a religious order, be it Christian or Buddhist, the change in status is marked by the ritual act of a change in name. Customs vary across religious congregations as to the manner of name assignment. In some cases, new sisters suggest their own name preference, such as their favorite saint, the name of a parent (if it is a saint's name), or a saint after which they would like to be named; in other cases, the name is chosen by a leader, which could be the name of a sister who had died in the congregation or the saint for which the parish is named. In all cases, final approval rests with the superior of the community. Typically a saint's name or a title of Mary or Christ is chosen.

Priests in most religious orders (e.g., Dominicans, Redemptorists, Passionists) who take vows of poverty, chastity, and obedience similarly change their names and assume a biblical or saint's name. A priest in charge of a diocesan church is not required to change his name and generally assumes the name of "Father" plus his given name (e.g., Father James, Father Bob).

Name-changes and the assignment of titles are also practiced within Buddhism. My colleague tells me that, while variations occur across different schools and different traditions (Japanese, Tibetan, Korean), in one particular school of Zen Buddhism, gradual stages of progression are marked by name-changes chosen by the Zen master. At the Kwan Um School of Zen, both Koreans and non-Koreans acquire these names: Nancy Brown became Zen Master Dae Bong, Gye Mun Sunim became Zen Master Bon Haeng, and Barbara Rhodes became Zen Master Soeng Hyang. Those who have studied and become dharma teachers are given a title as well as a new name. *Ji Do Poep Sa Nim*, or JDPSN (Korean for "dharma master"), would be given to a student who has been authorized to teach *kong-an* practice and lead retreats, whereas the title *Ji Do Poep Sa*, or JDPS, would be assigned to teachers who are monks or nuns.

The legendary South African jazz pianist and composer Abdullah Ibrahim was born Adolph Johannes Brand. With a modified anagram of his name, he became known in the music world as Dollar Brand, playing in the Dollar Brand Trio. It was only after his spiritual conversion to Islam in his forties that he changed his name officially to Abdullah Ibrahim.

The precedents for spiritual transformations associated with renamings are scattered through the Old and New Testaments of the Bible. In each of these cases, the change in name is imposed, not self-chosen.

Before his conversion to Christianity, Saul of Tarsus was a Jewish rabbi, a zealous Pharisee who persecuted the followers of Jesus without remorse. On the road to Damascus—his plan was to persecute any Christians that he might find in the synagogues there—Saul was struck down by a light that left him blind. He heard the voice of Jesus in a vision and was informed to go to Damascus, where he would be told what to do. Jesus called out to one of his disciples in that city named Ananias and commanded him to attend to Saul, who had been fasting for three days. Ananias's response is well known:

> "Lord," Ananias answered, "I have heard many reports about this man and all the harm he has done to your holy people in Jerusalem. And he has come here with authority from the chief priests to arrest all who call on your name."
>
> But the Lord said to Ananias, "Go! This man is my chosen instrument to proclaim my name to the Gentiles and their kings and to the people of Israel. I will show him how much he must suffer for my name."
>
> Then Ananias went to the house and entered it. Placing his hands on Saul, he said, "Brother Saul, the Lord—Jesus, who appeared to you on the road as you were coming here—has sent me so that you may see again and be filled with the Holy Spirit." Immediately, something like scales fell from Saul's eyes, and he could see again. He got up and was baptized, and after taking some food, he regained his strength. (Acts 9:13–19)

With this transformation, Saul, whose home town was Tarsus, the capital city of the Roman province of Cilicia, and who was the son of a Roman citizen, assumed the Roman cognomen Paulus and became the

Apostle to the Gentiles, famed for his doctrine and teachings, captured in the epistles he wrote to the churches he founded.

❊ ❊ ❊

Many centuries before Paul, Abram, son of Terah, sits in his tent. His father has encouraged him to begin a move from the city of Ur to the land of Canaan, but they have stopped at Haran. Who was this man to whom God appeared? We have few facts. We do know that after seventy years of a mundane existence, living with his barren wife Sarai, performing the daily rituals of his life, he is visited by God.

This righteous man hears a voice. It is a call to which he must respond; he must say yes or no to the trial presented to him with all the sacrifices such a decision will entail. He is challenged to accept the summoning. (Here is another example of a call[ing] that demands a response.) He must leave his country, the native land of his extended family and the house of his father; he must travel to a new land to which he will supposedly be directed; and he must establish a new life for himself and his family with no promise of future certainty or stability.

Lech lecha, God commands. "Get thee out," or "go, leave," in the sense of "separating or taking leave of." So Abram begins a journey, an internal and external passage that will become an emotional and spiritual disengagement from his father and a break from the bonds of his father's house. Abram rarely settles down; he is in constant movement: coming to Canaan, going down to Egypt, going south again, then north to Beersheva, to Sodom and Gomorrah, to Jerusalem to sacrifice his son, and to Hebron to bury his wife.

When he is ninety-nine years old, God appears once more, and again Abram is humbled by the presence of this divine force and forced to hear the call. And these mighty words echo through the generations in the hearts and souls of all children of the desert: "As for Me, this is My covenant with you: You shall be the father of a multitude of nations. And you shall no longer be called Abram, but your name shall be Abraham, for I make you the father of a multitude of nations. I will make you exceedingly fertile, and make a nation of you; and kings shall come forth from you" (Gen. 17:4).

Sarai, the wife of Abraham, remained childless for a very long period of time. For safe passage, Abraham passed this beautiful woman off as his sister and gave her as a wife to the Pharaoh of Egypt. Later, she encouraged her husband to bed Hagar, her Egyptian handmaiden, so that through her, Abraham's kingdom may be "built up." After Hagar gave birth to Ishmael and was told by an angel that her seed would be numerous, Hagar returned to Sarai.

It was after Ishmael's birth that God once again appeared to Abram, telling him not only that his name would now be Abraham, but that Sarai's name would also be changed: "As for your wife Sarai, you shall not call her Sarai. I will bless her and indeed, I will give you a son by her" (Gen. 17:15). Abraham burst out laughing at the thought that his ninety-year-old wife would bear him a child, and so his son was named Isaac (Yitzchak), which means "he will laugh." Isaac is the only patriarch whose name would not be changed.

❃ ❃ ❃

The story of the patriarch Jacob's nocturnal struggle by the river Jabbok is also well-known. Isaac, the second patriarch, was rumored to have favored Jacob over his older twin, Esau. Esau (which means "hairy") was so named by his mother, Rebecca, because at birth he was "red all over like a hairy garment." The younger twin, Jacob, had been born with his hand grasping Esau's heel, as if he had been trying to pull Esau back into the womb so that he could be the firstborn.

To supersede his brother and in collusion with his mother, Jacob stole his older brother's birthright by pretending to be Esau, receiving the blessings of inheritance from his father in his place. Note that Jacob derives from the letters *a-k-v*, which can be read as *akev*, meaning "heel," a reference to his holding his brother's heel at birth, but also *akov*, meaning "crooked," an allusion to this impersonation of Esau to steal his brother's birthright. Many years later, after incurring his brother's wrath, Jacob returned to his home in Canaan with his large family and sizable livestock. There he enlisted God's help as the impending meeting with his brother drew nearer and his fear increased. He showered his brother with gifts of flocks of camels, sheep, and cattle, sending his family ahead to cross the river while he stayed behind for the night. It was then that he was "left alone, and a man wrestled with him until the break of dawn" (Gen. 32:25).

Commentaries abound on this ambiguous encounter between Jacob and this other with whom he has striven, referred to at first as a "man" and later as "beings, divine and human." Scholars point out that the man may have been Esau, the Prince of Esau, or the heavenly angel assigned to Jacob, his own inner being, or the angel of God. In any case, it was this mysterious adversary who could not free himself from Jacob's clutches and who asked of Jacob his name. When he replied "Jacob," the other said, "Your name shall no longer be Jacob, but Israel, for you have striven with beings divine and human, and have prevailed" (Gen. 32:29).

Israel derives from the root *sar* and *serarah*, which connote power and authority and which imply "perseveres with God." It is interesting that Jacob also asked his adversary his name and the other replied, "Why do you ask my name, for it is unknowable," suggesting that the wrestler's name was the name Jacob gave to the site, Peniel, or "the face of God," because "I have seen God face-to-face, yet my life has prevailed" (Gen. 10:10).

* * *

It is not uncommon today for people to acquire new names. Within a parade of alternative festivals—religious festivals, pagan festivals, arts and crafts festivals, pioneer festivals, and Renaissance fairs, with such exotic names as the Shambala Festival featuring music and art in Northamptonshire or the Green Man Festival of music, art, and theater nestled in the enchanted forests of Wales—people transformed by their experience transfigure themselves through the symbolic act of changing their name. Removed from the formal tradition of any religious or spiritual order, these name-changes occur informally and at will. They are attempts to signify a new beginning and an alternative or altered personality.

A yoga teacher informed me that her name was Ananda, a name given to her by a yogic spiritual leader. "My guru chose this name for me at a ten-day retreat. I did not question this choice, but accepted it very willingly. I was honored. However, when I told my parents, they struggled with this and still call me by the name they gave me at birth, which is Rebecca." Another man told me about his boss's friend who had visited a psychic when her luck took a consistently negative turn. The psychic apparently told her that she would have to change her name in order to reverse her fortune. She then went on to give the woman a new name with the appropriate "energy" but with a very particular spelling: Dyann (instead of Diane).

A friend of mine sent me an article that she had come across on the Internet with the headline "When the New You Carries a Fresh Identity, Too." Like the search for eternal youthfulness touted by the marketers of the cosmetic industry, the search for everlasting happiness is now being promised by a name-change, a simple act of self-direction. The twenty-six-year-old Cheryl Strayed, née Nyland, created her surname around the time of her divorce. Caught up in a time of personal turmoil with the loss of her mother a few years earlier and a pending divorce, she decided that the lack of attachments provided her with an opportunity to redefine herself. As Strayed, author of the best-selling 2012 memoir *Wild: From Lost to Found on the Pacific Crest Trail*, explained in the article:

> Naming myself was symbolic in many ways. It signified to me how it was I had to take full responsibility for my life. I had to create my own happiness, to build my strength, to be the engine of my momentum. Choosing my own name struck me as both a positive act and a powerful one during a time when I felt uncertain and weak.[5]

While women have increasingly opted to keep their maiden name after marriage, challenging the Western tradition of assuming their husband's surname, this particular trend of name-change among young women is less about image-making or cachet and more about a newfound freedom associated with a symbolic change. No longer bound by the name of one's family or husband, they feel a kind of metamorphosis, suggesting that, like the name-changing made by celebrities, the process can be transformative and profitable. Perhaps even therapeutic? As the article goes on to note, "After all, aren't we all celebrities of a kind thanks to the so-called social media?"[6]

Many women experience a sense of freedom after an egregious period of marriage and divorce and immediately perform a symbolic act to mark the end of an unhappy period and the beginning of a new, more positive one. Men do not feel the same need to mark a change in their life because they do not "take on" a new name in marriage.

Julianna Norrie, the owner and host of Maple Ki Forest Spirit Waters, a retreat center in a wilderness-like setting near a tiny hamlet in southern Ontario, is a warm and open woman with a robust laugh. When I met her, she told me that her maiden name had been Szeider (pronounced like "cider"). Her family had immigrated from Germany to Hungary in the 1700s; it was likely, she said, that her name had been changed in the course of the family's travels, *Sz* being a typical Hungarian spelling for *S*. During her adolescence and young adulthood, she had been called different names by friends and relatives—Julie, Judy, and sometimes Juliana. When she and her husband divorced, she made a decision to return to her birth name, Juliana, changing the spelling to Julianna.

"No more Julies or Judys," she said. "I like to call everyone I meet by their full name. So if I meet a Mike, I call him Michael, or Pete, Peter. At the same time, I decided to keep my husband's surname, Norrie, in spite of the disappointed reactions from some friends and family. I feel it flows naturally out of Julianna, and I like the soft sound of it. And, hey, besides, having been macrobiotic for over fifteen years, it reminded me of nori, an edible Japanese seaweed that I was eating a lot back then."

Name-changing can also be the portal to a new life in a new country. It opens a door to new possibilities and infuses life with new hope and potential. My friend Anastasiya, a Russian emigrée now called Stacy, described how she had modified her surname when she arrived in Canada. "For me it was to be a new beginning—a new home, a new country, a new career, a new life. I did not want to be reminded of my previous life, not that it had been bad. I simply wanted a fresh start, and I thought it should also include a change of name."

Another young woman I met on a plane told me the following story about her name:

> I was the second-born child and the only child of my mother's marriage to her second husband. She would go on to have a third child with a third husband. While I was Canadian, I lived for many years in France on a working visa while retaining my Canadian passport. When I met the American man I thought I was going to marry, I decided to move to the United States with him. However, getting a green card was almost impossible, so my boyfriend's father said he would help by adopting me.
>
> When my father, with whom I did not have a close relationship, heard about this through my half-brother, he blew up. He felt completely rejected by me. Because his marriage had been fraught with so much tension and acrimony, he interpreted my change in name as complete desertion and abandonment. I tried to explain my reasons for this action, but he could not be convinced, accusing me of punishing him like my mother had.

> As a result of this guilt trip, I let it go and eventually I went to the states on a temporary study visa for six months. The romantic relationship didn't last, so maybe it was not meant to be, as they say. I had never wanted my father to feel punished by me. I guess I knew my intent was honorable, but I guess he felt insecure in our relationship.

This can be compared with the positive reaction by parents in the following story of a woman I also met while on holiday. Her husband had been named after his uncle (his father's elder brother), who had died tragically in the Second World War. The weight of this name had struck her husband when he visited his uncle's tombstone during his adolescence. In bearing witness to the trianomen that he carried— William Stephan Tupkal—he felt a certain shame that he had not lived up to the ideal set by his father's brother and therefore the name he carried, even though nothing had ever been said. After considerable deliberation, he changed his name twenty years after he had been married, adopting his wife's patronymic. So he became Tup William Montgomery, thus incorporating the names of both families. Having never had sons, his parents-in-law were thrilled to have someone to carry on their name.

* * *

Sometimes name-changing can be a deliberate choice to hide an ethnic identity, like the deliberate erasure of a history that is fraught with intolerable weightiness and psychic pain. In these cases, the name has become an encumbrance and curse. Such was the case with the pioneers of my own profession, psychoanalysis. The father of psychoanalysis was born Sigismund Schlomoh Freud but later dropped Schlomoh and replaced Sigismund with Sigmund to avoid anti-Semitic jokes and discrimination.

Like Freud, Michael Balint, a notable Hungarian psychoanalyst, also changed his name. Born Mihály Maurice Bergmann, this son of a practicing physician in Budapest, at the age of seventeen and against his father's wishes, changed his name to Mihály Bálint, a popular Hungarian name at the time. Subsequently, he also changed his religion from Judaism to Unitarian Christianity. Other well-known Hungarian analysts also changed their names to more Magyar-sounding names, apparently a trend at the time: Otto Rosenfeld, a protégé of Freud, became Otto Rank during adolescence, and Sandor Fraenkel became Ferenczi.

According to one interpretation, Hapsburg Jews wished to change their German-sounding names to more Hungarian-sounding ones during a short period of national revival. Erik Erikson, acclaimed for his writings on the stages of psychosocial development, was born in 1902 in Frankfurt, Germany. His Danish-born mother, Karla Abrahamsen, came from a prominent Jewish family in Copenhagen. At the time of her son's birth in Germany, Karla Abrahamsen had not seen her husband, the Jewish stockbroker Waldemar Isidor Salomonsen, for several years. She decided to retain this man's name for her son, even though it was suspected that Erik was his mother's child from an extramarital union with a Danish lover (hence Erik).

In later life, the young psychoanalyst admitted to never having seen his birth father or his mother's first husband. Erik's young mother raised him by herself for a time before marrying a pediatrician, Dr. Theodor Homberger. The fact that Homberger was not his biological father was concealed from him for many years. In 1908 Erik Salomonsen became Erik Homberger and in 1911 was officially adopted by his stepfather. The details of his birth were kept a secret from him until he was an adult. Being a tall, blond, blue-eyed boy raised in the Jewish religion, he was teased by the children at temple school for being a Nordic; when he went on to grammar school, he was teased for being a Jew. Later, in an independent gesture, he chose the name Erikson. It was subsequently rumored that Erikson's theoretical preoccupation with identity formation stemmed from concerns about his own past.

13

INVOLUNTARY NAME-CHANGING

Names travel. They come by rail, they come by steamship, they come by bus. They come in pairs: mothers and fathers, husbands and wives, brothers and sisters. They come in families, large and small, with screaming infants, sniffling children, or reluctant teenagers; they come in droves, and they come one by one. They come risking their lives or to bury their pain in the soil of a new land. They come in flight from oppressive regimes that dictate every movement and demand total allegiance and loyalty. They come to escape the persecution of war and battle, the threats of violence and vice. They come to escape the sword of dogmatism at their throats and the shackles of prejudice, racism, and bigotry around their feet.

They come seeking a better life, for their children, for their grandchildren, and for their own remaining years. They choose to live, exiled and in exile, coerced voluntarily and voluntarily coerced. They come seeking the ideals of a democracy that guarantees them safety and freedom from harm. They come with tears of pain and tears of joy, prepared to erase the past in a journey into the unknown.

They are the Boat People from Cambodia, Laos, and Vietnam; they are the Holocaust survivors from Poland, Germany, Austria, Romania, Greece, and elsewhere. They are the tortured from Chile, Argentina, and Uruguay; they are the victims of oppression from Iran and Iraq, Syria and Palestine.

And with what do they come, these inquisitive settlers, these sanguine immigrants on the run? With what do they fill their suitcases, their pockets, satchels, and backpacks? How do they choose what to bring to a new homeland? How much time and energy went into their decisions?

Some come treasuring a ring, a gemstone that belonged to a parent or an aunt. Some come with one suitcase brimming with clothes and linens, a dowry to bring to the country in which they shall now be wed. Some bring a treasure: a tablecloth, a gold-threaded caftan, a sprig of myrtle, a jar of sand.

Some come empty-handed, forced to flee with no memento, no souvenir with which to reclaim the past they are leaving, choosing to bury the suffering, the sleepless nights, the tortured lies and lying, the falsehoods they can no longer swallow.

And some come with the name of a contact scribbled in a foreign language on a scrap of paper tucked in a pocket.

✳ ✳ ✳

At a bed-and-breakfast in Stratford, Ontario, I complimented the hostess on the comfort of the pillows I had slept on.

"Where did you get them? Are they a particular brand?" I asked.

"No, they're just feather pillows," she replied quickly.

And as I took another sip of coffee, she added, "No, wait a second. Those pillows are special feathers, very special feathers. When my grandparents were fleeing Hungary to Austria at the end of the Second World War, fearing the onslaught of the Russians, my grandmother wrapped her china dishes to take with her. Imagine! She packed her chinaware and wrapped them with feather pillows and duvets to protect them from breakage and stored them in trunks. In fact, my grandparents were stopped at the border and ended up in a German refugee camp, but eventually made their way to Canada."

Later that morning I met her ninety-year-old mother, who confirmed the story in greater detail. "Yes, we put those things in there to protect what mama wanted to keep. It was what was so valuable to her."

The forced removal of people from one country to another, like the herding of cattle, is the movement of the displaced, the dispossessed, the tortured, the persecuted, and the oppressed. It is the torturous removal of one's name and the adoption of another, a rebranding, that can be for many the final step in a series of humiliating and disruptive upheavals. Stories of survivors of such trauma abound in the archives of

memoir, film, and poetry. They are the springboard for public awareness and inspire social action.

But no matter from where and with what, they land on new soil, a
land that will become their new haven of hope. They come with dreams
and aspirations, their hearts filled with desire and faith in a better life
than the one they left behind. And no matter from which point of
departure, or whether legally or illegally (smuggled past guards at border crossings), they must arrive at a port of embarkation. And once they
arrive at their particular promised land, or at least better land, they each
carry a name—a name that may be old or new, a name given them by
force, by conviction, or by convenience, but nevertheless a name that
will be inscribed on a piece of paper bearing a string of letters. And at
this port of entry, they will encounter a civil servant, an official, who will
take down the details of their demographics, recording that name, along
with their citizenship, language, and, in the past, ethnic origin and
religion. And they will leave that place of arrival classified and stamped,
approved of or denied.

Sometimes, a change in name occurs at a border crossing due to the
transliteration of letters from an unfamiliar script. Sometimes it is with
shock and awe that one discovers on a piece of official paper the
changed spelling of a name, a deformation in the familiar print of letters
that represents one's signature. But at that moment, there is no time for
misgivings. New life soon begins with the toil and demands of the
immigrant experience: the search for housing and a space to live; the
search for work to support a family who awaits abroad or lies sleepless
each night, tossing and turning with uncertainty and fear; and the
search for social contacts and for community to become introduced to
this strange and foreign culture. Days loom large with projects and lists
of things to accomplish. Hopes and dreams are replaced with frustration, irritation, and hardship. But for many, the immigrant experience
holds out the promise of a better life once the initial phases of accom-
modation and integration have been accomplished.

❋ ❋ ❋

What is the experience of these newcomers? How does the lived
reality clash with the anticipation of promise and hope? What awaits in
terms of the livelihood and the economics not only for themselves, but
also for their children, those already born and those whose future lives
in waiting? And finally, what does one want and what can one change?

These are some of the questions raised in an interesting book, *Changer de nom* by Nicole Lapierre, a sociologist who undertook a study on name-changes in France. Focusing on the situation of Jews, North Africans, and Armenians in France during the 1900s, she considers the stakes and the costs of name-change for these immigrants.

While liberty, equality, and fraternity are the guiding principles of all egalitarian societies, Lapierre discovered the reality is often different from the expressed ideals. To carry an identity card with a foreign-sounding name often translates into disillusion and disenchantment. In the hopes of seeking refuge from countries of persecution and oppression, many immigrants she interviewed came with the aspirations of a new life and a better world for their children. Instead, they encountered ongoing prejudice, closed doors, and explicit or implicit prejudice. After all, consider the following list of names: Witold Lutoslawski, Jacques Finkelsztajn, Dikran Kouyoumijan, Abdelmalek Sayad, Mahmoud Ben Addis, Anatolia Kernivachian.

To name is a rite of the collective, announcing admission to group membership. To pronounce one's name is, in many cases, to automatically reveal one's ethnic origin. For some immigrants, a renaming is a clandestine rite of passage, an attractive alternative for those who have been scorned or shunned or whose name has led to forced limitations and exclusions. To rename is to escape being a discredit, to erase or remove a stigma, to obliterate a difference, or to sanction an affiliation. It is to establish admission to a society without the projected and often real status of being a pariah, a second-class citizen or an outcast.

Imagine the agonizing ordeal that would lead a family to change their name. Envision the determination to contest and oppose a diminutive social status assigned on the basis of one's name. A refusal to bow down to the tenacious stranglehold of racial intolerance and discrimination. A decision to reverse outrightly the respect for one's ancestral name is to assert one's identity by alternate means. For these people, the change to a banal and neutral name is a means of protection against an oversimplistic or a priori reading of one's ethnic identity. In these cases, is it possible that name-changing is a subterfuge, a subversion of their identity for the quest of equality and freedom from the stigma of prejudice?

In several of the vignettes recorded by Lapierre, we hear the voices of young men and women who refuse to be so strongly identified with their names, insisting that their ethnic identity goes beyond the label or the name. In fact, they insist on the interiority of their identity, the force of an internal singularity of heritage that cannot be removed in spite of any attempts at erasure. Yet even by blotting out any overt traces of ethnicity in their written or spoken name, they cannot eliminate the power of their ancestry; the truth of their past inevitably remains locked within. The historical examples of the Marranos, those Jews living in the Iberian Peninsula at the time of the Spanish Inquisition who were forced into conversion but whose Judaism remained concealed within the privacy of rituals, is only one of innumerable examples where a collective attempt at ethnic or religious erasure survives within a community.

According to many individuals interviewed by Lapierre, the desire to reduce racial and ethnic identifications interfering with opportunities for success in xenophobic societies outweighed any attachment to an ethnic-sounding name. In my encounters at work, I have learned that Canada is not exempt from such prejudice and discrimination. Several of my patients have modified and shortened their names, eliminating the awkward and strange-sounding mixture of consonants. They claim the Anglicization of their name made a huge difference when seeking employment and applying to university.

✴ ✴ ✴

On Rosh Hashanah, the Jewish New Year, my friends, family, and I sit around the table after a traditional meal of roast chicken and gefilte fish, honey cake and apples dipped in honey. We wish each other the hopes for another year of health, happiness, and creativity. We offer the blessings over candles and bread and wine.

We can now sip, feast, and schmooze, a group of friends sharing an annual ritual. This year, I cannot refrain from mentioning my writing project on the name, and in no time, there are more anecdotes.

> You know, my father was one of eight children who all escaped during the war at different times. Each of them carries a different name.
>
> ✴ ✴ ✴
>
> I just learned about the original spelling of my name. I always thought it had been Klezner, but I learned that originally it had been Kleszczynska. Somewhere along the way, it was changed because it was too difficult to pronounce.

* * *

My uncle had a very long name with five consonants in a row. The port authority said to him: Too long; make it short. He and his five siblings now share the surname "Short." So now I am beginning to wonder about the popularity of this common surname.

* * *

I had an Italian friend whose father changed his name to a more Jewish-sounding one when he arrived in Canada. How's that for a switch? He went from Franco Adamoli to Frank Adam, modifying his name by dropping a few letters. Years later, no longer ashamed of his Italian heritage, in fact quite the contrary, he reverted back to the original name.

* * *

I remember hearing about the story of a community of Jews from Russia who wanted their children to have English-sounding names in order to be more easily assimilated into North American culture. As a result, sons were named Marvin, and within a short time, the name Marvin became associated by these new communities with Russian Jews. Just proves how difficult it is to erase one's ethnic identity.

* * *

I know a young man who told me the story of his family name Steinberg, which translated in English would mean "mountain of stone." His paternal grandfather of Polish descent had emigrated to Israel and when his Israeli-born father married a *sabra* [native Israeli], he decided to change his name to Har-Even, a literal translation from the Polish. [In Hebrew, *har* means "mountain" and *even* means "stone."] This young man was planning to remove the hyphen, condensing it to Hareven, because he said it felt "too split." He may even consider a further modification of his name, as he feels the name does not suit him. He's a sensitive and thoughtful person and claims he does not like the heaviness of its sound or meaning and one day plans to remove the weight of the "stone" [*even*] by shortening the name to Haran. Haran is a biblical name: It was the name of Abraham's brother, a man whose roots are common to the ancestry of all Jews, including Jesus, as well as a toponym for the place Abraham and his father temporarily settled on their journey from Ur to the land of Canaan. It translates into English as "mountaineer," an active name suggestive of movement and strength.

Jackie reminds us of the legendary tale no longer known whether fabled or real. An elderly Polish Jew has been advised to choose an

American-sounding name when he arrives from Warsaw so that the civil
state authorities will not incorrectly translate his name. He asks advice
from a baggage handler, who proposes the name Rockefeller. He repeats this name several times, but when he arrives at the desk of the
officer in charge, he can't remember it. When asked his name, the
elderly Jew replies in Yiddish, "*Shoyn fargesn!*" ("I've already forgotten
it"), and so he ends up with the very American-sounding name, with
Gaelic origins: Sean Ferguson.

We laugh, we joke, we share stories of name-changes, we who live in
a democratic country where freedom to change our names at will is
written into law.

A few months after this evening, one of my friends e-mailed me an
article on name-changing that had appeared in the Israeli newspaper
Haaretz. The article highlighted the trend of both European Ashkenazi
and Mizrachi (of Middle Eastern or North African origins) Jews to
Hebraize their surnames. According to Professor Aaron Demsky,
founder and director of the Project for the Study of Jewish Names at
Bar-Ilan University, Tel-Aviv, name-changing reflected the immigrants'
desire to reject the diaspora and the names they were forcibly given.
After considerable thought and attention, even rabbis and high-ranking
politicians changed their names.

Most immigrants to Palestine from 1881 onward Hebraized their
patronymics as a way of turning the page and beginning a new chapter.
Like all new immigrants, they wanted to burn the bridges to the diaspora legacy with all of its baggage. In fact, I recently read that over 28,000
names were changed between 1921 and the founding of the state in
1948. The fathers of modern Zionism—David Ben-Gurion (Gruen),
Levi Eshkol (Shkolnik), Eliezer Ben-Yehuda (Perlman), Yitzchak Ben-
Zvi (Shimshelevich)—apparently all changed their names in order to
express a kind of ideological identification with Zionism. Then in the
1950s, Ben-Gurion, as defense minister, insisted that anyone who represented the state of Israel in a formal capacity, such as athlete, a
diplomat, or a military man, had to have a Hebrew surname.

Demsky writes, "The beauty of names is that they reflect changes in
history and fashion in a society. Each person carries with him historical
baggage that is reflected in names, but to a certain extent, a name is also
a matter of fashion. There are those people who in the throes of immi-

gration and with the aspiration to build and fulfill [the Zionist dream] said, 'Let's change our name.'" [1]

I was initially struck by this cavalier attitude to names, as Jews have always insisted on the importance of ancestry and lineage. However, as Demsky also points out, surnames for Jews have never been sacred, and, historically, changing them has occurred in the migrations of Jews from place to place. A surname as a mark of social identification was considered far less significant than it was to become later. For Jews, what remained critical was that the Hebrew name still retain its primary importance.

However, as we shall see shortly, this attitude towards name-change is not shared by everyone. In fact, this article's viewpoint was not even shared by all of its readers. One person angrily commented on this facile shedding of names and history, raising the question, "Who are the self-hating Jews?"

* * *

On October 18, 2009, at the Jewish Museum in Paris, and on November 1–3, 2009, at the Hebrew University in Jerusalem, an international and multidisciplinary colloquium was held on the question of the proper name, sponsored by several French and Israeli organizations. A documentary entitled *Et leur nom, ils l'ont changé* (And Their Name: They Changed It) formed the basis of the colloquium, which culminated in the book *La force du nom: Leur nom, ils l'ont changé*. The documentary describes seven families who changed their surnames:

- Fainzylber/Fazel
- Wolkowiicz/Volcot
- Frankenstein/Franier
- Sztejnsztejn/Stenay
- Finkelsztejn/Fine
- Rozenkopf/Rosen
- Rubinstein/Raimbaud

All of these families felt compelled to modify their names after the Second World War in order to *franciser* (Frenchify) their name so that their children could carry a name that would not identify them as Jews and the families would be prevented from once again becoming victims of anti-Semitism. What is significant is that several third-generation children, those born with the changed name, participated in this documentary as a way of learning about their family names.

The Nazis eliminated the names of Jews and branded them with numbers as a form of dehumanization. As noted by one author, killing the bodies meant killing names, and killing names meant killing the Symbolic. By killing the names, the Nazis amputated and sealed off the flaws they perceived in the Jews. Although these name-changes referred to above were decided by the survivors, to prevent discrimination and harm, it is the offspring who are now challenging and questioning the masking of their identity through a name that conceals and hides a part of their ethnic identity.

The dilemma is that the legal system in France, as in most European countries, prevents the return to names that are *à consonance étrangère* (foreign-sounding names). This has raised a number of questions regarding what it means to have a name that comes from abroad and what it means to be a French citizen. Céline Masson, the principal organizer and coeditor of the book *La force du nom*, emphasizes the inherent importance of the accent of names. In a lyrical overture to the book, she writes movingly about the singularity of each name in its sonority, the uniqueness of pronunciation, the savor of the name in the mouth, the literal vibrations of our own name voiced, and the names of others that link us, through sound, to the weight of our ancestors. She adds that names, like faces, identify us, reminding us that these names stick to our bodies, and when we try to get rid of them, they return like significant carriers of our origins.

In Canada and the United States, such a law does not exist and it is possible for anyone to change their name at will, within the constraints of certain legal procedures. Every American and Canadian citizen, and every applicant for citizenship under those countries' immigration laws, is offered common-law, free-speech rights to take and use a name as long as it is not offensive or confusing, does not incite violence or racial hatred, or is not taken for some unlawful purpose such as fraud, flight from the law, evasion of debt or bankruptcy, or the commission of a crime. As long as the name is not a number, hieroglyph, or visual symbol, the new name becomes as legal as the one given at birth.

Yet, especially when it has been imposed involuntarily or chosen reluctantly, name-changes carry emotional weight. As discussed in the colloquium mentioned above, the concealed original will emerge through the traces left behind, especially if the change was made ideologically or forced politically.

In order to examine the impact, we must first ask some questions: What is one hoping for by the changing of one's name? What does one want or anticipate by such a dramatic and symbolic act? What are the motives for the alteration? Are we speaking about a wholesale name change or a modification in the spelling? Was the change imposed under threat or duress, or was it voluntarily chosen and adopted?

When a name-change is tied to a historical event, a social situation, or the affirmation of integration into society, the outcome is often favorable, especially for the generation who made the choice. Similarly, when the change is motivated by the anticipation of obtaining a diploma, entrance into a professional life, moving into a new region, marriage, and the prospect of having children, the stakes, while high, are likely to be positive.

And yet, there are many who disparage and oppose any modification for whatever reason. Given the high value placed on the patronymic in our society—men die, but the name lives on, as someone once said—these critics claim that any alteration is a betrayal of one's family roots, a disloyalty to one's ancestors. They accuse such individuals of a lack of courage and bravery in the face of adversity, without acknowledging the opprobrium and negative judgment that is often caused by carrying an obscene or ridiculous surname, or one that puts a target on the back of those whose ethnicity sets them apart. These critics fail to see that modifying or changing a name is not the same as putting on a mask or forging a new identity. It is a desperate attempt to overcome obstacles, to acquire a passport for freedom from prejudice and to avoid chronically misplaced social and professional barriers. Pierre Pachet, a well-known writer and university professor in Paris, paid tribute to his father by breaking the silence of his father's voice in his book *Autobigraphie de mon père* (Autobiography of My Father). Giving expression to an imaginatively reconstructed life of his father, Pachet offered his own interpretation of his family history, which is the story of the wandering Jew.

His father, born Simcha Apatchevsky in 1895 into a Russian Jewish family, finds himself in Odessa after the Russian revolution in 1905 (a precursor to the Bolshevik revolution of 1917) and continues his travel westward until he reaches Bordeaux in January 1914, becoming a university student on the eve of the outbreak of the First World War. He lives there with his family, his wife giving birth to his son Pierre in 1917, and dies shortly thereafter. Pachet writes, taking on his father's voice:

> My name is Simcha, which means "joy" in Hebrew. I can't prevent myself from bringing this together with the name of one of my illustrious contemporaries, of whom I have been so critical, Sigmund Freud for that is also the sense of his name [Freud means "joy" in German]:. My son suggested another homonym: the Irish novelist James Joyce, whose name would also have the same signification. I attribute no other value to this trilogy [Simcha-Freud-Joyce] than derision: it suffices to see our photographs, or my face, to understand that these names did not bring us luck, unless you consider that the joy stayed well hidden in us. An irony of destiny to which I am very sensitive. Another point, my name is feminine, which exposed me to a lot of jibes.[2]

In the interview with Lapierre in *Changer de nom*, Pachet mentions the announcement board written in his father's script and placed outside his father's medical office during the Vichy regime. In large, bold letters, it broadcast to the public: "Change of name. Docteur S. Pachet. Ex-professor at the school of dental surgery and stomatology of Paris. I respectfully inform you that from now on he carries the name of 'PACHET' instead of D'Apatchevsky." Pachet says the statement was intended as a declaration of pride in the face of the political situation in France, but also claims that it was a saving grace for him, adding, in his own words:

> The change of name is a chance, it simplifies, it detaches the imaginary roots and permits one to be furtive, to pass to circulate . . . Salman Rushdie once declared: "I look at my feet, I don't see any roots growing out of them on the bottom." The name, in any case, is only a part of one branch of filiation, it is only attached to a branch, not a root. But it is tied to the weight of familial patriotism, which in itself is linked to a larger patriotism, that makes that one is, for example, the Pachets . . .[3]

Pachet, who has returned to the subject of his identity in several of his writings, adds that he both does and does not completely inhabit his name, that the change of name has created a sense of "decentering" for him. On the other hand, he claims that even if no one else is aware of the original change, this is always a place where one can be "master of the name" because only the bearer of the name knows the truth of it.

❊ ❊ ❊

Name-changing seeps through the branches of the family tree. Changes made under a shroud of secrecy, forbidden names forfeited under threat of persecution, forced conversions made at the time of one generation—all filter down the limbs and branches. And like all secrets, eventually, the truth is exposed. Children learn surreptitiously about their family heritage. Clandestine research, furtive conversations made at family reunions and gatherings, probes by the more inquisitive often reveal certain truths about family history. Family secrets explode or implode. They shock and disturb the familiar narrative.

Imagine the discovery of your name—not the one you have lived, breathed, pronounced, and written; not the one that informs your being with a particular texture of light and darkness. Imagine that you are told that this group of letters you called your name is not your name because the man you thought was your father is not in fact your father. When confronted by an alternate reality, the solidity of the birth name, which denotes a particular substantiality of being—these lips, this hair, these eyes, this body, which I inherited from my father—undergoes a radical upheaval.

The discovery of one's hidden ethnic roots, often linked to a modified or truncated surname, can also be a beneficial or informative self-discovery. Dow Marmur, rabbi emeritus of Toronto's Holy Blossom Temple, wrote an article in a Toronto newspaper describing three types of Jews: Jews by birth, Jews by faith (or conversion), and Jews "by surprise," or those who discovered their Jewish roots later in life and only recently have "come out" with pride and interest.[4]

Madeleine Albright, the former U.S. Secretary of State, is one of the latter. She was born in what is now the Czech Republic to Jewish parents who apparently kept her Jewish identity and family faith from her. Though she may have suspected it for a long time, it was only recently that she decided to acknowledge it publicly.

A few years ago, the Polish-Jewish Heritage Foundation of Canada hosted Romuald Waszkinel, a Polish priest and professor of French at the Catholic University of Lublin. Waszkinel recounted that, as his mother was dying when he was in his thirties, she told him that his birth parents were Jews who gave him to her and her husband days after he was born and hours before they were taken by the Nazis to the gas chambers. When he finally found surviving relatives in Israel, he pressed them for details about his family. He was allowed by Pope John Paul II, who had been his teacher at university, to hyphenate his name with that of his late father, Jakub Weksler. He now spends time in Israel, where he continues to affirm his Christian faith while celebrating his Jewish descent.

* * *

Many psychoanalysts, and particularly those of a Lacanian persuasion, are vehemently opposed to any change of one's name. They believe that tampering with any of the letters, such as the addition or subtraction of a consonant or vowel, or the alteration of a syllable (for example, the change in spelling from Sheila to Sheilagh or from Rosen to Roazen) inevitably will lead to difficulties, if not in the generation of those who initiate the change, then in those that follow. They claim that any tinkering with a name creates a certain psychological instability that reverberates within one's identity. For these analysts, the name is "written in one's body."

According to the French psychoanalyst Pierre Legendre, whose work is cited in Lapierre's book, this outright condemnation among psychoanalysts arises from certain misreadings of the concept of the name-of-the-father as discussed in chapter 11. As noted, this symbolic function of the role of paternity is different from the social function of the proper name (or patronymic) in general. These two concepts closely overlap without being identical. Unfortunately, individuals whose decision to modify or change their family name based on a history of persecution have been subject to criticism and prejudice by professionals and nonprofessionals alike who have misunderstood and misapplied these psychoanalytical terms.

Legendre reminds us that nomination and the act of name-giving function differently in distinct cultures and societies and during distinct historical periods. He points out that this rich diversity in the forms of nomination does not interfere with the father's role as a universal denominator in its function; that is, that important "third" who intervenes in the primary mother-child duo, instituting a kind of "totemic principle" or taboo. This paternal function creates not only a psychological cut or separation between the mother and child, but also, with the assignment of his name, a symbolic cut that will not be lost. Even in cases where the mother adopts the father's name, she continues to carry, in the presence of its absence, the name of her father, as we see in the case of divorced women who revert to their maiden name.

In other words, while the patronymic system may vary from culture to culture, being a variable method of naming, it serves a structurally necessary role, as we saw earlier, in the psychic development of men and women. Therefore, the "disorder" referred to by some analysts occurs as a result of confusion between the system of naming, which varies, and the necessary function of the paternal metaphor, which is universal. Legendre argues that the father's function ensures that the name, modified or not, is still a master component in the "montage of filiation." The imperative to differentiate ourselves is, after all, an imperative of the human condition: one name for each of us.

I agree that changes to the proper name, that permanent inscription in the history of the subject, cannot be modified without an impact, be it major or minor, significant or inconsequential, but that personal impact is not automatically pathological.

Name-changing *in extremis* is well-intended—to protect succeeding generations from the weight of a name that has caused oppression, persecution, and discrimination. Yet, today, family arguments flare and recede. In some families, children accuse their parents of a deformation and amputation of their names, while in others, children sympathize and appreciate the sentiment under which the decision was made. Some parents are horrified and hurt to think they are being faulted when they were simply trying to save their children from undue pain and suffering. They feel their children do not appreciate how, on the basis of a name, one could be classified, declassified, or over-classified, and that such verdicts could disqualify the bearers of these names from equal opportunity in society.

Some adult children—whether they have attacked their parents for "selling out" and "giving in to the enemy" or appreciate their parents' rationale and motivations—have decided to revert to their original family name.

For example, a friend of mine whose name had been modified to eliminate an Arabic sound felt that the new name was inauthentic and somehow left a hole in the chain of affiliation or family connection. "By removing the ethnic syllable," she said, "it removed a part of the ethnic identity of my family. I know it hurts my parents to hear me say this, after all the suffering they experienced in their past, but for me, the change is a form of lie. I do not want to hide or conceal my identity. Instead, I want to announce it to the world."

Meanwhile, some of those involved in this debate argue that it is only "the privileged"—those with the good fortune to have never experienced the full extent of racial hatred as manifested during and following the Second World War—who are in a position to be more public about a name that exposes ethnic identity.

In my own case, the modification in the spelling of my family's name led me to explore the roots of my father's patronymic and to learn as much as I could about the discussion surrounding this decision. My father and his siblings chose to change the family name when most of them were in their twenties and setting up their own businesses.

As a young adult, I liked the fact that my name concealed my Jewish roots and that I could remain somewhat opaque in my encounters. I smiled to myself when people thought I might be Mediterranean, enjoying the exoticism that such origins implied. Later, I began to resent the intrusiveness of questions about my identity and felt this information was too personal to share with my inquisitors. Saying that I was Canadian and so were my parents provoked quizzical looks. Caught off guard by the question, I also knew what they were really asking: What is your ethnic background?

In examining the repercussions of this modified name, I became more aware of the way in which the concealment of my ethnicity led me to make certain decisions and not others. While I seriously considered putting back the missing letters of my name, for the time being I have decided to leave it in its truncated form. One day, I may choose to revisit this decision and revert to the original spelling.

❅ ❅ ❅

Another category of voluntary name-change is sometimes ignored or consciously dismissed: changes by those for whom the weight of their name has become unbearable—by the children of parents who, in the name of some ideology, have committed abominable acts against humanity.

Recently on the Internet I came across the work of the Israeli filmmaker Chonoch Ze'evi, whose documentary *Hitler's Children* had recently been released. Ze'evi's film investigates the lives of the children of Hitler's inner circle, bearing family names that evoke horror and revulsion for acts that we equate with the incarnation of pure evil: Himmler, Frank, Goering, Hess.

Bettina, the grandniece of Herman Goering, is perhaps the most open and publicly known living relative of the Nuremberg group of war criminals. A doctor of Oriental medicine, she said in an interview, "The eyes, the cheekbones, the profile . . . I look just like him. I look more like him than his own daughter."[5] Following a troubled adolescence and early adulthood, with several nervous breakdowns, Bettina made an earnest attempt to cope with the legacy of guilt associated with her name. Her odyssey to cleanse herself of the family's tarnished past landed her in Israel, where a documentary, *Bloodlines*, about her relationship with a child of Holocaust survivors, was featured.

At the age of thirty, she underwent the drastic measure of having her fallopian tubes tied for fear of creating another monster. Her only brother, independently of her decision, decided to have a vasectomy. While close to her brother, she is estranged from the rest of the family. "It's all a part of this guilt," she said.

Katrin, the granddaughter of Ernst Himmler and the grandniece of Heinrich Himmler, the SS and Gestapo commandant and the man responsible for the execution of the Final Solution, is now an author, notably of *Die Brüder Himmler: Eine deutsche Familiengeschichte*, published in English as *The Himmler Brothers: A German Family History*. For many years she did not speak German outside of Germany. In the film *Hitler's Children*, she admits to the ongoing shame and humiliation she feels. Her marriage to an Israeli man, the son of Holocaust survivors, resulted in a complete rupture with her own family.

Niklas is the son of Hans Frank, Nazi Germany's chief jurist and governor-general of occupied Poland's German Government Territory. From 1939 to 1945, Hans Frank instituted a reign of terror against the civilian population, becoming directly involved in the mass murder of Polish Jews. Niklas, a gifted writer and novelist best known for his book *In the Shadow of the Reich*, now travels to German schools to disseminate the message of his book and provide forums for discussion. It is his way of spreading "his hatred toward his parents." Monika Hertwig (née Göth), the daughter of Amon Leopold Göth, the sadistic commandant of the Plaszów concentration camp in Poland, describes the severe beatings she received from her mother when she dared ask how many

Jews her father killed. She is also an actor in the film *Inheritance* (by director James Moll, 2008), in which she narrates her family story and her curiosity about her father and his past.

Many German men refused to accept their given name Adolph following the Second World War, choosing to use their middle name or adopt a completely different one instead. I met a man who shared his family's story with me. His parents, escaping their country, had sent the children ahead to relatives already settled in Canada, and joined them after the war following an arduous escape route through Europe during the war. This man, now a grandfather, could not accept his given name, Adolph, especially in a country where postwar Germany was considered the "evil enemy." Instead, he stopped using this name and became Bill. "I bleached out any possible association to my homeland, especially in the community in which we had settled. I told my parents they would have to just put up with my decision if they wanted me going to school every day. Fortunately, they were understanding."

* * *

And finally, there is one more class of individuals for whom a name-change is tantamount to a new identity. These are not the victims of persecution, of prejudice, of racial hatred, or children of Nazis, fascist monsters, or communist assassinators. These are not the wanted, the convicted, or the thrill-seekers whose involvement in espionage or undercover work has created a new identity for them. Nor are these the artists and writers, superstars and superheroes of our culture whose names are illuminated in the media.

No, these are the men and women whose lives are mentioned in the Lives Lived column of Toronto's *Globe and Mail*, whose stories are told in the pages of other newspapers, the ones whose obituaries fill the back pages of all newspapers, the ones who got up every morning and like clockwork performed their everyday activities, coming home to their families and loved ones or to their empty apartments. These are the same men and women who struggle daily with the burden of depression and anxiety, suicidal ideation, and panic attacks. They could be our friends or friends of our children or parents, the shopkeepers or service people with whom we interact each day, the members of our choir, our book club, or our fitness center, the men or women who shuffle by our homes regularly to pick up a newspaper or a carton of milk.

The stories of these individuals are those most often encountered in the privacy and confidentiality of the offices of social workers, psychiatrists, and psychoanalysts. For them, name-changing is one desperate way of dealing with the weight of a family name contaminated by personal history: serious family dysfunctionality, including the depravity of sexual abuse or incest. In these and other less extreme cases of family degradation and humiliation, the symbolic and legal act of name-changing remains the only option to be rid of traumatic identifications.

In my own practice, I have treated an individual for whom, in the course of his analysis, the weight of his name required of him a minor modification in spelling, in order to create a distance or cut from his family. He felt the persistence of this act to be the only way he could successfully move forward in his life. Certainly, many other patients have used their analysis as a means of exploring all the ramifications of their proper name. As both a science and art of the particular, psychoanalysis provides a space in which the history and narrative of each person can be confronted. For the name we bear is not just inherited, but inhabited.

14

A HOUSE IS NOT A HOME

I own my name, for it is my own private residence. Like my physical house, this dwelling has many rooms in which I can roam. Sometimes, I choose to open the curtains and interact with the people with whom I share my life; at other times, I close the shutters and retreat into my space, seeking solitude and contemplation. At times, I venture into the basement where I have placed the fragments and relics of my childhood residence, that house which served as an underpinning for this current one. Or I play with the toys in the attic, opening treasure boxes and old chests of discarded dreams. I try on the fur hats and woolen coats stowed away in a cedar-scented closet, wrapping myself in a past before my time.

In the empty rooms of this home, I place the suitcases of mementos, souvenirs, and reels of conversations—the accumulated tokens of a life spent at moments lying on a beach of a northern Ontario lake, working in a children's mental health clinic, relaxing on a rooftop in Istanbul, living in an apartment with red and blue kitchen cupboards, driving to an office building facing a laneway with daffodils sprouting every spring. In the library are lined up the trove of books I have read and continue to read. Here and there I pull out a book full of underlined passages, those perfect sayings that have influenced my thoughts and attitudes.

This house, truncated from the original before my birth, is the one I inhabit, sometimes proudly and at other times reluctantly. Within these walls reside my private space, a place of contemplation and unknown mystery. Facing out is the name I carry to welcome the world, Mavis Carole Himes, the name of greetings and life stories. Facing in is *Malkah bat Leib v'Miriam*, my Hebrew name, the one used in rituals and Jewish customs. And reaching out to me from the past is Malkah Heimovitch, my unabridged name, an inscription that marks my subjective truth.

For all of us, the place from which we begin to speak, this intimate house, is fundamental, creating a psychological foundation from which we build our connection with the world. It is a developing space of growth, a realm of familiarity, and a shelter that becomes our home. It ensures that we each have a sphere of utmost intimacy, shaped by the summary of our distinct memories and experiences. Surrounded by the structure of our family with its particular cultural landscape and character, anchored in the tradition of past generations, our name is initiated through the rituals practiced by our ancestors and sustained by their values over time.

As both a gift and an inheritance from our parents, we gradually come to occupy our name as a unique personal dwelling place And yet this house stands in relation to a community, a neighborhood in which it has been built. As an inheritance, we make changes to our house, adding personal touches and remodeling it to fit our purposes. Not without conflict and indecision, ambivalence and doubt, we tear down and rebuild, modifying it to make it our own. And thus it is that, while given to us as an inheritance, this house also becomes our home.

When we were adolescents, my sister, in fury over what she perceived as an outrageous demand or complaint, would rail at our mother, "I didn't choose to be born! It wasn't my decision that you had me! So now you have to deal with me and my shortcomings! I didn't choose you, I didn't choose this family, and I certainly didn't choose this name."

When we are born, we move into our parents' home, our first place of residence. This first domicile quickly becomes a physical and mental space, the one in which we will build our foundation. Our initial state of helplessness and defenselessness makes us totally dependent on our parents with whom we share this first space. We move about the shared rooms in an exchange of comings and goings. While our mother and father are attuned to our physical and emotional needs and demands, they too create demands, insisting that we comply with their rules.

As we mature and require less of our parents' presence, we move into the other rooms, fastening onto the walls our banners and mementoes, the newfound souvenirs of encounters with friends and strangers, trinkets found along the way. We begin to paint the walls of our rooms with shades of our favorite colors from a newly discovered palette. We stretch and flex our limbs, trying to reach the outer boundaries of our house. We retreat into the basement or the attic as a place of solitude and silence to escape the influence and constraints of those others with whom we continue to live. We watch them troll the rooms, looking for evidence of our independent means and ways, struggling between encouraging our endeavors and continuing to limit our freedom. We try to make our mark; we struggle to create a spot, a space for ourselves that we can call our own. This is my house with my signature written on its walls. This is the house in which I celebrate my existence.

For most of us, the modeling and construction of this place that we will call home is a long and arduous process. It entails construction and reconstruction, temporary walls and false staircases, moldings and fixtures that are installed and then replaced. Yet the foundation is always there: the basement of our dreams and hopes, the first stirrings of desire, the echoes of those first embraces with the loved ones of our infancy.

Sometimes, we wish to remove ourselves completely from our family constellation. Sometimes, we want to imagine a different landscape with pastel walls and multicolored carpets, or with bold paintings and soft lighting. Or sometimes, we desire a family with different players.

✳ ✳ ✳

When I was in grade two, I told my best friend, Susan Ritz, that I had seven brothers living in Africa. I fabricated a list of names that I can no longer recall. I created a host of characters that went along with this imaginary family living several oceans away. Many years later as a student of psychoanalysis, I discovered that I was not unique in my musings of a fabricated past.

Freud wrote about this exact phenomenon and called it the family romance—a personal fantasy and imaginary construction we create to embellish or modify our family relationships and background. Some may imagine they are the children of royalty adopted by parents of humble origins, while others may believe they are the children of peasants rescued by wonderful godparents and brought to a kingdom imbued with riches.

Sometimes we play with the thought of a name-change as a game of fantasy and possible intrigue. Sometimes we may even play with the thought of being someone else, of being unfettered from our past with its strong identifications and perceived constraints. When I was an adolescent and staying with my sister and parents at a resort, I told a girl I met there that my name was Rosa. I liked the sound of what reminded me of a beautiful red rose. I maintained the false name until my sister heard me respond to this name and broke the spell.

And when I was twenty-five and escaping the pain of a relationship break-up, I traveled to Mexico for a sun-filled holiday adventure. High above the clouds, traveling at eight hundred kilometers an hour, in this no-man's-land where anything and everything is possible, I conversed with the handsome man in the seat beside me, telling him, "My name is Maya." This name flew out of my mouth as if it had been there waiting to emerge. Maya, the illusory veil of chimera, the exotic Hindu goddess whose dance of multiplicities deceives and distracts us from life's true essence, tricking us into mistaking her movements for reality. Maya of the Greco-Roman world, a goddess of the earth and the youngest daughter of Atlas who shines with her sisters in the night's sky in the constellation known as the Pleiades. Celebrated in her named month as the goddess of spring and rebirth, the one who brings forth the tulips and the daffodils, the fragrant cherry blossoms and the wild grasses. Without any moorings to the land below, I was adrift on a flight of fancy. I became a foreigner with a different passport, a manufactured history, and a new identity. I was surprised at the ease with which I could create and sustain a newfangled version of myself. When we landed, I said good-bye to my flight companion and once again slipped into the skin of Mavis Himes.

Today, the temporary forging of a new identity is a game commonly played among men and women on the dating circuit. The social media network with its tendrils of communication winds its way into daily encounters and provides a facile way to create new identities. In this world of aliases, genuine names are avoided to protect oneself from harassment and the abuse of confidentiality. However, the anonymity of a different or modified name also permits us to embellish our profile by adding to or subtracting from our personal résumé.

* * *

Are we, in fact, bound to our name by duty or by desire? Is it a blessing or a curse? Is it possible to remove our personal moniker and assume another one? And if so, are certain psychoanalysts correct in stating that a name-change always brings with it serious repercussions, as suggested in the previous chapter? Is it possible to retain our proper name and still change the identifications cemented to it by our history? Can we lift the weight of a name that has become overburdened?

We have seen how our proper name is always an invocation or summoning to life, a wake-up call to which we must respond. The catch or snare is that this call, this beckoning to life, always comes from others, typically our parents, preventing our choice in the matter and making us susceptible to their desires. We are dependent on these adults, for better or for worse, to determine our name, this appellation that will stick to us like a second skin from birth to death. As we grow up and have opinions about the way the world is or the way we think it should function, when we begin to say *Yes, I like this; No, I do not like that*, we rarely consider our name in such objective ways. We may not like our given name and prefer to be called by our middle name, a nickname, or a modified version of the original, yet we take for granted that this is the name we will carry forward to the end of our time.

However, on a more profound level, the fact that our name comes from others external to ourselves at a *first* moment and then must be interiorized at a *second* moment, has certain implications. Not only must we act in response to the call to life, but we also must appropriate our name and make it our own. As Goethe writes, "What that hast acquired from thy fathers, acquire it to make it thine own."[1]

We each must come to accept our name, making it our own. In most cases this process is automatic, but not always without some struggle or inner tension. By accepting and taking our name, we step into a communal world of speech and accept the socio-cultural norms and rules of convention represented by our parents and society.

The name bestowed upon us therefore forces us to acknowledge certain positions that we may outgrow and change. In the course of our lifetime, we may decide to question and challenge the positions of our parents; we will re-create our own values and morality and voice our opinions about the death penalty, hostage-taking, the battle of the sexes, and the causes of war.

Can we perhaps say that in order to fashion it into something of our own making, we must forget about our name and temporarily lay it to rest? That we must forget the associations and identifications attached to it, the desires and fantasies of our name-givers who had some vision or idea of who they wanted us to become? That we must forge it into a refuge of comfort and authenticity that becomes that safe home in which we grow and develop?

We all hope to become as freethinking and freewheeling as we desire. But can we? Is it so easy to establish our autonomy without being weighed down by our name? By our identifications? By our family values? By our symptoms and quirky behaviors? Are we not all forced to accept the process of transformation required to inherit our name?

* * *

Names are rarely neutral. There is pride or there is shame; there is a bond or there is a rupture; there is a positive association or there is a negative dissociation: There is curiosity, there is gratitude, or there is regret.

Some wear a distinguished name that easily opens doors. For them, the proper name is an advantage, a blessing that requires and demands nothing, which, on the contrary, automatically ensures prosperity and triumph. The history of family success and a "good family name" are fortunate attributes that are welcomed from birth. But is it possible that the children of powerful men and women with renowned names not only experience pride and honor but also self-doubt and inadequacy? Do they need to establish themselves independently so that they can *put their own name on* their actions and successes? And what exactly does it mean to *live up to one's name*?

Royal families are certainly prisoners of their names. Consider the fresh face of the late Diana, Princess of Wales, born Lady Diana Frances Spencer, who seduced the world with her charm but whose regal stature was sometimes questioned as a result of her behavior.

Currently in Canadian politics, Justin Pierre James Trudeau, the eldest son of Margaret Sinclair and Joseph Philippe Pierre Yves Elliott Trudeau (known simply as Pierre Trudeau), has been elected as leader of the Liberal party. Trudeau the father, the fifteenth prime minister of Canada, who held this office from the late sixties to the early eighties, was the most acclaimed Canadian politician of his time both at home and abroad. His multiple achievements, including the patriation of the

Canadian Constitution and institution of the Charter of Rights and the introduction of the Official Languages Act, have been well documented. His legacy of personal idiosyncrasies have made him a controversial figure, both revered and criticized.

In a recent newspaper interview, Trudeau the son claimed that his father was "extremely strong intellectually and academically, but it left him a little short on some of the interpersonal skills, the emotional intelligence." In the same interview, he described himself as the opposite of his father, being strong on emotional intelligence and weak in "intellectual intelligence."[2] Comparisons of the two men are unavoidable: They are both fearless; they are both actors and performers. Trudeau Senior was a strong leader because of his educational and experiential credentials; Trudeau Junior has a fiery personality that may or may not be able to get things done. Is his name a blessing and a curse? Will the Trudeau name turn out to be an advantage or disadvantage at the voting polls?

At times we feel our ancestry is a prison from which we wish to escape; at other times we hide behind these imaginary chains that keep us locked into our comfortable patterns, excusing and blaming our fears and resistance on family loyalties and the demands of allegiance. Some of us cannot escape the tyranny of our distinction as Bob Sr. or Bob Jr. I was reminded of this while reading *In Red*, a novel by the Polish writer Magdalena Tulli. Describing the claustrophobic life of a community in an imaginary small village, Tulli recounts the naming of a family of townsfolk: "The Looms married late. Their wives each gave them an only child, a boy who was always given the name Sebastian. Each of them was able at the right moment to replace his predecessor in such a perfect manner that Sebastian Looms endured in the memory as a single person."[3] No distinction, no possibility of creating an identity, no will or possibility of escape.

"You know, I have the same name as my father and my grandfather," someone once told me. "We are all John Emerson Black and we all have the initials J.E.B. My father was called by his first name, but I am called by my second name. There was nothing to distinguish me from my father, so I insisted on calling myself Emerson. Funny, though, I gave my son the same middle name and he gave his son the same middle name. So now the Emerson lives on."

I once read about a particular clinical case of a young woman in treatment with a French analyst. The analyst describes how a mother married to a man of a different culture and religion was determined to name her son something that would represent this child for her, in order to make her son hers and hers alone. She decided that she had found the perfect name—Amoi—a name that would be the equivalent of "mine" in English.

In my own practice, a patient of mine told me about her friend Louise, nicknamed Lou, who named her firstborn son Louis and her daughter, born two years later, Luella. We can imagine the confusion of names that may arise from such similarities, where the abbreviation of names would all be Lou, but we can also wonder about the motivation and needs of a woman who needed to name all her children with names that so closely resembled her own.

❊ ❊ ❊

Juliet of Shakespearean fame is cursed with her name. For her, to be a Capulet means to be prevented from her love affair with a Montague, a member of a rival family. A long-standing history of feuds between the two families casts a darkness over these "star-cross'd lovers." And so we hear the plaintive cry of fair Juliet beseeching her new lover to forego the bond linking him to his name:

> O Romeo, Romeo, wherefore art thou Romeo?
> Deny thy father and refuse thy name,
> Or; if thou wilt not, be but sworn by my love,
> And I'll no longer be a Capulet . . .
> 'Tis but thy name that is my enemy,
> Thou art thyself, though not a Montague.
> What's Montague? It is nor hand, nor foot,
> Nor arm, nor face. O, be some other name
> Belonging to a man.
> What's in a name? That which we call a rose
> By any other word would smell as sweet.
> So Romeo would, were he not Romeo called,
> Retain that dear perfection which he owes
> Without that title. Romeo, doff thy name,
> And, for thy name, which is no part of thee,
> Take all myself.[4]

Naive Juliet tries to convince her lover to change his name, forcing him to accept the insignificance of this arbitrary grouping of letters, this word forged of an indifferent convention. And Romeo, so besotted himself, is prepared to reject his family name and vows to deny his father and be "new baptized" as Juliet's lover. Poor Juliet wants to ignore the name branding of her beloved Romeo with its imposed restrictions. Not only does she wish to crush the weight of their family names, but she also wishes to overcome the social mores and prescriptions of a well-brought-up female of her time: chastity, submission, and obedience. After all, Juliet was much more constrained in her expression of sexual desire or yearning than most women of her time.

In her own way and in her own words—"Come, gentle night: come, loving black-browed night / Give me my Romeo"—Juliet smashes social convention, rebelling against the confinement of her social class and family values. Predetermined and arranged marriages were normative in Elizabethan times, when this play was written, while family and dynastic mergers were more typical of the Italian Renaissance. As a consequence, the secret marriage between Romeo and Juliet would have been forbidden. By indulging her desire and openly acting on her own values, by defying the "ancient grudge" between the Montagues and the Capulets, Juliet expresses the age-old conflict between old forms of identity and new forms of desire, between the law of the father and the desire of the individual.

In this way Juliet behaves very much like Antigone, daughter of Oedipus and sister of Polynices, who, in the play *Antigone*, by Sophocles, requests to bury her brother within the city walls. Since his actions made him the aggressor in a fight with his brother Eteocles, Polynices was forbidden to have a proper burial within the city. Antigone decides to transgress the dictates of her uncle Creon, the king of Thebes, who representing the law (*nomos*) of the polis, threatens her life should she persist in her demand. In the end, by pursuing her desire, she also loses her life. By defying the decree of the unrelenting king, she is apprehended at the burial site and condemned to exile in a cave by her uncle, where she takes her own life by hanging.

In a different setting many centuries later, but with a parallel dilemma, we can hear the melodies of poor Tevye, the iconic milkman in *Fiddler on the Roof*, pleading with his daughters the necessity of following tradition in a world of change and uncertainty. In trying to convince them, he appeals not only to a religious tradition, but also to a loyalty to the clan or tribe. In the early 1900s in Tsarist Russia, the patriarchal plea, no longer in this case related to an inheritance of nobility, but tied to the tradition of ancestry, is another incarnation of the same message: the binding power of familial expectations and the demands of ancestral lineage.

The struggle is that each of us carries a desire to speak our own voice, to write our own story, and to create our own signature, while still acknowledging a debt to our past and our family history.

❈ ❈ ❈

Alexander Stille is one of many authors who have written about their struggles with their name and the turbulence caused by their family history. The words that his "sprawling history of his family's trek across the 20th century is a study in the plasticity of identity" caught my eye in a literary review. According to this review, *The Force of Things*, a family memoir by this American journalist and professor, uncovers "clandestine revelations" of his family history that include multiple identities, shifting and sliding within a certain indeterminacy. We read that, prone to these oscillations and new appropriations of identity,

> . . . his Byelorussian dentist grandfather covered up his background and found a fraudulent way to make himself a pioneer of the Italian nationalism movement through a conniving patient who was the mistress of the Fascist poet laureate, Gabriele d'Annunzio.
>
> His father didn't learn he was Jewish until he was twelve years old, having assumed as he wrote Christmas letters to the baby Jesus that he was a full-fledged Italian Catholic. But then, naturally enough in wartime Italy, his almost accidental Jewishness became the defining element in his life. Though he went to school with Mussolini's sons and goosestepped in the blackshirt youth movement that welcomed Hitler to Rome, he was still sent packing.
>
> "He was angry when he discovered that he was Jewish," says Stille. "And then ashamed at being angry. And then twenty years later when courting my mother, he lies to her about being Jewish. He feels a need to hide that side of himself to win approval."[5]

But then we learn a more fundamental fact about this half-Jewish, half-Italian memoirist. His father, Ugo Stille, began life as Mikhail Kamenetski. Stille, the German word for "silence," was a pseudonym adopted by both his father and a close friend to conceal their true identities to the readership of the Mussolini era. Even though his father's friend died, Ugo Stille retained the name. Alexander comments on how his name, begun as a camouflage, artificially constructed because of certain events, became real once it acquired a history. He continues to ponder the impact of this on his identity.

❖ ❖ ❖

In the privacy of my consulting room, I hear the words of men and women who are strained and constrained by the struggles of family dynamics. Their words speak for themselves:

> My mother's legacy was her mental illness. This is my inheritance—a disease that was undiagnosed, unnamed, untreated, and unacknowledged within the family. My great-grandmother had electroshock treatments in the forties, and then my grandmother took Lithium in the fifties, and my mother was on Prozac in the sixties. My other grandmother took enough Valium to be stoned half the time and appeared at my aunt's funeral like a complete zombie. And now I have to take Wellbutrin and Clonazepam to stay stable myself.
>
> So this is my family legacy. So why would I want to carry this name? My surname is a noose. I want to detach myself from this history. I wish my name were just Martha. Why do I have to carry this name that reminds me of this weight that I do not want? I want no surname so that I can just be me. Martha Blank. Martha with no affiliation, no bonds, no expectations.

❖ ❖ ❖

> I grew up in the home of a strict Portuguese Catholic family. The home was impregnated with magical beliefs. "If you are not careful, this will happen to you," my mother would always say. "Be careful, the evil eye is watching." Superstitious remedies and cures for a number of ailments, talismans to ward off evil eyes, and amulets strung about the house—all of these permeated the household atmosphere.
>
> When my mother announced that I would be cursed with bad children if I did not behave as a "good daughter," I believed that this would be my fate. And so, in spite of my scientific training, I still find myself falling back on certain of these irrational beliefs. Now that I have three children, I still feel doomed. So now I end up always feeling relief when negative things happen, as if I am ensuring that these events will ward off anything worse. As long as I am somehow

being punished, I know I am warding off anything else and I can make sure that my children and I are safe from that godammed evil eye.

◦ ◦ ◦

My mother inherited my papa's dirt, the permanent grime under his fingernails, the calluses and rough skin on his hands, and the smell of sweat coming home from a day at the steel plant. Not the kind of washed-off dirt of a weekend gardener or the sexy colors of an artist's palette. No, this was the dirt and stink of poverty and hard work, back-breaking and endless.

My mother was determined to lift herself out of that quagmire; her fortitude and resolution, persistence and obstinacy, drove her forward until she acquired a position of success in an advertising company. I am not my mother's daughter—I am weak and lack her determination—but I suffer from the guilt that I am not living up to her name, the name of her success. I am not free of my name. It carries the weight of my grandfather's toil and exertion.

A patient whose birth was nearly fatal to her mother's health was given the name Lachesis (meaning "destiny") by her father, a name representing one of the goddesses of fate, chosen in gratitude for his wife's survival. "And what of my destiny, my fate?" she wonders as she struggles to come to terms with what she perceives as the weight of this particular name.

My name is an exotic name: Lachesis. It is a name of hope, opportunity, and optimism. I feel as though I can never fulfill the expectations of my name . . . And my middle name is Audrey after Audrey Hepburn, but who can live up to that talent? Perhaps my mother could, but I can't. I suppose my father hoped I would become like her, but I didn't. If I had been a boy, I would have been named Matthew, which means "gift of love," but instead I am this fate of destiny for my mother . . . My name separates me. Separation is like death. I was over there, different. Even in my family, I was the odd one out, like I wasn't supposed to be there.

Another patient, whose conflicts with her mother resurfaced in an intense manner following her mother's remarriage, spoke in anger one day about her given name. According to what she had been told, she was named by her mother, who had already divorced her father prior to her birth. As a result, she felt cut off from any connection or identity with her biological father.

> My mother gave me a name and then took it away, just like the relationship with my father. She had it and then she ended it. She had wanted to name me Scarlett after Scarlett O'Hara, the Southern belle in *Gone With the Wind*, but then she thought that would be too weighty a name to carry so she renamed me Nicole, or Nikki, as I am now known. Why did she tell me this? It would have been easier if she had never mentioned this fact to me, as now I still feel that I am implicitly carrying the name of Katie Scarlett O'Hara-Hamilton-Kennedy-Butler, the protagonist of that damned movie. I have watched it so many times, and I can't say that I am attracted to this woman who is outwardly confident yet inwardly insecure, seductive and coquettish, yet shy and retiring. I have given up on men altogether; it's as if any attraction to a man makes me vampish or too alluring. My affections are more directed towards women, although even then I have some reticence.

* * *

In the washroom of a restaurant, I hear two women talking. As one is washing her hands, the other is applying Chanel red lipstick to her wide lips. Having accomplished a perfect application, she stares in the mirror and says to her friend, "When I was a kid, Marilyn Monroe was popular and so my mother named me Marilyn. I always thought I had to be glamorous."

We know that in spite of the inheritance of our name, there often is a gap between the name we are given and what we make of it. Each of us interprets and reinterprets the understanding of our history and parentage, and the meanings we attach to our name. Fortunately, because of the unique status of the name as a signifier, the meanings attached to it are fluid and have the capacity to be modified, or to use another expression, the capacity to be disentangled from their original signification or intent.

But how do we become free of the weighted history of our ancestry? How do we maneuver through the heaviness imposed by our name, or can we even do so? And how do we fulfill Goethe's directive to appropriate our name? How do we engage with our heritage without being weighed down by it? How do we break the chains of tradition, those customs, beliefs, and practices handed down from generation to generation? How do we integrate the possibility of familial and tribal continuity and loyalty with individual differences and rebellion?

This same issue of identification appears in any creative situation in which there is a mentoring relationship. How does one move beyond one's teacher, mentor, trainer and develop one's own style, or to use our vocabulary to make a name for oneself independently of one's guide?

In an attempt to encourage originality and inventiveness, Francis Jean Marcel Poulenc, the twentieth-century French composer, advised his students to "spit on your parents and teachers." He subsequently added, parenthetically, "before you worship them." This adage would seem opposed to the more usual one of learning the "tried and true" before experimenting on your own.

One direction to search for answers to the questions posed above is to consider the examples of those who indeed have been successful in their attempts to "possess their name." Freud revolutionized our way of thinking, making a name for himself in the history of Western thought. The theoretical underpinnings of the Freudian revolution are thoroughly woven into the fabric of our thinking.

Freud shocked the world when he wrote about the Oedipal myth, claiming that a little boy was enamored of his mother and wished to eliminate his father; that all children had sexual strivings and desires, impulses for which they could not be held accountable; and that sexual fantasy was the underpinning of the libido, the energy driving the id, that cauldron of seething passion. He revolutionized our thinking with his discovery of the unconscious, making man no longer master of his own house. As one author writes, "Freud descended into the basement of his house, into the cellar of the psyche; and there he found the irrational, demonic and the mythical secrets in the heart of reason."[6] Freud uncovered and exposed heretical desires at the origins of each man and woman.

In the development of his theory, Freud wrote and rewrote, rejected and accepted, demolished and restored, refuted and reaffirmed his earlier writings. Like all brilliant scientific thinkers, he challenged even his own ideas with his inquisitive mind.

But Freud's making a name for himself involved more than public recognition and acknowledgment, more than the revolutionary production of an entirely new field. For the founder of psychoanalysis, there was also a symbolic renomination, a remaking of his own name. Freud's was a long struggle of personal conflict and radicalism—a lifetime process that he worked out in his own self-analysis, in his letters to William Fliess, his major interlocutor for many years, and in his own writings.

Born Solomon Sigmund, son of Jakob, Freud had his own personal conflicts about both his Jewish identity and his relationship with his father. According to Marthe Robert, in her *From Oedipus to Moses: Freud's Jewish Identity*, Freud's ambivalence was the catalyst of the origins of psychoanalysis and a central link to his writing on the Oedipal complex.

Freud's ambivalence can perhaps be symbolized by a particular family incident. For Freud's thirty-fifth birthday, in 1881, his father presented him with a leather-bound copy of the actual Bible from which Sigmund had studied as a child. Inscribed in the front was a lengthy dedication to his son, written in Hebrew and drafted in the style of a *melitzah*, a form of writing that is made up of biblical fragments and phrases and rabbinical commentary fitted together to create statements other than those intended by the author. Here is the literal translation by the historian and scholar of Jewish studies and culture, Yosef Hayim Yerushalmi, in his book *Freud's Moses*:

> Son who is dear to me, Shelomoh. In the seventh in the days of the years of your life the Spirit of the Lord began to move you and spoke within you: Go, read in my Book that I have written and there will burst open for you the wellsprings of understanding, knowledge and wisdom. Behold, it is the Book of Books, from which sages have excavated and lawmakers learned knowledge and judgment. A vision of the Almighty did you see; you heard and strove to do, and you soared on the wings of the Spirit. Since then the book has been stored like the fragments of the tablets in an ark with me. For the day on which your years were filled to five and thirty I have put upon it a cover of new skin and have called it: "Spring up, O well, sing ye unto it!" And I have presented it to you as a memorial and as a reminder of love from your father, who loves you with everlasting love. Jakob Son of R. Shelomoh Freid [*sic*] In the capital city Vienna 29 Nisan [5]651 6 May [1]891.[7]

In the writing of this inscription, father Jakob makes a number of allusions by transposing and inserting biblical quotations and references that only someone versed in Hebrew studies could appreciate. But more significant is that Jakob, bound to his Jewish faith and tradition, is admonishing his son Shelomoh to return to his ancestry and to reconcile with his Jewish roots.

As the father reminds him, Freud had studied Jewish texts as a child but at some point had abandoned the Book of Books, while his father retained it and kept it for safekeeping. Now in his prime, Jakob returns the childhood copy of the Bible with a plea to his son, a dramatic call to return to the originally shared values of his father and to the traditional legacy of his lineage—"a memorial and a reminder of love," to which Freud never adhered. Psychoanalysis was to be born over the next number of years with the publication of Freud's first seminal work, *The Interpretation of Dreams*, in 1900, a few years after his father's death in 1896. We know that Freud continued his internal struggle with his father in his writings on his dreams, his letters to Fliess, and the recurring theme of the father-son bond in his theoretical works.

Shelomoh ended up developing a new science of the human mind, and followed this quest with a burning passion to the end of his days. The son of traditional Jewish parents, he insisted on breaking ground and smashing preciously treasured tenets of thinking, ever risking the scorn, the chastisement, and the prejudices of his professional and family communities. For example, his work on *Moses and Monotheism*, in which he claims that Moses was an Egyptian, led to charges of heresy and slander, not only within his own sphere but also in the larger public. And yet, in spite of himself, Freud placed tremendous significance on the text of speech and of dreams in the formulation of his theories, revealing a thread that, in spite of himself, linked him to his predecessors. Towards the end of his life, Freud wrote in his *Autobiographical Study*:

> I was moved, rather, by a sort of curiosity, which was, however, directed more towards human concerns than toward natural objects; nor had I grasped the importance of observation as one of the best means of gratifying it. My deep engrossment in the Bible story (almost as soon as I learned the art of reading) had, as I recognized much later, an enduring effect upon the direction of my interest.[8]

Perhaps Freud took his own words to heart: "The hero is the man who resists his father's authority and overcomes it." Freud was able to rid himself of his deep-rooted identifications and link with his family's tradition, a first step in the symbolic rewriting of his name and his personal history. But did this rewriting necessarily entail a break with the chain of generations? Can we see in the writings of psychoanalysis and the elaborations not only a rupture but a revolution around a critical axis?

Every discipline has its renegades and revisionists who are audacious, speculative, willful, and controversial. The visions of these revolutionaries challenge those around them to listen and take heed. In the fields of knowledge with which I am most familiar, we might consider: James Joyce, Franz Kafka, Jorge Luis Borges, and Georges Perec (literature); the Greek thinkers Plato and Aristotle, along with Ludwig Wittgenstein, Walter Benjamin, and Roland Barthes (philosophy); Claude Lévi-Strauss (anthropology); John Cage, Luciano Berio, and Arvo Pärt (musical composition); Robert Lepage (theater); Karl Heinrich Marx (social science and economics); Elizabeth Cady Stanton, Susan Brownell Anthony, and Betty Friedan (women's studies); along with my personal mentors, Freud and Lacan.

❅ ❅ ❅

Perhaps you think I am suggesting that we all become revolutionaries and heretical thinkers. Or perhaps you feel a pressure to become an unconventional leader in your own field. Let me dispel such thoughts. As a mentor of mine once said, "We strive for an ideal but we live in the real world." While the people I cite are exemplary, it is not their life's work or oeuvre per se that is significant, but their courage to challenge and confront inner constraints, which allowed them to move beyond themselves. In this antagonism between tradition and revisionism, the name becomes a metaphorical fulcrum.

I am reminded of a patient who had a dream in which she visualized a huge open space with buffalo running wild, as in the scenes of a Clint Eastwood western. In the foreground, she sees a group of horses corralled. As she begins to free-associate in response to the dream, she says, "You know, they were beyond the Pale, those buffalo, but not the horses who were penned in."

I question this phrase "beyond the Pale," and she continues, "Within the Pale, there are laws that have to be obeyed, but you have to be a subject of the land, a citizen of the state, to belong. The cost for protection is submission and subjection to these laws of the land. Outside the Pale, there is a lawlessness—a recklessness and a wild freedom."

Her associations led her to insights about the sense of enclosure and restraint she felt in "being a good girl," complying with everyone's demands and wishes. Her desire: to be free, to live life wildly, to think outside the box.

Yes, outside the Pale is unbridled energy that cannot be contained, the freedom of choice and only the self-imposed laws of restraint. With this freedom comes the fear of excess, of going too far, of losing one's bearings. How do we trust that we can move towards the unknown, that territory of freedom, liberated from the certainty of familiarity and safety? Is it possible to travel beyond the protection and certainty, the safety and security of a known master? To wander farther afield into unknown territory for the sake of a wager? Is there the chance to emerge from the depths like a defiant Prometheus unbound?

The story of the giving of the Tablets of Law is a biblical reference to how the struggle for autonomy and independence from a significant other is only won after a struggle with the law of the father and not without consequences. The first Tablets of Law presented by Moses to the people awaiting his return from Mount Sinai were two pieces of stone. Fashioned by God and inscribed with the Ten Commandments, they represented a covenant between law-giver and his people. However, an impatient and insolent group of people awaited him on his return.

> As soon as Moses came near the camp and saw the [golden] calf and the dancing, he became enraged; and he hurled the tablets from his hands and shattered them at the foot of the mountain. He took the calf that they had made and burned it; he ground it to powder and strewed it upon the water and so made the Israelites drink it. (Exod. 32:19–20)

With the first set of tablets smashed and broken, Moses appealed to God and begged forgiveness on the behalf of his people. The Israelites were spared but not fully pardoned at first. In a gesture of good faith, God agreed to carve out another set of tablets, only this time it was to be a joint human-divine effort. A second set of tablets (referred to as "the tablets of stone" or "the tablets of the covenant") inscribed with the Decalogue was formed and once again presented to the Israelites. Certain considerations ensued: "He does not remit all punishment, but visits the iniquity of parents upon children and children's children, upon the third and fourth generations" (Exod. 34:7).

Which makes sense. After all, are parents not responsible as role models to ensure that their children are well taught and well informed? However, can we interpret this story in another way? Is there a positive spin to this cautionary tale? To establish our own autonomy and to change the laws, to turn the world upside down, to damn the jailers and censors, do we not need to counteract the prison guards and demons that we carry around within us? Do we not need to create an upheaval and break with the status quo? To even go so far as to err and learn by failure?

There is a price to be paid for a true renomination. Another biblical reference that may be helpful in describing this process of symbolic renomination, a process that is necessarily linked to a struggle and/or revolution, is the act of creation in Genesis, or, more specifically, the Kabbalistic processes used to describe creation: *tzimtzum* (contraction), *shevirat ha-kelim* (the shattering of the vessels), and *tikkun* (repair).

Tzimzum describes the first step in the process by which God withdrew into his own essence, creating an area in which creation could begin. *Shevirat ha-kelim* describes the process when God began to pour his Light into the vessels (*ha-kelim*) that he had created in the empty space left by his self-contraction. However, because these vessels were not strong enough to hold the power of God's Light, they shattered (*shevirat*) randomly. The third step, *tikkun*, is the process of gathering and raising the sparks of God's Light that were carried down with the shards of the vessels.

In a like manner, renaming (or reappropriating our name) involves *deformation* or splitting from *formation/nomination* and a *(re)creation/ (re)nomination*. For the name to be read or received otherwise than it was given at birth—that is, to make it one's own ("to make a name for oneself")—there must be a cut or a temporary rupture, a "breaking of the vessels." It is only through this dramatic renewal that the appropriation of one's name can become a movement from the other to the self. Emptied or released from the heaviness of its initial identifications and released from its referential bondage, the name can become as neutral as a common noun.

* * *

My granddaughter Ashley and I are walking hand in hand on a beach by Puerto Viejo, a small laid-back town on the Atlantic coast of Costa Rica. She is a thoughtful young woman who radiates an openness towards life. She is explaining some principles of Waldorf teaching, which she has been studying and practicing, an alternative educational practice based on a humanistic philosophy developed by the Austrian philosopher Rudolph Steiner. "You know," she says, "children in the Waldorf system are introduced to the letters of the alphabet and even the basics of language arts through creative play and self-expression. Rather than the formal methods of the regular school system, we believe that the basics of reading and writing should also flow from an integration of body, soul, and spirit."

I look at her quizzically.

"Let me give you an example, Grandma. Every letter of the alphabet can be associated with a different movement and gesture, like this." She flings her arms outwards with an unself-conscious freedom that personifies her open spirit for me. "See, this is an *A*. *A* for Ashley. And so each child learns the spelling of his name through these various physical movements. It's what we call eurythmy, Grandma; we call it learning to dance your name." *Eurythmy*, from the Greek root meaning "beautiful" or "harmonious rhythm," a term used by Greek and Roman architects to refer to the harmonious proportions of designs. I am reminded of the tradition of Orthodox Jews who introduce their children to Torah through a pairing of honey and letters or words. It is hoped that, by placing a drop of honey on their tongue or hand after pronouncing a word, they will associate the sweet taste of honey with the sweetness of learning.

If we fully own that house of letters we call our name and into which we are born, then it becomes a home, a place of comfort and solace. We can choose to embrace it or leave it, replace it or modify it, accept it with resolution or reject it with silent rancor. In time, we may come to create a name for ourselves that is unencumbered of negative associations, identification, and/or a burdensome past.

Each of us is split between duty and desire—a duty to fulfill certain obligations and live up to our name and a desire to maintain our own individuality. Inevitably we will encounter times when we are bound to break and destroy the laws enforced by our fathers and mothers, either surreptitiously or openly. And for this, we carry the burden of guilt imposed by our ancestry, by an implicit contract with the law of our fathers. Yet in the best of outcomes, we learn to dance our name not only at the beginning of our life, but a second time when we have truly appropriated it for ourselves.

APPENDIX: THE LANGUAGE OF NAMES

Onomastics, the study of proper names and their origins, includes anthroponymy, [which is] concerned with human names, including personal names, surnames and nicknames. . . . The study of proper names . . . has a wide-ranging scope encompassing all names, all languages, all geographical and cultural regions. [1]

When I was four years old, my sister began attending kindergarten. In my preschooler's mind, I imagined that my sister was spending her mornings in a classroom constructed of books—books piled up high to the ceiling, chairs and desks made out of books glued together, multi-colored stacks of books, their spines all facing outwards like the ones in overstuffed used bookstores I now love to frequent. I no longer remember where in my active imagination I placed the toys my sister mentioned to my parents, the areas of sand play and water play, the building blocks and crayons. For it was this literary mansion that so captivated my attention. My fascination led to incessant questions about my own attendance at this wonderful place in anticipation of the time I too would be big enough to attend the learning place of words and books.

When I pursued my graduate studies in psychology, I gravitated to the field of language acquisition, that complicated process we all seem to master so effortlessly. I became fascinated by the facility we all have to acquire our mother tongue. So for my doctoral dissertation, I chose to investigate one aspect of this complex process, the verbal patterns of communication between mothers and their children. By videotaping mother-infant pairs at three different periods within a year span, I ex-

plored the language strategies mothers automatically use to engage
their children.

The acquisition of language is truly a baffling process. As language-
learning beings, we take the complexities of this astonishing feat for
granted. It is only when there is a breakdown in the process (such as
aphasia) that we marvel at how each of us accomplishes this develop-
mental milestone. Some of us repeat this process and become language
learners again as adults, taking on the task of acquiring a second or third
language. Not only must we learn the new phonological sounds and
semantics of words, but we must also master syntactical and grammatical structures, those rules that permit certain word groupings to form
sentences. Initially, when we listen to a new language, strings of foreign
sounds become parsed into smaller units until we gradually begin to
recognize, decode, and understand them. Conversely, as we begin to
speak, we must put together those phonemes and morphemes into the
construction of meaningful units of words, phrases, and eventually sentences.

The capacity for speech and language is the gift of our humanity, a
capacity that our kindred mammals do not share. Man holds an exceptional and inimitable status in the world of living beings. Like his animal
cousins, man is that individual of appetites, of instincts, and of cravings
for food, for sex, and for satisfaction of his needs. Man desires a full
belly and a bellyful of laughs, a wet mouth and a mouthful of pleasure, a
sexy partner and a partner for sex. Yet what distinguishes man from his
animal predecessors is his capacity for generative speech and language
(and here I am not speaking about communication). Man's faculty to
generate thoughts and to create endless streams of words in infinitesi-
mal combinations is the unique talent of speaking beings—*Homo sapiens.*

Homo sapiens is symbolic man: the orator, the spokesperson, the
scribe, the literary negotiator, the storyteller. Like my imaginary childhood image, speech and language constitute a symbolic house in which
man resides, a house of words developed, constructed, and transmitted
by an extraordinary history of civilization. This symbolic reality incorpo-
rates all of the activities that flow from a wellspring of letters, numbers,
and symbols.

What is it that allows man to speak and generate language? Words
and their constituent parts are dependent on the physical apparatus of

our mouth and jaw to be conveyed. Until letters are spoken or voiced, they remain the carriers of pure *non-sense*, curly waves or straight stick-men littered on a sheet of paper. And it is only when consonants are combined with vowels, allowing the flow of air through the vocal tract, that these letters grouped together and lined up side by side like a brigade of marching soldiers can be spoken in any meaningful way. It is the breath occurring through vocalization that parses and interrupts the murmuring flow of sound, thereby creating units of meaning.

We breathe life into these dead consonants—the gutturals, labials, and fricatives—to make them sing and dance for us, to create meaning and to inhabit our world through language. In specific combinations, these groupings open into a universe of sense. From a change in one letter of a *word*, there is before us a *world* of difference. Words bring division, order, conflict, the creation of life and the creation of death. Opposites and similarities, homonyms, antonyms, and synonyms. We enter the theater of life through these letters, words, and thoughts. As the Arabic poet Mahmoud Darwish writes so beautifully in his memoir *In the Presence of Absence*, describing the power of this house of letters and words:

> Letters lie before you, so release them from their neutrality and play with them like a conqueror in a delirious inverse. Letters are restless, hungry for an image, and the image is thirsty for a meaning. Letters are empty clay so fill them with the sleeplessness of that first con-quest. Letters are a mute appeal in pebbles scattered on the open path of meaning. Rub one letter against another and a star is born. Bring a letter close to another and you can hear the sound of rain. Place one letter on top of another and you will find your name drawn like a ladder with only a few rungs.[2]

Before I continue, let me introduce a few terms. Nomenclature is the term that applies to either a list of names and/or terms, or to the system of principles, procedures, and terms related to naming. Nomina-tion is the assigning of a word or phrase to a particular object or proper-ty and derives from the Latin *nomen* (name) and *calere* (to call).

The act of naming is a human attempt to inhabit the illimitable vastness of existence with its mysteries, to capture a degree of order and control over the wildness and unpredictability of life. We name things in an attempt to "hold on(to)" or "pin down" our attachment to complex ideas or concepts that elude our grasp, requiring a harness of some magnitude. And with the straps in place, we can transmit these ideas and concepts to others with a shared vocabulary. It was not until we named a cluster of stars that we could see the constellations of Orion, Taurus, and the Big Dipper.

Words simplify and categorize our reality; common nouns or names label all those forms, shapes, objects, and people that constitute our personal and collective universes. The act of naming solidifies our reality, bringing order to chaos. Tree is the word we give to the concept of tree, therefore we can recognize and learn something about a tree. By naming we separate and identify elements of our world. Apple is a fruit that grows on a tree; it is separate from a pear that is another fruit that also grows on a tree.

In *Through the Looking-Glass, and What Alice Found There* (the sequel to *Alice's Adventures in Wonderland*), Alice innocently ponders the question of names. In her charmingly naive fashion, she points out the impossibility of a world without names:

> "This must be the wood," she said thoughtfully to herself, "where things have no names. I wonder what'll become of *my* name when I go in? I shouldn't like to lose it all—because they'd have to give me another, and it would be almost certain to be an ugly one. But then the fun would be, trying to find the creature that had got my old name! That's just like the advertisements, you know, when people lose dogs—'*answers to name of "Dash": had on brass collar*'—just fancy calling everything you met 'Alice,' till one of them answered! Only they wouldn't answer at all if they were wise."
>
> She was rambling on in this way when she reached the wood: it looked very cool and shady. "Well, at any rate, it's a great comfort," she said as she stepped under the trees, "after being so hot, to get into the—into *what*?" she went on rather surprised as to being unable to think of the word. "I mean to get under the—under the— under *this*, you know!" putting her hand on the trunk of the tree. "What *does* it call itself, I wonder? I do believe it's got no name— why to be sure it hasn't!"[3]

Alice quickly realizes that she no longer knows who or how she is. It is only when a fawn comes along and encourages her to move into another field that the situation is cleared up. The fawn gives a sudden bound into the air, shakes itself free from Alice, and cries out in delight,

"I'm a Fawn! and dear me! you're a human child!" It is following this outcry that Alice remembers her own name in relief.

In today's society, we can appreciate how much we are dependent on common names to label, classify, and share our collective world when we consider the expanding universe of social media: tweet, web, spam, blogger, etc. In the midst of either radical or progressive change, we are forced to adapt to our new reality by creating new terms and names to reflect the ever-evolving world of industry, technology, and science. We also appropriate old words and create new usages for them. We borrow and extend the meaning of words, stretching the canon of language like an elastic band. For example, the English language is infused with the word *name* . . .

We *put a name to* when we report an event or creation; we *call someone names* when we are displeased or annoyed or when we want to insult an opponent or rival (Plain Jane); we *give our name to* a discovered disease (Lou Gehrig's), a new construction (Trump Tower), or a cutting-edge creation (the Frank Gehry museum). And *by the name of*, we call or label a person, a pet, or a favored treasure.

We say that something *has one's name on it* when we want to suggest that something is so aptly suited to a person or to imply that someone is destined to receive something. We *have in one's name* when we hold or contain something in our possession. We own, register, complete, or devise an activity or event *in all but name* when we feel something exists in a particular state minus the formal requirements. *In someone's name*, we bequeath money, donations, or gifts as a way of granting something on behalf of someone; *in the name of*, we perform an act using the name of a specified person or organization. And *in name only*, we describe something that does not actually happen in reality.

If we are lucky and exceptional in our life projects, we may *make a name* for ourself; we acquire public recognition and acknowledgement—by peers, by a professional community, and/or by the public at large. For some, to *be a name to contend with* is a challenge of public success and fame.

Common measures of status, fame, and fortune in our Western world are often associated with namings—*to be named* in a certain magazine or newspaper; to be considered or referred to as a *big name* in theater or film, the sciences, or the arts; to *have to one's name* a certain credit or cachet is to have in one's possession something to be desired.

There are those with endowments who have a building, a museum, or a foundation *in one's name*. And if you are lucky enough to have your success and fame acknowledged, you might *give your name to* a new discovery or organization, thereby transforming your name from a proper noun into an adjective, such as the Picasso museum, a Kafkaesque film, the Epstein-Barr virus, or the Hubble telescope. Some names have worked their way into the vernacular of everyday speech: Geez Louise, Even Steven, Dapper Dan, Don't know from Adam, For Pete's Sake, Plain Jane, Handy Andy.

I have read somewhere that there are three levels of fame. The first is when you go somewhere and someone recognizes you; the second is when you go somewhere and everyone recognizes you; and the third is when you go somewhere and someone recognizes you but can't believe it is you in the flesh. *Is that really Penelope Cruz? I can't believe it is really her!* In today's culture, to make a name is what is encouraged in every field of endeavor. I turn on the radio and I hear that Justin Trudeau, the son of one of Canada's former prime ministers who was well-loved and revered by many, *brings his name to the table*, that Stevie Wonder now *has his name in lights*, and that Margaret Thatcher is *really a name to conjure with* these days.

According to linguistic theory, common names can be placed on one shelf in a cupboard of linguistic categories, while proper names slide underneath as a subcategory. While both common and proper names are used for identification, the further subset of proper names holds a particular position within the category of nouns.

Curiously, the proper name has always been a troubling paradox for linguists and philosophers of language, psychoanalysts, and anthropologists alike. We can join this debate by asking: What differentiates the proper name from the common name or noun? What exactly is so *proper* about the proper name? What is its *proper* use? Is the granting of a proper name to an individual a matter of convention or is it an attempt to capture a certain essential character or trait? What are the rules and practices that underlie the formation of names? Are proper names merely a more refined or particular means of classification? Is there something immutable about the name?

Perhaps we can blame the Greeks for a certain confusion in this regard. After all, as the French philosopher and ancient Greek historian Jacques Brunschwig reminds us, it was the Stoics, those contrarian philosophers, who, for reasons connected to their analysis of language, created a new genus *onoma* (or name), which was then further divided into two species: the *idion onoma* (or common name) as opposed to the *koinonion onoma* (or proper name). And it was this split that would engage academics and scholars in ongoing discussions over their differences. To complicate the picture, in the French language, with its roots yoked to Latin, there is only one word, *nom*, that means both noun and name, whereas in English we use the two terms. In English, we can still refer to the man (the noun) and Socrates (the name), whereas in French there is only one word (*nom*) to refer to both situations.

Given that it was the Greeks who were the major culprits of this debate, let us turn our attention to that most argumentative and brilliant of philosopher-kings, Plato, who wrote the well-known dialogue *Cratylus* on the topic of proper names. In fact, Plato's own name, according to the philosopher Diogenes Laërtes, was Aristocles after his grandfather, but his wrestling coach, Ariston of Argos, dubbed him Platon, meaning "broad," on account of his robust figure. According to other sources dating from the Alexandrian period, Plato derived his name from the breadth (*platytês*) of his eloquence or from the width (*platys*) of his forehead.

Now, imagine living in Athens in 360 BCE. In the ancient agora, the town square, we are standing in front of the Stoa of Zeus, the temple-like structure commemorating the victory of the Greeks over the Persians. We admire the magnificent Doric external columns and the Ionic inner ones as we approach the bronzed statue of Zeus Eleutherios, the liberator, with his outstretched arms. The heat is assaulting and so we decide to sit down on the steps of the stoa in the shade.

Three men appear in view. As they saunter over, we recognize the man with a mane of white hair and recessed eyes as Socrates. He is accompanied by two other men: One is short and appears slovenly; the other, distinguished by his height and his demeanor, is clutching a sheaf of papers. The latter is Cratylus, a Greek philosopher mentored by the renowned Heraclitus of Asia Minor, whose teachings on the constant flux and motion of life were well regarded at the time. A self-assured man, pompous and erudite, and a master of discourse, Cratylus stares down at his intellectual opponent with contempt. His opponent is none other than Hermogenes, the son of Hipponicus and brother of the wealthy Callias. Hermogenes, a man of little talent, learning, or property, bearing a name of grandeur yet ignorant of the basic tenets of philosophy, is nevertheless an inquisitive subject, a seeker of truth, and an investigative soul.

The two men sit down a few meters from us and within minutes begin speaking in high-pitched tones so that we can overhear their words. They seem to be engaged in a passionate debate within the presence of the ever moderate and wise man of learning, Socrates. The topic under dispute: the truth or "correctness" of names. It appears that for Cratylus, names are appropriate to their objects insofar as they describe them. For example, the Greek word for "man," *anthrôpos*, breaks down into *anathrôn ha opôpe*, "one who reflects on what he has seen," a fitting description for a species in unique possession of what the Greeks considered both eyesight and intelligence. According to Cratylus, this name reflects the distinguishing characteristics of man and so is an apt description that fits the referent.

This approach, termed linguistic naturalism and embodied in Cratylus's thinking, is pitted against the linguistic conventionalism of Hermogenes, who we overhear saying:

> I cannot convince myself that there is any principle of correctness in names other than convention and agreement; any name you give, in my opinion, is the right one, and if you change that and give another, the new name is as correct as the old—we frequently change the names of our slaves, and the newly-imposed name is as good as the old: for there is no name given to anything by nature; all is convention and habit of the users;—such is my view.[4]

It is not surprising that Hermogenes would argue against a naturalist position. After all, what could possibly be natural, or even proper, about his name Hermogenes, which means "offspring of the god Hermes," which implies "of the same kind as Hermes"? How could such a simple man carry the name of such a resourceful and verbally adept god, a contriver of tales and speeches, and a messenger of the gods?

"I am no true son of Hermes for I am no good at speeches," he moans. "This cannot be. My name can only be a product of random conventionality." For Hermogenes, it is merely a convention that certain phonemes are assigned to certain referents, and it would be equally valid and acceptable to switch the names for "man" and "cow" if a community so decided.

In the ensuing dialogue, Socrates logically dissects the issues in detail. Ever the devil's advocate, he first seduces Hermogenes into believing that he is in agreement with a naturalist position by providing extensive etymological evidence and insight into historical linguistics. With a torrential outpouring of examples of the names of mortals and gods, he seduces his listeners into a belief in the embedded meanings of names. There is Orestes, the man of the mountains, who is described as having the brutality, fierceness, and mountain wildness suggested by his name. There is Agamemnon, admirable for remaining "steadfast," who is described as patient and persevering in the accomplishment of his resolutions. There is the mighty Zeus, whose name Socrates mentions is divided into *zena* and *dia*, both signifying the nature of God. And there is Tantalus, or Tantalos, the most weighted down by misfortune, whose life was full of ill-luck and whose death includes the weight of a stone suspended (*talanteia*) over his head.

However, in spite of his lengthy catalogue of examples, Socrates eventually concedes that names of men, unlike those of the gods and heroes, are deceptive because they do not necessarily reflect the shared characteristics of those lofty ancestors but merely reveal mortal parental desires and wishes. Speaking as somewhat of a linguist, he concludes that names may be correct and even significant but that they necessarily and inevitably become "twisted in all manner of ways." By making proper names independent of their inaugural moment and acknowledging their modifications over time, Socrates undermines and ousts the positions of both Cratylus and Hermogenes.

Today, it is easy to identify names that might fall into either category: those that are ordinary and appear to have no semantic meaning versus those that appear to be more appropriate and semantically meaningful. As examples, we might say that Faith, Dahlia, and Prudence are Cratylic names, whereas Susan, Timothy, and Kevin are not. However, this simplistic division does not account for all those names whose derivation or etymological reference tie them to meanings of Greek, Latin, or Hebrew origins, or those names infused with particular significance.

In fact, as Socrates points out, perhaps it is more accurate to say that over time and in certain places, names grow in associations, both positive and negative. Certain names become popular and acquire the status of popular icons, whereas other names become corrupt and temporarily removed from social circulation. The original meaning of such German-sounding names as Adolph or Heinrich in the postwar Western world may have been Hermogenean at one time, but today carry a particularly negative connotation. The historical entanglement of names and the complex circumstances in which they can become charged with meaning and signification prevent any clear-cut divide between these two categories.

The history of words and its incorporation into everyday discourse shows us how certain common names become branded. When a new scientific discovery emerged triumphant, it was with a proper name that it was awarded and rewarded: the Franklin stove, the Geiger counter, the Gallop poll, the Morse code, the Newtonian telescope, and in the field of psychology, the Rorschach test. Many common nouns have become so well integrated in our everyday vocabulary, we have forgotten that the original source was a named individual: bloomers after Amelia Bloomer, cardigan after James Brudnell, 7th Earl of Cardigan, jacuzzi after Candido Jacuzzi.

I was surprised to learn that many food items that are part of our regular diet have been named after people's preferences or idiosyncrasies: Baco noir, a hybrid grape, named after its breeder, Maurice Baco, coined to flatter the maître d'hôtel to Louis XIV, Louis de Bechamel, Marquis de Nointel (1630–1703), who happened to also be a financier and ambassador; Caesar salad, named after Caesar Cardini (1896–1956) or one of his associates who created this salad at the restaurant of the Hotel Caesar in Tijuana; pavlova ("light as Pavlova"), a meringue and fruit dessert named after Anna Pavlova (1881–1931), the Russian ballerina; and Oh Henry!, the candy bar introduced by the Williamson Candy Company in Chicago in 1920, named for a young man who frequented the company store and was often commandeered to do odd jobs with that call of his name.

Let us look at another place in which proper names are given considerable attention. Just as new parents must decide on a name for their newborn, so are authors faced with the process of nomination in giving birth to their characters and introducing them to the public. They take tremendous care to ensure that just the "proper" name is chosen to reflect the disposition and temperament of the men and women who will inhabit their pages. In the introduction of his insightful book *Literary Names: Personal Names in English Literature*, the author Alastair

Fowler highlights the notion that not all literary names can be easily categorized into one group or another (i.e., Cratylic or Hermogenean), citing the delightful dialogue between Humpty-Dumpty and Alice as an example:

> When Humpty-Dumpty demands what Alice's name means, she wonders "must a name mean something?" "Of course it must," says Humpty positively: "my name means the shape I am—and a good handsome shape it is, too. With a name like yours, you might be any shape, almost."[5]

Fowler points out that "Humpty-Dumpty" was then still descriptive of "a short, dumpy, hump-shouldered person," and that Alice would assume that he was an egg, based on her familiarity with nursery rhymes. He believes that Lewis Carroll—that is, C. L. Dodgson, the mathematical logician (two names for two distinct identities)—knew that names could not easily be categorized as meaningful or meaningless, so that "Alice" and "Humpty-Dumpty" each had their own histories and meant different things at different times.

The choice of names for literary characters is an excellent example of the way names are not only *denotative*, designating a particular person, but also *connotative*, conjuring up rich associations. The creation of names is never random or indiscriminate, but systematic and built on current social values and implicit associations. Many authors choose names that carry specific meanings in order to strengthen a theme or underline a personality trait. For example, some names might reflect allusions to particular characteristics, such as the hypocritical Silver in *Treasure Island* that "may shine brightly but is not true silver."

It is obvious to most readers that by the end of a well-written book, one feels that the character fits the name and vice versa. In the case of the classics, we associate certain personality traits with legendary characters: the mysterious, brooding, and romantic Mr. Rochester born by the pen of Charlotte Brontë; Josef K., the universal and timeless Everyman of Franz Kafka; the deductive reasoning powers of Sherlock Holmes; or the funny, feisty, and passionate Anne of Green Gables.

I cannot resist sharing with you the impact of what the master craftsman and literary genius James Joyce has managed to convey by his inventive list of names that are fanciful, evocative, and overdetermined. Combining satire and burlesque with associations and classical references, we are immediately struck by the following wedding list of guests in *Ulysses*, so astutely noted in Fowler's book:

> Lady Sylvester Elmshade, Mrs. Barbara Lovebirch, Mrs. Poll Ash, Mrs. Holly Hazeleyes, Miss Daphne Bays, Miss Dorothy Canebrake, Mrs. Clyde Twelvetrees, Mrs. Rown Greene, Mrs. Helen Vonegadding, Mrs. Virginia Creeper, Miss Gladys Beech, Miss Olive Garth, Miss Blanche Maple, Mrs. Maud Mahogany, Miss Myra Myrtle, Miss Priscilla Elderflower, Miss Bee Honeysuckle, Miss Grace Poplar, Miss O Mimosa San, Miss Rachel Cedarfrond, the Misses Lilian and Viola Lilac, Miss Timidity Aspenall, Miss Kitty Dewey-Mosse, Miss May Hawthrone, Mrs. Gloriana Palme, Mrs. Liana Forrest, Mrs. Arabella Blackwood and Mrs. Norman Holyoake of Oklahoma Regis graced the ceremony by their presence.[6]

Conversely, as Fowler points out, we also appropriate the characteristics of literary characters into our personal stock of shorthand. Perhaps no greater a writer than Shakespeare has instilled into our vocabulary a number of dramatic creations that have become emblematic and stereotypical of certain qualities: the ambitious and greedy Macbeth, the doubting Hamlet, Shylock the penurious Jew, and Sir John Falstaff, "the fat knight of great wit . . . spectacular resilience; fierce subversive intelligence . . . carnivalesque exuberance." The assumptions we make, both true and false, about names in literature also remind me of the preconceived notions we make about people in our everyday lives based on our associations to their names. I was reminded of this when I recently met a friend of my mother's named Annette.

"Annette Joanne Funicello," I said innocently, "that's the only other Annette I ever knew."

With a disparaging look, she said, "Oh, no. Please, not her." For me, this actress who played the most cherished of the Mouseketeers in the Mickey Mouse Club had been an icon of energy, laughter, and life. Little did I know that she had also battled multiple sclerosis for over fifteen years and had died a few months before this encounter.

In the same way that we conjure up a world of associations and memories when we hear the scratchy voice of Bob Dylan crooning, "Lay, lady, lay, lay across my big brass bed," or The Beatles earnestly singing "I wanna hold your hand," so too do names retrieve a world of sensual memories laced with the sights, smells, and sounds of times past. With certain names, not only do we re-create the past, but we imbue them with personalities and imaginary projections, placing them in an unwritten syllabus of metaphors, making them "proper" to the people who carry them.

In spite of Socrates' conclusion, and the rich associations that are now fixed to certain names, we have still not addressed the question of what is unique and particular about the proper name. Today, the debate is less about how a name has been assigned, but rather the distinctive characteristics of the proper name. In other words, what distinguishes the proper name from the common name?

If we shift from the fallout from Plato's seminal text and the eloquence of Socrates' arguments and fast-forward to the contemporary world, we can see that Western philosophers of language and logicians line up under the banner of one of two camps regarding theories of the proper name. The first is the *descriptivist theory*, notably heralded by such philosophers as Gottlob Frege, Bertrand Russell, Ludwig Wittgenstein, and John Searle; and the second is the *causal theory of reference*, championed predominantly by the preeminent American philosopher and logician of the twentieth century, Saul Kripke.

Those who argue for a *descriptivist* position claim that the meanings of proper names are identical to the descriptions associated with them by their speakers. The name Socrates refers to the man who was a Greek philosopher, the man who lived from 469 to 399 BCE, the protagonist of Plato's dialogues, and the man who was executed for heretical ideas. This theory takes the meaning of the name *Socrates* to be a collection of descriptions and takes the referent of the name to be the thing that satisfies all or most of these descriptions or cluster of properties. Bertrand Russell, whose theory would also be termed *descriptivist*, claimed that the proper name is a term that designates something particular. This particular designation is what distinguishes the proper name from the abbreviated description of a common noun. The proper name is "a word for the particular"; there can only be one Socrates, and he is designated by that name.

By contrast, causal theory states that a name's referent becomes fixed by an original act of naming or a "dubbing." When this happens, the name becomes attached to the person or thing in a permanent way as a *rigid designator* of that object. Irrespective of the later uses of the name, it will always remain linked to the original, in spite of any coincidental etymological connections. In other words, any proper name, even those that appear to refer to an obvious referent as a *linguistic naturalist* like Cratylus would suggest, has been transmitted through an indefinitely long series of earlier uses that can be traced back to an original or "baptismal" naming.

Let me illustrate with an example. The fact that a proper name is a *rigid designator* as opposed to a *bundle of descriptors* means that a proper name refers to the object in every country in which the object exists, while most descriptions designate different objects in different languages. This means that Marilyn Monroe refers to the same person in every possible world in which Monroe exists, while the blond actress and sex icon of the 1950s who emblazoned movie screens around the world could also refer to Ursula Andress, Raquel Welch, or Brigitte Bardot.

Both these positions fall apart if we consider the function of the proper name in everyday conversation. We tend to think of common names (nouns) as referring to multiple objects. While we may not necessarily have in mind the same table when we label an object by the word "table," we all agree that there can be many tables of different shapes, sizes, and colors. By contrast, when we refer to Albert Schweitzer, we are designating the one and only, the unique medical missionary who went to Africa to practice medicine. If we say that the proper name is singular, unambiguous, and denotes only one individual, then what can we say about the several Allan Browns, Abdul Mahmouds, or Sung Lees that all share the same name yet refer to several different people?

In a similar way, let us consider the argument that a common noun always refers to a class or an "all," so that all men named John is a general form, whereas John Smith is unambiguous and refers to the man whose proper name is John Smith. Yet even in this case, there are multiple John Smiths that would be difficult to distinguish on the basis of the full proper name alone. Secondly, it is argued that the proper name is a linguistic unit that can only function as a subset of nouns and can never be used in different grammatical forms, such as adverbs or adjectives. Yet today there are names such as And, Or, and the musical group The Who. And we certainly and with regular frequency turn proper names into adjectives and common nouns: Kafkaesque, Victorian, Copernican, Darwinian. In my field of psychoanalysis alone, we

refer to theories that are Freudian, Lacanian, Kleinian, Jungian, Bion-
ian, or Kohutian, to name a few.

A third argument is that we refer to a *common* name when we want
to imply that we all share the same meaning of its word usage. For
example, a telephone is an instrument of communication that transmits
sounds across a wire, and we all conform to this shared understanding
of its meaning. Similarly, a common noun is usually considered to be a
word that has a semantic connotation, or "means something," such as a
dog or a cat. As noted above, we refer to a *proper* name when we imply
an exclusivity of reference that does not contain any "meaning." But
how then do we explain such proper names as Joy, Grace, and Rose or
Goldman and Singer, whose spelling without capital letters constitute a
basic part of our everyday lexicon of nouns? A stronger counterargu-
ment is the class of those names that have entered our vocabulary
because of their universal associations, such as *a* Shylock or *a* Dr. Jekyll,
or *a* Machiavellian principle.

Working in a different field of study, Sir Alan Henderson Gardiner,
an Oxford philologist and Egyptologist, eventually developed an alternative theory about common and proper names that overcame some of
these noted problems. While developing a method for documenting
and cataloguing hieroglyphs, those primitively drawn symbols, he began
jotting down his ideas in his scribbler and eventually wrote a little-
known but controversial book on the theory of names. As an alternative
to the two theories mentioned above, Gardiner argued that proper
names are to be distinguished by their particular sound, or *sonant dis-
tinctiveness*. While acknowledging that some proper names do have
meaning, his focus was on the significance of the characteristic sound
qualities that give names a unique meaning of their own. From this, we
can infer that my name is Mavis Himes and will be understood and
translated and pronounced in all languages as Mavis Himes, even if it is
spelled as Heims, Hymes, Chaims, or Heimz. As such, it will always be
identified by the unique sound with which it is uttered.

This notion goes along with the considerable shock and dismay that
one feels when trying to translate the proper name of a character from
one language to another by a literal translation of meaning: e.g., Louis
Brasfort for Louis *Armstrong*; Oliver *Pierre* for Oliver *Stone*; or Sigmund *Joy* or Sigmund *Pleasure* for Sigmund *Freud(e)*. It is clear that we
can definitely say that all names are characterized by their sound qual-

ity. This immunity and immutability from literal translation as a key feature of the proper name makes its articulation sacred and permanent for its bearer.

NOTES

1. AN INVITATION INTO BEING

1. Gaston Bachelard, *The Poetics of Space*, trans. Maria Jolas (Boston: Beacon Press, 1994 [1958 in French]), 4–5.

2. Edmond Jabès, *The Book of Resemblances*, vol. 2, *Intimations of the Desert*, trans. Rosemarie Waldrop (Hanover, NH: Wesleyan University Press, 1978), 21.

3. Homer, *The Odyssey*, trans. Ennis Rees (New York: Modern Library, 1960), 119.

2. NAMES WITH POWER

1. Irving Zeitlin, *Ancient Judaism* (Cambridge: Polity Press, 1984), 7.

2. Michael Ondaatje, *Divisadero* (London: Bloomsbury Publishing, 2009), 181.

3. Jacob Neusner, "The Phenomenon of the Rabbi in Late Antiquity," *Numen* 16, 1969: 1–20, as referenced in Stuart Weinberg Gershon, *Kol Nidrei: Its Origin, Development, and Significance* (Northvale, NJ: Jason Aronson, 1994), 53.

3. GO OUT AND NAME

1. David Meghnagi, *Freud and Judaism* (London: Karnac Books, 1993), 64.
2. Boris Feldblyum, "Understanding Russian-Jewish Given Names," *Avotaynu* 13 (2), 1997: 3.
3. Stephen Wilson, *The Means of Naming: Social and Cultural History of Personal Naming in Western Europe* (London: University College Press, 1998), 245.
4. Nahum M. Sarna, *The JPS Torah Commentary: Genesis* (Philadelphia: Jewish Publication Society, 1989), 7.

4. NAMES AND NOMADS

1. Charles Raddock, *Portrait of a People*, vol. 1 (New York: Judaica Press, 1965), 7.
2. Jeremy Leigh, *Jewish Journeys* (London: Haus Publishing, 2006), 78.

5. CHOOSING NAMES

1. "Naming Rights," *Globe and Mail* editorial, January 4, 2013.
2. Thomas Carlyle, quoted in Da'ud ibn Auda [David B. Appleton], "Periodic Arab Names and Naming Practices," 2003, http://heraldry.sca.org/names/arabic-naming2.htm.
3. ibn Auda, "Periodic Arab Names and Naming Practices."
4. Peter Oliva, *The City of Yes* (Toronto: McLelland & Stewart, 1999), 186.

6. CELEBRATING NAMES

1. Yuri Rytkheu, *The Chukchi Bible*, trans. I. Y. Chavasse (Brooklyn: Archipelago Books, 2011), 134.
2. Ibid., 361.
3. Rau: the sun, the lord. Wa: a child, birth, the existent.
4. Ma: the mother, mouth, cavity, water, nature.
5. Ba: the father, spirit, nonexistent.

6. Ibrahim al-Koni, *Anubis: A Desert Novel* (Cairo: University of Cairo Press, 2007), 6–7.

7. THE STRANGE FATE OF NAMES

1. Justin Kaplan and Anne Bernays, *The Language of Names* (New York: Simon & Schuster, 1997), 104.

2. Karl Abraham, "On the Determining Power of Names," in *Clinical Papers and Essays on Psychoanalysis*, trans. H. C. Abraham and D. R. Ellison (London: Hogarth Press, 1955 [1911]), 31.

3. Catherine Millet, *Dalí and Me*, trans. Trista Selous (Zurich: Scheidegger & Spiess, 2008), 166.

4. Ibid.

5. Adriana Cavarero, *Relating Narratives: Storytelling and Selfhood*, Warwick Studies in European Philosophy (London: Routledge, 2000), 19.

8. TRANSMISSION AND INHERITANCE

1. C. J. Tyerman, "Flags and Stories," review of *To Follow in Their Footsteps*, by Nicholas Paul, *The Times Literary Supplement*, June 14, 2013.

2. Ibid.

3. Stephen Greenblatt, *Will in the World: How Shakespeare Became Shakespeare* (London: Pimlico / Random House, 2005 [2004]), 358.

4. Ibid., 79.

5. Emily Landau, "The Amazing Adventures of Michael Snow: An Uncensored History of Toronto's Most Notorious Art Star," *Toronto Life*, March 27, 2013, http://torontolife.com/city/the-amazing-adventures-of-michael-snow.

6. Téa Obreht, *The Tiger's Wife* (New York: Random House, 2011), 283.

10. THE FAMILY TREE OF LIFE

1. Gilles Deleuze and Félix Guattari, *A Thousand Plateaus: Capitalism and Schizophrenia* (London: Continuum [1987] 2003), 18.

2. Cynthia Rimsky, *Poste Restante* (Madrid: Ediciones Lastarria, 2011), as quoted in Penny Siganou, "Like a Tourist in Exile: Imagery, the Ephemeral and Returning in Cynthia Rimsky's *Poste Restante*" (unpublished graduate student paper).

3. Deleuze and Guattari, *A Thousand Plateaus*, 25.

4. King George letters patent, as published in the *London Gazette* on December 14, 1917, http://www.heraldica.org/topics/britain/prince_highness_docs.htm#1917_2.

5. Queen Elizabeth II letters patent, as published in the *London Gazette* on August 30, 1996, http://www.heraldica.org/topics/britain/prince_highness_docs.htm#1996.

6. Harry Ostrer, *Legacy: A Genetic History of the Jewish People* (Oxford: Oxford University Press, 2012), 218–19.

I I. IN THE NAME OF THE FATHER

1. "Potlatch Ban: Abolishment of First Nations Ceremonies," *Working Effectively with Aboriginal Peoples Blog*, October 16, 2012, http://www.ictinc.ca/the-potlatch-ban-abolishment-of-first-nations-ceremonies.

2. Max Müller, as quoted in Sigmund Freud, *Totem and Taboo*, in *The Standard Edition of the Complete Psychological Works of Sigmund Freud*, vol. 13 (London: Hogarth Press, 1960 [1913]), 110.

12. VOLUNTARY NAME-CHANGING

1. "Jane Siberry," *Wikipedia*, last modified September 11, 2015, https://en.wikipedia.org/wiki/Jane_Siberry.

2. Matt Soniak, "How 8 Famous Writers Chose their Pen Names," *Mental Floss*, June 14, 2014, http://mentalfloss.com/article/51195/how-8-famous-writers-chose-their-pen-names.

3. Donna Rifkind, "A Fictional Character," review of *Joseph Anton: A Memoir*, by Salman Rushdie, *New York Times*, October 12, 2012, Sunday Book Review.

4. Fanny Mendelssohn, letter to her father, July 16, 1820, published in Sebastian Hensel, *The Mendelssohn Family (1729–1847)*, 4th rev. ed., 2 vols. (London: Sampson Low, 1884), as quoted in "Fanny Mendelssohn," *Wikipedia*, last modified October 23, 2015, https://en.wikipedia.org/wiki/Fanny_Mendelssohn.

5. Megan Wood, "When the New You Carries a Fresh Identity, Too," *New York Times*, February 15, 2013, http://www.nytimes.com/2013/02/17/fashion/much-in-common-but-in-name-only.html?_r=0.

6. Ibid.

13. INVOLUNTARY NAME-CHANGING

1. Efrat Neuman, "In the Name of Zionism, Change Your Name," *Haaretz*, April 17, 2014, http://www.haaretz.com/weekend/week-s-end/.premium-1.566809#.

2. Pierre Pachet, *Autobiographie de mon père* (Paris: Editions Autrement, 1994), 121 (translation by author).

3. Ibid., 300.

4. Dow Marmur, "Surprise, You're Jewish," *Toronto Star*, September 16, 2012, http://www.thestar.com/opinion/editorialopinion/2012/09/16/surprise_youre_jewish.html.

5. Allan Hall, "Hermann Goering's Great-Niece: 'I Had Myself Sterilised So I Would Not Pass on the Blood of a Monster,'" *Daily Mail*, January 20, 2010, http://www.dailymail.co.uk/news/article-1244754/Hermann-Goerings-great-niece-tells-Hitlers-Children-I-sterilised-I-pass-blood-monster.html.

14. A HOUSE IS NOT A HOME

1. Goethe, *Faust*, part I, scene IV.

2. Richard Gwyn, "The Contender: The Appeal of Justin Trudeau's Emotional Intelligence," *The Walrus*, July/August 2013, 26–30.

3. Magdalena Tulli, *In Red*, trans. Bill Johnston (Brooklyn: Archipelago Books, 2011), 12.

4. William Shakespeare, *Romeo and Juliet*, Folger Library Edition (New York: Simon and Schuster, 1992), 71–72.

5. John Allemang, "An Intimate Epic," *Globe and Mail*, April 29, 2013.

6. Susan Handelman, *The Slayers of Moses: The Emergence of Rabbinic Interpretation in Modern Literary Theory* (Albany: State University of New York Press, 1982), 199.

7. Yosef Hayim Yerushalmi, *Freud's Moses: Judaism Terminable and Indeterminable* (New Haven and London: Yale University Press, 1991), 71.

8. Sigmund Freud, *An Autobiographical Study*, vol. 20 of *The Standard Edition of the Complete Psychological Works of Sigmund Freud* (London: Hogarth Press, 1960 [1925]), 8.

APPENDIX: THE LANGUAGE OF NAMES

1. "Nomenclature," *Wikipedia*, last modified October 27, 2015, https://en.wikipedia .org/ wiki / Nomenclature.

2. Mahmoud Darwish, *In the Presence of Absence*, trans. Sinan Antoon (Brooklyn: Archipelago Books, 2011), 28.

3. Lewis Carroll, *Alice's Adventures in Wonderland and Through the Looking-Glass,* 150th Anniversary Edition (New York: Penguin Books, 2015), 152–53.

4. Plato, *Cratylus*, The Internet Classics Archive, http//classics.mit.edu.Plato/cratylus.html.

5. Alastair Fowler, *Literary Names: Personal Names in English Literature* (London: Oxford University Press, 2012), 2.

6. Ibid., 218.

BIBLIOGRAPHY

Note: Most full proper names of well-known people in this book have been retrieved from the Internet. Some have been obtained from resource materials. Most etymological definitions have been retrieved from the *Oxford Dictionary of English Etymology* or from the website *Online Etymology Dictionary*.

Abraham, Karl. *Clinical Papers and Essays on Psychoanalysis.* Translated by H. C. Abraham and D. R. Ellison. London: Hogarth Press, 1955 [1911].

Ahmed, Leila. *A Border Crossing: From Cairo to America—A Woman's Journal.* New York: Penguin Books, 2000.

Allemang, John. "An Intimate Epic." *Globe and Mail*, April 29, 2013.

Bachelard, Gaston. *The Poetics of Space.* Translated by Maria Jolas. Boston: Beacon Press, 1994 [1958 in French].

Barkhatova, A., and T. Burkova. *The Romanovs: Tsars and Emperors.* St. Petersburg: Abris Art Publishers, 2007.

Barney, Rachel. *Names and Nature in Plato's Cratylus.* New York: Routledge, 2001.

Beider, Alexander. *A Dictionary of Jewish Surnames from the Russian Empire.* Teaneck, NJ: Avotaynu, 1993.

———. "Names and Naming." In *YIVO Encyclopedia of Jews in Eastern Europe.* New Haven, CT: Yale University Press, 2005.

Bell, Catherine, et al. "Recovering from Colonization: Perspectives of Community Members on Protection and Repatriation of Kwakwawa'wakw Cultural Heritage." In *First Nations Cultural Heritage and Law: Case Studies, Voices, and Perspectives.* Edited by Catherine Bell and Val Napoleon. Vancouver: University of British Columbia Press, 2008.

Benjamin, Walter. "On Language as Such and on the Language of Man." In *Reflections: Essays, Aphorisms, Autobiographical Writings.* Edited by Peter Demetz and translated by Edmund Jephcott. New York: Schocken Books, 1978.

Berger, John. *This Is Where We Meet.* New York: Vintage International, 2006.

Blanchot, M. *The Infinite Conversation.* Translated by Susan Hanson. Minneapolis: University of Minnesota Press, 1993 [1969 in French].

Cardinal, Marie. *In Other Words.* Translated by Amy Coper. Bloomington: Indiana University Press, 1995.

Carroll, Lewis. *Alice's Adventures in Wonderland and Through the Looking-Glass,* 150th Anniversary Edition. New York: Penguin Books, 2015.

Cavarero, Adriana. *Relating Narratives: Storytelling and Selfhood*. Warwick Studies in European Philosophy. London: Routledge, 2000.

Christou, Panaghiotis, and Katharini Papastamatis. *Greek Mythology: The Trojan Wars and the Odyssey*. Florence: Casa Editrice Bonechi, 2008.

Darwish, Mahmoud. *In the Presence of Absence*. Translated by Sinan Antoon. Brooklyn: Archipelago Books, 2011.

Deleuze, Gilles, and Félix Guattari. *A Thousand Plateaus: Capitalism and Schizophrenia* . London: Continuum, 2003 [1987].

Efron, John. *Defenders of the Race: Jewish Doctors and Race Science in Fin-de-Siècle Europe*. New Haven, CT: Yale University Press, 1994.

Feldblyum, Boris. "Understanding Russian-Jewish Given Names." *Avotaynu* 13 (2), 1997: 3.

Fishbane, Michael. *Sacred Attunement: A Jewish Theology*. Chicago: University of Chicago Press, 2008.

Fowler, Alastair. *Literary Names: Personal Names in English Literature*. London: Oxford University Press, 2012.

Freud, Sigmund. *The Interpretation of Dreams*. Vol. 4 of *The Standard Edition of the Complete Psychological Works of Sigmund Freud*. London: Hogarth Press, 1960 [1900].

———. *The Psychopathology of Everyday Life*. Vol. 6 of *The Standard Edition of the Complete Psychological Works of Sigmund Freud*. London: Hogarth Press, 1960 [1901].

———. *Totem and Taboo*. Vol. 13 of *The Standard Edition of the Complete Psychological Works of Sigmund Freud*. London: Hogarth Press, 1960 [1913].

———. *An Autobiographical Study*. Vol. 20 of *The Standard Edition of the Complete Psychological Works of Sigmund Freud*. London: Hogarth Press 1960 [1925].

Fuks, Betty. *Freud and the Invention of Jewishness*. Translated by Paulo H. Britto. New York: Agincourt Press, 2008.

Gadamer, Hans-Georg. *Truth and Method*. 2nd rev. ed. New York: Continuum International, 2004.

Gardiner, Sir Alan. *The Proper Theory of Names: A Controversial Essay*. Rev. ed. London: Oxford University Press, 1954 [1940].

"Genealogy and Family History." Libraries and Archives Canada. http://www.bac-lac.gc.ca/eng/discover/genealogy/Pages/introduction.aspx.

Gershon, Stuart Weinberg. *Kol Nidrei: Its Origin, Development, and Significance*. Northvale, NJ: Jason Aronson, 1994.

Gollob, Herman. *Me and Shakespeare: Adventures with the Bard*. New York: Anchor Books, 2003.

Green, Arthur. *Radical Judaism: Rethinking God and Tradition*. New Haven, CT: Yale University Press, 2010.

Greenblatt, Stephen. *Will in the World: How Shakespeare Became Shakespeare*. London: Pimlico / Random House, 2005 [2004].

Gwyn, Richard. "The Contender: The Appeal of Justin Trudeau's Emotional Intelligence." *The Walrus*, July/August 2013, 26–30.

Hall, Allan. "Hermann Goering's Great-Niece: 'I Had Myself Sterilised So I Would Not Pass on the Blood of a Monster.'" *Daily Mail*, January 20, 2010. http://www.dailymail.co.uk/news/article-1244754/Hermann-Goerings-great-niece-tells-Hitlers-Children-I-sterilised-I-pass-blood-monster.html.

Handelman, Susan. *The Slayers of Moses: The Emergence of Rabbinic Interpretation in Modern Literary Theory*. Albany: State University of New York Press, 1982.

Harari, Roberto. *How James Joyce Made His Name: A Reading of the Final Lacan*. Translated by Luke Thurston. New York: Other Press, 2002.

Hartman, David. *A Living Covenant: The Innovative Spirit in Traditional Judaism*. Woodstock, VT: Jewish Lights Publishing, 1998.

Heller, Aron. "Nazi Leader's Grandniece, Jewish Woman Find Peace." *USA Today*, October 31, 2008.

Hensel, Sebastian. *The Mendelssohn Family (1729–1847)*. 4th rev. ed., 2 vols. London: Sampson Low, 1884.

Hesiod. *Theogony: Works and Days*. Translated by M. L. West. Oxford: Oxford World's Classics, 1999.

Himes, Mavis. *The Sacred Body: A Therapist's Journey*. Toronto: Stoddart Publishing, 2002.

———. "What's in a Name? Reflections on a Lacanian Perspective." *Journal for Lacanian Studies* (3) 2, 2005: 209–21.

The Holy Bible, New International Version. International Bible Society. Colorado Springs, CO: Biblica, 1978.

Homer. *The Odyssey*. Translated by Ennis Rees. New York: Modern Library,1960.

Howatson, M. C., ed. *The Oxford Companion to Classical Literature*. Oxford: Oxford University Press, 1989 [1st ed., 1937].

ibn Auda, Da'ud [David B. Appleton]. "Periodic Arab Names and Naming Practices," 2003. http://heraldry.sca.org/names/arabic-naming2.htm.

Jabès, Edmond. *The Book of Questions*. Vol. 1. Translated by Rosemarie Waldrop. Hanover, NH: Wesleyan University Press, 1964.

———. *The Book of Questions: El, or the Last Book*. Translated by Rosemarie Waldrop. Hanover, NH: Wesleyan University Press, 1984.

———. *The Book of Resemblances*. Vol. 2, *Intimations of the Desert*. Translated by Rosemarie Waldrop. Hanover, NH: Wesleyan University Press, 1978.

Jacobs, Joseph. "Names (Personal)." In *Jewish Encyclopedia*. http://www.jewishencyclopedia.com/articles/11304-names-personal.

Jones, Edward P. *The Known World*. New York: HarperCollins, 2003.

Kaplan, Justin, and Anne Bernays. *The Language of Names*. New York: Simon & Schuster, 1997.

Kapuściński, Ryszard. *Travels with Herodotus*. New York: Random House Vintage, 2007.

King George V letters patent, as published in the *London Gazette* on December 14, 1917. http://www.heraldica.org/topics/britain/prince_highness_docs.htm#1917_2.

Klein, Richard G. "The Names of the Analysts," Freud 2 Lacan, updated July 1, 2015. http://www.freud2lacan.com/docs/FREUD-NAMES_OF_THE_ANALYSTS.pdf.

Koni, Ibrahim al-. *Anubis: A Desert Novel*. Cairo: University of Cairo Press, 2007.

Kripke, Saul. *Naming and Necessity*. Cambridge, MA: Harvard University Press, 1972.

Kristeva, Julia. *Strangers to Ourselves*. Translated by Leon S. Roudiez. New York: Columbia University Press, 1991.

Kuper, Adam. "Persons Who Become Relatives." *Times Literary Supplement*, July 12, 2013.

Lacan, Jacques. "The Function and Field of Speech and Language in Psychoanalysis." In *Ecrits: A Selection*. Translated by Bruce Fink. New York: W. W. Norton, 1966 (2004 [1953]).

———. *The Seminar of Jacques Lacan: Book III, The Psychoses, 1955–1956*. Translated by Russell Grigg. London: Routledge, 1993.

———. *The Seminar of Jacques Lacan: Book XII, Crucial Problems for Psychoanalysis, 1964–1965*. Translated by Cormac Gallagher. Unpublished manuscript. Seminar 4, 3.

Landau, Emily. "The Amazing Adventures of Michael Snow: An Uncensored History of Toronto's Most Notorious Art Star." *Toronto Life*, March 27, 2013. http://torontolife.com/city/the-amazing-adventures-of-michael-snow.

Lapierre, Nicole. *Changer de nom*. Toulouse: Editions Eres, 2012.

Leigh, Jeremy. *Jewish Journeys*. London: Haus Publishing, 2006.

Linn-Williams, Susann. *Folk Art*. London: Flame Tree Publishing, 2006.

Marmur, Dow. "Surprise, You're Jewish." *Toronto Star*, September 16, 2012. http://www.thestar.com/opinion/editorialopinion/2012/09/16/surprise_youre_jewish.html.

Masson, Céline, and Michel Gad Wolkowicz, eds. *La force du nom: Leur nom, ils l ' ont changé*. Paris: Desclée de Brouwer, 2010.

Meghnagi, David. "A Cultural Event within Judaism." In *Freud and Judaism*. Edited by David Meghnagi. London: Karnac Books, 1993.

Millet, Catherine. *Dalí and Me*. Translated by Trista Selous. Zurich: Scheidegger & Spiess, 2008.

Milner, J-C, A. Banfield, and D. Heller-Roazen. "Interview with Jean-Claude Milner." *Journal of the Jan van Eyck Circle for Lacanian Ideology Critique* 3 (2010): 4–21.

Monk, Ray. "Looking for Wittgenstein." *The New York Review of Books* 15, no. 10 (June 6, 2013).

Moreau Ricaud, Michelle. "Un changement de nom chez un analyste hongrois: Le cas de Michael Balint." In *La force du nom: Leur nom, ils l'ont changé.* Edited by Céline Masson and Michel Gad Wolkowicz. Paris: Desclée de Brouwer, 2010.

Morris, Errol. "What's in a Name? (Part 1)." *Opinionator* (blog), *New York Times*, April 29, 2012. http://opinionator.blogs.nytimes.com/2012/04/29/whats-in-a-name-part-1/?_r=0.

"Naming Rights." *Globe and Mail* editorial, January 4, 2013.

Néret, Gilles. *Dalí.* Cologne: Taschen, 2007.

Neuman, Efrat. "In the Name of Zionism, Change Your Name." *Haaretz*, April 17, 2014. http://www.haaretz.com/weekend/week-s-end/premium-1.566809#.

"Nomenclature." *Wikipedia*, last modified October 27, 2015. https://en. wikipedia .org/ wiki / Nomenclature.

Obreht, Téa. *The Tiger's Wife.* New York: Random House, 2011.

Oliva, Peter. *The City of Yes.* Toronto: McLelland & Stewart, 1999.

Ondaatje, Michael. *Divisadero.* London: Bloomsbury Publishing, 2009.

Ostrer, Harry. *Legacy: A Genetic History of the Jewish People.* Oxford: Oxford University Press, 2012.

The Oxford Dictionary of English Etymology. Edited by C. T. Onions. Oxford: Oxford University Press, 1966.

Oz, Amos, and Fania Oz-Salzberger. *Jews and Words.* New Haven, CT: Yale University Press, 2012.

Pachet, Pierre. *Autobiographie de mon père.* Paris: Editions Autrement, 1994.

Pandolfo, Stefania. *Impasse of the Angels: Scenes from a Moroccan Space of Memory.* Chicago: University of Chicago Press, 1998.

Perec, Georges. *Wou le souvenir d'enfance.* Paris: Denoel, 1975.

Plato. *Cratylus.* The Internet Classics Archive. http://classics.mit.edu/Plato/cratylus.html.

Polack, Gillian. "Languages in Medieval England." http://www.triviumpublishing.com/articles/languages.html .

Porge, Erik. *Les noms du père chez Jacques Lacan.* Toulouse: Editions Eres, 2013 [1997].

"Potlatch Ban: Abolishment of First Nations Ceremonies." *Working Effectively with Aboriginal Peoples Blog*, October 16, 2012. http://www.ictinc.ca/the-potlatch-ban-abolishment-of-first-nations-ceremonies.

Queen Elizabeth II letters patent, as published in the *London Gazette* on August 30, 1996. http://www.heraldica.org/topics/britain/prince_highness_docs.htm#1996.

Rabinowitz, Isaac. "'Word' and Literature in Ancient Israel." *New Literary History* 4 (1972): 119–30.

Raddock, Charles. *Portrait of a People.* Vol. 1. New York: Judaica Press, 1965.

Rifkind, Donna. "A Fictional Character." Review of *Joseph Anton: A Memoir*, by Salman Rushdie. *New York Times*, October 12, 2012, Sunday Book Review.

Rimsky, Cynthia. *Poste Restante.* Madrid: Ediciones Lastarria, 2011.

Robert, Marthe. *From Oedipus to Moses: Freud's Jewish Identity.* Translated by R. Manheim. New York: Doubleday, 1976.

Rosenstein, Neil. *The Lurie Legacy: The House of Davidic Royal Descent.* Teaneck, NJ: Avotaynu, 2004.

Rothenberg, Benno. *Sinai: Pharaoh, Miners, Pilgrims and Soldiers.* Bern: Kümmerly + Frey, 1979.

Rottenberg, Dan. *Finding Our Fathers: A Guidebook to Jewish Genealogy.* New York: Random House, 1977.

Rytkheu, Yuri. *The Chukchi Bible.* Translated by I. Y. Chavasse. Brooklyn: Archipelago Books, 2011.

Safi, Omid. *Memories of Muhammad: Why the Prophet Matters.* New York: HarperCollins, 2009.

Sarna, Nahum M. *The JPS Torah Commentary: Genesis.* Philadelphia: Jewish Publication Society, 1989.

Sedley, David. *Plato's Cratylus.* Cambridge: Cambridge University Press, 2003.

Seung Sahn. *Wanting Enlightenment Is a Big Mistake: Teachings of Zen Master Seung Sahn.* Compiled and edited by Hyon Gak. Boston: Shambhala Press, 2006.

Shakespeare, William. *Romeo and Juliet.* Folger Library Edition. New York: Simon and Shuster, 1992.

Shalev, Meir. *Beginnings: Reflections on the Bible's Intriguing Firsts.* New York: Harmony Books, 2011.

Shepherdson, Charles. *Vital Signs: Nature, Culture and Psychoanalysis.* New York and London: Routledge, 2000.

Shokek, Shimon. *Kabbalah and the Art of Being: The Smithsonian Lectures.* London: Routledge, 2001.

"Siberry, Jane." *Wikipedia,* last modified September 11, 2015. https://en.wikipedia.org/wiki/Jane_Siberry.

Siganou, Penny. "Like a Tourist in Exile: Imagery, the Ephemeral and Returning in Cynthia Rimsky's *Poste Restante"* (unpublished graduate student paper).

Sileika, G. Paul. "Just Call Me Paul." *Globe and Mail,* January 21, 2014.

Soniak, Matt. "How 8 Famous Writers Chose their Pen Names." *Mental Floss,* June 14, 2014. http://mentalfloss.com/article/51195/how-8-famous-writers-chose-their-pen-names.

"Spanish Naming Customs." *Wikipedia,* last modified September 27, 2015. http://en.wikipedia.org/wiki/Spanish_naming_customs.

Tulli, Magdalena. *In Red.* Translated by Bill Johnston. Brooklyn: Archipelago Books, 2011.

Turkle, Sherry. *Psychoanalytic Politics: Freud's French Revolution.* New York: Basic Books, 1978.

Tyerman, C. J. "Flags and Stories." Review of *To Follow in Their Footsteps,* by Nicholas Paul. *The Times Literary Supplement,* June 14, 2013.

United Synagogue of Conservative Judaism. *Etz Chaim: Torah and Commentary.* New York: Jewish Publication Society, 2001.

Volkov, Solomon. *The Magical Chorus: A History of Russian Culture from Tolstoy to Solzhenitsyn.* Translated by A. W. Bouis. New York: Alfred Knopf, 2008.

Waal, Edmund de. *The Hare with Amber Eyes.* New York: Farrar, Strauss and Giroux, 2010.

Weil, François. *Family Trees: A History of Genealogy in America.* Boston: Harvard University Press, 2013.

Wilhelm, Rabbi Y. Z. *What's In a Name: Laws and Customs Regarding the Naming of Children and Related Topics.* Brooklyn: S.I.E. Publications, 1998.

Wilson, Stephen. *The Means of Naming: Social and Cultural History of Personal Naming in Western Europe.* London: University College Press, 1998.

Wood, Megan. "When the New You Carries a Fresh Identity, Too." *New York Times,* February 15, 2013. http://www.nytimes.com/2013/02/17/fashion/much-in-common-but-in-name-only.html?_r=0.

Woodstock, George. *The Marvellous Century.* Markham, ON: Fitzhenry & Whiteside, 1989.

Yerushalmi, Yosef Hayim. *Freud's Moses: Judaism Terminable and Indeterminable.* New Haven and London: Yale University Press, 1991.

Young-Bruehl, Elizabeth, and Christine Dunbar. *One Hundred Years of Psychoanalysis, A Timeline: 1900–2000.* Toronto: Caversham Productions, 2009.

Ze'evi, Chonoch. *Hitler's Children.* Produced by Maya Productions (Israel) with Saxonia Entertainment (Germany). First viewed publicly in Israel in May 2013 and since shown at a number of film festivals.

Zeitlin, Irving. *Ancient Judaism.* Cambridge, UK: Polity Press, 1984.

INDEX

ABOUT THE AUTHOR

Mavis Himes, PhD, is a psychoanalyst and clinical psychologist in Toronto where she maintains a full-time private practice. She is also clinical consultant at Wellspring, a cancer center for patients and their families. Himes is the director of Speaking of Lacan Psychoanalytic Group, a Toronto-based forum dedicated to the study of Lacanian psychoanalysis. Her previous book, *The Sacred Body: A Therapist's Journey*, is about her work with cancer patients; as well, she frequently contributes to professional journals and books about psychoanalysis.